JUICE

RADICAL TAIJI ENERGETICS

SCOTT MEREDITH

JUICE

ISBN-13: 978-1478260691

ISBN-10: 1478260696

Interior Design: The Fast Fingers, http://www.thefastfingers.com

DEDICATION

To the memory of the genius master jeweler,
WANG ZONGYUE（王宗岳）
who cut, polished and set
the radiantly mysterious gem, Taiji.

To the greatest Taiji master of his generation,
BENJAMIN PANG JENG LO（羅邦楨）
who is in no way responsible
for any part of this wild book.

很抱歉請原諒我先斬後奏式的貿然行事

TABLE OF CONTENTS

NOTES

All translations from the Chinese and Japanese (ancient and modern, literary or technical), appearing in this book are the original copyrighted work of the author unless otherwise explicitly sourced. The Zheng Manqing quotation on p. 18-19 is by Douglas Wile, (*Zheng Manqing's Uncollected Writings on Taijiquan, Qigong, and Health*).

Most Chinese characters are traditional, with occasional variation including adoption of simplified characters, based on common usage, personal preference, and accepted historical precedent in names, among other criteria.

Most Chinese transliterations are Pinyin, with occasional variation including adoption of Wade-Giles and other variants, based on common usage, personal preference, and accepted historical precedent in names, among other criteria.

All sketches are 100% original artwork produced for this book, copyright 2012 Scott Meredith. Anatomical diagrams are derivative artwork copyright 2012 Scott Meredith, derived in part from licensed 3rd-party graphic materials.

Sometimes the 3rd person plural form of pronouns is used for singular to include both genders, at other times I use the gender-contorted singulars; s/he, him/her, and his/hers.

DISCLAIMER

All practices, processes, and methods described in this book are provided for entertainment purposes only. All martial arts practices including Taiji entail risks including, but not limited to, permanent disability and death. The reader is fully responsible for his or her own health and welfare. Never engage in Taiji or any other physical practice except under the immediate and ongoing oversight of currently certified and licensed health care professionals. Before beginning any activity, you must undergo a comprehensive physical and psychological examination by a qualified, currently licensed health care professional, and comply strictly with your health care provider's guidelines and recommendations following this examination. Do not attempt anything described in this book without the full knowledge, consent, and personal supervision of a qualified, currently licensed physician or other qualified health care professional. If you experience any pain or difficulty when engaging with the ideas presented in this book, stop immediately and consult your healthcare provider. This book is not meant to be used, nor should it be used, to diagnose or treat any medical condition. For diagnosis or treatment of any medical problem or concern, consult your physician. The publisher and author are not responsible for any specific health or allergy needs that may require medical supervision and are not liable for any damages or negative consequences from any treatment, action, application or preparation, to any person reading or following the information in this book. References are provided for informational purposes only and do not constitute endorsement of any websites, books, or other sources. While best efforts have been used in preparing this book, the author and publisher make no representations or warranties of any kind and assume no liabilities of any kind with respect to the accuracy or completeness of the contents and specifically disclaim any implied warranties of merchantability or fitness of use for a particular purpose. Neither the author nor the publisher shall be held liable or responsible to any person or entity with respect to any loss or incidental or consequential damages caused, or alleged to have been caused, directly or indirectly, by the information or programs contained herein. Protect yourself at all times.

PREFACE

The shuddering echo of the Gion temple bell
tolls the impermanence of all things.
The brilliant-hued flowers of its double-trunked tree
affirm the sole truth, that what flourishes must fall.
Like a springtime evening's wisp of dream,
the strong are broken at last
to end as dust before the wind.

- Heike Monogatari (13th century C.E.)

Taiji, to me, isn't primarily for health, nor for self-defense and martial arts, nor is it for reducing stress in daily life through mind-body balance, or any of the other clichés. To me, Taiji is *performance art*. That conjures visions of pretty poses in the park, on a sunny spring morning. Or the flashing fists and flailing silk tassels of a Chinese New Year's day Kung-Fu show. But those are shallow spectacles, mere theatrics. I'm talking here about the *deep* performance art which reaches the soul. *Deep* performance art is when I send a man who outweighs me by 70 pounds stumbling or hurtling backwards with a soft touch. *Deep* performance art is when I seem to evade like smoke the rough grasp of somebody far stronger than myself. Even if that same person could seriously harm me were we to fight "for real", even if onlookers may smirk that he's having to "play my game", even if he could stalk me tomorrow with an Uzi and blast me into Swiss cheese – still, just for an instant, when I see that questioning look in his eyes, when I hear that note of amazement in his voice:"How'd you *do* that …?""What *was* that…?"then I know I've achieved art's deepest purpose - opening a quick window on wonder: *Is there something else?*

FABLE

Long ago in a far-away land, the King yearned for the deepest secret of the Art, to gain its powers and pleasures. He summoned the realm's greatest wise men and most learned scholars to a royal audience in the high tower. As they jostled and murmured before the golden throne, the King commanded them: *Silence! I desire for myself the powers and pleasures of the Art. But long, hard practice does not befit a King. I won't knock for empty years outside the Art's door, rather will I batter it down with Knowledge alone! I give you, my wisest scholars, wizards, and magi, one year to distill for me the boiled essence of the Art, as short and simple as may be. Go now, and work well - lest your heads pay the forfeit of your task.*

When the leaves had browned, and greened, and browned again, the King assembled the wise men and commanded: *Tell me the Art's great secret, as short and simple as may be.* So the oldest and wisest of them bent low before the great throne, and his arms trembled as twigs in the storm, yet he held high a small scroll, saying: *O King, we have squeezed and scraped and squashed the Art down to but a single word, that your Majesty can easily gain for Himself the powers and pleasures it may yield.*

The King spread the scroll and read the single word that held all the Art. That word was merely this:

Relax

And the King said: *You have done well to be so brief with the Art's great secret. But I can't use it. This word alone does not make the Art mine. I therefore grant you another year to boil down the Art's essence for me. Give me no more than a single sentence - yet sufficient that I may have the powers of the Art, and the pleasures thereof. And mind well that your heads shall pay the forfeit of your task.*

So it came to pass that after the snows had fallen, and melted away in the earth, and fallen again, the King summoned the wise men and commanded: *Tell me the Art, as short and simple as may be. Give me the one sentence - sufficient that I may have the powers of the Art, and the pleasures thereof.* The oldest and wisest of them bowed deeply before the throne and his arms trembled the more greatly (for another year had passed) but his face beamed as he handed up a scroll to the King, saying: *Sire, we have smacked the Art down to but a single sentence, that your Majesty may have the Art's powers and pleasures.*

The King spread the scroll and read the sentence that held all the Art. That sentence was merely this:

Mind leads the energy from feet to hands.

And the King said: *You have done well again, to be so brief with the Art's great secret. Yet still - I do not understand it! I can't use it, and this sentence alone does not make the Art mine. I grant you one last year to bring me the boiled essence of the Art, as short and simple as may be - no more than a single volume - but sufficient that I may have the Art as my own, and truly your heads shall pay the forfeit of this final task.*

After the birds had flocked away to the South, and returned to nest, and flocked away South again, the King summoned the wise men and commanded: *Now show me the Art, as short and simple as may be, no more than a slim book, but sufficient that I may have the Art's powers and pleasures for my own.* The oldest and wisest of them bowed deeply before the golden throne and his back was humped and his arms shook but his face shone as he held up a book, saying: *Your Majesty, we have compacted the Art down to this book, of many words and sentences, but no more and no less than required, so that Your Majesty may finally have the powers and pleasures of the Art.*

The King read the title of this book that held all the Art, and it was merely this:

JUICE: Radical TAIJI Energetics

And the King roared: *Off with their heads!* (For the King despised frippery). And he flung the book out the tower window into the peat bogs below.

For long years the leaves greened and browned, the snows fell and melted, the birds flocked and nested and flocked again. And Time crushed the castle into dirt, and the great King was forgotten and for uncounted eons dust blew across the empty hills.

But then a new kingdom arose, ruled by a new King. One morning the King's boatman brought him a book, saying: *Great King, I have found this ancient book in the mud of our quay and thinking it may be a precious relic, would now tender it to your Majesty.*

All the day, alone in the great chamber of audience, the King riffled the book, pondering. Then the King called the wisest men of the realm to assemble, and commanded: *I do not understand this book at all, yet I feel it may hold deep secrets that I would have for my own. You, the wisest scholars, wizards, and magi of the realm, are granted a year to bring me the boiled down essence of this book, as short and simple as may be, and take care - lest your heads pay the forfeit of your task.*

So after the snows had fallen, and soaked away in the sun, and fallen again, the King summoned the wise men and commanded: *Tell me the book's wisdom, as short and simple as may be, that I may have it as my own.* So the oldest and wisest of them bowed deeply before the great throne and his arms trembled but his face was proud as he held up a scroll to the King saying: *O King, we have scraped and squeezed and squashed the book down to but a single sentence, that your Majesty may easily have for Himself its powers and pleasures.*

The King spread the scroll and read the single sentence that held the book's entire wisdom. That sentence was merely this:

Mind leads the energy from feet to hands.

And the King said: *You have done well to be so brief with the book's great secret. Yet it is too long and wordy, too much complication for my royal mind. You have a final year to bring me the essence of that sentence, shorter and simpler, that I may most easily have the book's powers and pleasures as my own. And truly shall your heads pay the forfeit of this task.*

So after the birds had left in their great flocks for the South, and returned to roost, and flocked and roosted and flocked again, the King summoned the wise men and commanded: *Now show me the Book's wisdom, as short and simple as may be, that I may have it as my own.* The oldest and wisest of them bowed deeply before the great throne and though of hunched back and reed-thin arms yet proudly he held up a scroll to the King saying: *O King, we have mashed the Book's wisdom down to but a single word, that your Majesty may most easily have for Himself its pleasures and powers.*

The King spread the scroll and read the single word that held the Book's entire wisdom.

And that word was merely this:

Relax

And the King bellowed: *Off with their heads!* (For nobody likes a smartass).

CHAPTER 1:
WHAT, WHO, WHY

WHAT?

Boring! That's what. 'Boring' is the word that should spring to mind when you hear of yet another book on Taiji. Most Taiji books are vague, tepid, repetitive, derivative – real snooze fests. You know the sort - you typically read the first three pages, skim the rest of the first chapter, flip through the tortuous sequence of unusable posture photos, and end up reverently laying the book aside – til you *have time to get to it*. And yet ... Taiji is a wild, mystical, beautiful, radiant, powerful, sexy and generally awesome art. Books on Taiji should reflect and reinforce that.

If you're a Taiji beginner, or merely Tai-curious, this book will ring your ears and sting your eyes into full awareness of an amazing internal potential you've never known. *There's something inside you that you haven't yet experienced.* It may seem (due to the lack of form illustrations) that this book is targeted only to advanced Taiji students, but that's not the case at all. *This is the book I wish I'd had as a total newbie.* Even the parts a beginner can't fully understand yet describe true Taiji effects dramatic enough to inspire anybody.

If you're a Taiji veteran, on the other hand, ... you should run like hell! Just kidding. If you're a seasoned practitioner, this book will grab you by the heels and shake you upside down til you confess there may be more to the art than you've dreamt. I keep running into experienced players who've barely felt the internal energy – or who minimize that potential in favor of material stuff - the physical minutiae of posture and movement. This book should be a puff of fresh oxygen for them, as it's dead-centered on nothing but the radical energetics of the game.

Of course there are also those who swing the other way, assuming that only highly complex meditations will ever get you anywhere. Things like imagining maidens and warriors clothed in silver and gold, spinning giant waterwheels on either side of your sex center while you vertically rotate your eyeballs 360 degrees. Those methods are probably all good, and they are correct in that *energy follows mind*. We'd agree that training the mind is indeed the lion's share of the operation. But there are hundreds of these purely psycho-visual systems. How would you realistically evaluate them? Which would you focus on? We have limited time to work on ourselves. To me, Taiji has a unique beauty - a clean simplicity and directness not found in other Daoist energy practices. My idea of Taiji is using:

- *continuous light concentration*
- *lean and functional visualization*
- *minimal physical structure*

… to get you to the only thing that matters – your own radical energy.

Two kinds of 'what' need to be covered here: *What is Taiji? What is this book?*

What is Taiji? On the surface, it's a collection of standing martial arts postures, linked in a relaxed, slow motion sequence. But that's not my definition. Here's my executive summary:

Taiji is a discipline for training your mind to catch spirit power bounced from your feet to your hands.

Bravely spoken - but also kind of vaguely spoken, in that 'spirit power' isn't defined anywhere. Well, that's the mystery of Taiji. There are going to be a lot of terms like that in this book, but I'll do my best to insure that by the end you have a working feel for what you really need to know to radicalize your own practice.

I understand that some readers will shrink in horror from the executive summary statement above, because: "Oh but, Taiji is so much *more* than that! Taiji is about health, inner peace, spiritual balance, perfection of character, enlightenment and limitless undying love across the universe..." Others may be pissed that I haven't yet mentioned fighting and martial arts directly. Those reactions are both right and wrong. They're right in that Taiji can perhaps *lead* to all that other stuff. But the mechanism by which it does so, *the signature defining purpose and true result* of correct training stands as I've plainly stated it there. Accomplishing that energetic transmission is the work of Taiji. And it's plenty enough to keep you busy.

I shouldn't have had to write this book. There is nothing whatsoever original in here. The basic points have been clearly stated many times, many ways. They've been most cogently presented in the Taiji classic writings (太極拳經 *Taijiquanjing*), which is a compilation of brief essays by the greatest of all past masters, who've defined the art for all time. It's all clearly documented and there's no need for me of all people to say a single word more. At the same time though, everything I say here is original - because it's describing my personal experience with the art. How can the same set of notes, this book, be both utterly derivative and yet absolutely unique? Only one way: the ancient masters must have left us an objective description of an authentic human experience that anybody can accurately replicate, with a personalized twist, in his or her own body, mind, and soul.

I've written the book for the following reasons:

1. I'm disturbed that many people who've practiced Taiji for years or even decades haven't begun to understand that the point of the art is to engage the energy throughout the body by means of the mind. Some of these, even while claiming to accept the abstract idea of "internal energy" have obviously given up on the energy-centric practice altogether, secretly concluding that the cupboard is bare

5

and that going physical is the only way forward. I've noticed a creeping tendency, in the face of frustration at the *seeming* fraudulence of the ancient masters' claims, to do some destructive R&D on the art, reverse engineering it down to bio-mechanics and other physical, anatomical and structural stuff. Or else breaking it down to pure technique. That, above all, is what I hope to guard against, or the beautiful priceless gem of this art may be lost forever. Think of the ancient ivory spheres on display in the Palace Museum of China. These were carved from a single block of solid ivory, but nested in each are hundreds of embedded concentric balls, smaller and yet smaller within, at an ever more impossibly minute scale. The museum people have told me that this peak of craft mastery can no longer be replicated. Taiji may become like that, with only the appearance left to us, the inner craft lost and impossible for us to re-create for ourselves. The real art of Taiji, something more beautiful than *attack ships on fire off the shoulder of Orion,* and more dazzling than *the glitter of c-beams in the dark near the Tannhäuser Gate* may end up as a fading mystery … *lost in time, like tears in rain.*

2. Many of my students have requested the convenience of a detailed explanation of all the key teaching points of radical Taiji energetics bound up in one place. That's all this book really is – just my occasional teaching notes assembled and organized for the benefit of my students. It's actually targeted for eventual translation, when I get to it, on behalf of my Japanese students. For some reason there's a relative paucity of quality writing on deep Taiji principles available in Japanese, quite a contrast to the cornucopia available to readers of English.

Taiji is getting more popular all the time. Uncountable hundreds of millions of Chinese people practice it all across Asia. It's now spread through the West and the rest of the world. But most of that action is 'Senior Center Taiji', which is my translation of the gently disparaging term the Chinese themselves sometimes use for Taiji: *laorenquan* (老人拳), or literally 'old folks Boxing' (though possibly that flaccid image will be offset by Keanu Reeves' *Man of Tai Chi* movie). In any case it's clear that the practice is getting ever more popular.

As the Boomers age, they'll flock in their vast hordes, like pre-Columbian bison, to the Taiji parlors of the world. But little of what they'll learn has anything to do with the real essentials of original Taiji. Unless somebody takes action to set the record straight, it's going to become (it already *has* become?) just another folk dance. That somebody may have to be me, and the straightened record is this book. Right out of the gate, I want to emphasize the two things this book is *not*. This book is not a re-cloning of the well-honed and well-known chestnuts of traditional Chinese martial arts philosophy. Nor is it a primer on the mechanics of any one particular style or brand of Taiji. There are already loads of books out there on Taiji theory and mechanics.

Taiji *theory* books will walk you through the ancient literature and the high classical concepts, for the most part endlessly re-parroting the same austere profundities over and again. Undeniably, as a Taiji student, you should learn that stuff down to the ground, or you'll be crippled. It's just not my thing to spoon feed you that when so much material on it is already out there. Taiji *mechanics* books are unavoidably style-specific, crammed with endless photos of a given famous master doing his thing, each pic annotated with solid-rock boring specifications for your body, arms, legs, head, hands, feet … (where to put what when).

Both types of books have tremendous value, but another of those isn't needed. As I hinted in the opening above, most Taiji books tend to be on the dry side anyway. In fact, worse than dry – plain dull. It's odd when you think about it – an art which is supposed to be all about *flow* and *freedom* and *ecstatic immersion in nature's great Way* has produced so many authors and teachers who seem so stuffy, uptight, airless, lifeless, boring, prim, and pious about the whole thing. Though Taiji is indisputably a profound and mysterious art – something truly unprecedented in the whole litany of human accomplishment, it doesn't have to be whispered about prayerfully as though we're in church. The first step on the Taiji road is to loosen up a little. Nature's great Way – the Dao - may be cruel, but it's also whimsical. So this book is differently toned than most. I'm going to give you my personal, intuitive, anecdotal and experiential view of Taiji in my straight-forward style.

You will need to practice some type of Taiji form (series of linked postures) to get anything out of this book. It's like a book on trampolining – it won't do you much good if you have no access to a trampoline. Any Taiji form you may have learned, regardless of style, can be a perfectly good workbench for you as you step through the ideas presented here. Just trim to suit (either your form to my ideas or vice-versa).

And if you don't yet know a Taiji form? Then you'd better learn one! Just kidding… no hurry. You *will* ultimately want to learn one, to get much from this book. But take your time choosing a style and teacher. Digest the ideas and concepts here at your own pace. Even though I don't much get into style wars, nor do I rank-order the specific options out there, still you may find my general ideas useful in choosing the best practice mode for your goals.

The ideas I lay out here are Taiji universals. They're generic Brand X, applicable to any and all styles that attempt to follow the Taiji classic writings. In fact, this book is essentially just a collection of footnotes to those. As I said, I've tried to avoid full-on engagement in the style wars. When I do occasionally need to cite some specific aspect of Taiji, such as an example of a posture or movement, I'll haul up my favorite lab rat, the 37-move sequence synthesized by Professor Zheng Manqing around the mid-20th century (ZMQ37 hereafter). But that's just a convenience that I use now and again, for concrete exposition. You should view my mentions of ZMQ37 as you would any set of numbers used in a math textbook for a proof or example, but always with the phrase: "…without loss of generality".

Though I may seem chauvinistic at times, I feel that as long as a given style embodies the Taiji classic writings, it's all good. As of last check, the Wiki article *'List of tai chi chuan forms'* contained 86 unique entries for empty-hand forms alone, not counting weapons. As long as they all follow the Taiji classic writings, any one of those is as good as any other. I say that, yet I know that some readers will feel that I'm parochial, biased, and narrow-minded about the ZMQ37 style. I'd answer both yes and no. Yes, I am definitely parochial, biased and narrow-minded - but about radical energy-centric Taiji *overall*, as a truly unique and amazing human endeavor, not strictly about the ZMQ37 Taiji style *per se*.

I've actually dug deep and dirty trying to find something *better* than the ZMQ37 style for radical energy ignition. I've drilled into many other Taiji styles and schools, and more broadly into other martial arts and meditation methods and masters. I've found some spectacular and astonishing training out there. But at the end of the day, nothing holds a candle to the profoundly ecstatic *pleasure* deriving from the deep and delicate mindset of the ZMQ37 system (and any other system that scrupulously follows the Taiji classic writings) - *'soft wind, fine rain'*.

Once you've really soaked yourself in the relaxed Taiji energy, you can probably forget about *any* particular method, theory, practice, or style and be free. That's where this book aims to take you. The Daoist philosopher Zhuangzi said it first and best:

> *When the springs dry up and the fish are left stranded on the ground, they spew each other with moisture and wet each other down with spit - but it would be much better if they could forget each other in the rivers and lakes. Instead of praising Yao and condemning Chieh, it would be better to forget both of them and transform yourself with the Way.*

Or, in a more contemporary formulation, Deng Xiaoping also pretty well nailed it:

不管黑猫白猫, 能捉老鼠就是好猫

Doesn't matter if the cat's black or white, as long as it catches mice it's good.

But hey – I know what you really want. You want *drills*, right? Either psycho-visual stuff (like the gold-clad waterwheel maiden thing), or better - something *physical*. As long as it's specific, feels formulaic, something that feels *solid*. I understand. I really do. OK, here's one for you:

1.   Close your eyes
2.   Tap your heels together three times
3.   Think to yourself: 'There's no place like home'

Those *specifics* feel good, right? But this isn't a book of drills and exercises. I know that most travelers on the Way are constantly seeking new movements, forms, and postures as a boost to the next level. Amazon is littered with the corpses of martial arts books that are skewered by reviewers scorning them as offering *'no take-home methods here'*, *'nothing usable in my training'*, *'absolutely no specifics provided'*, etc. I laugh to remember that a few Amazon.com reviewers of my previous book (*Let Every Breath: Secrets of the Russian Breath Masters*, with Vladimir Vasiliev) after reading the dozens of step-by-step, minutely specified, fully illustrated *physical* drills in that book, complained: *not enough information, glorified pamphlet, sold the buyer short, only half the story,* and so on. I'd bet a free copy of this book that not one of those critics could correctly perform even the first basic exercise we covered: the slow pushup - one minute down, one minute back up - with perfect form and proper breathing. But instead of working deeper with the fundamentals explained in the other parts of the book, they wanted *more drills.*

Let's get clear: there are no physical drills or elaborate meditation sequences or anything of that ilk in this book. Qigong drills and other energy cultivation sets are widely available on DVDs, YouTube clips, books, websites, and any community center free class. Further, every weekend of the year, in every major city, some big name internal arts teacher is teaching a seminar that'll pack you to the gills with drills. But you don't need another way to wave your hands or stamp your feet.

Rather than 'practice *drills*', I call this a book of 'practice *ideas*'. This book is about *mindset*. If you don't understand the underlying conceptual approach to radical energetic practice, you won't reach the internal energy ecstasy no matter how many drills you rack up. Conversely, if you understand the energetic foundations of Taiji, *everything you do all day long* will qualify as authentic 24K uncut Taiji practice, as profound as anything in the Taiji classic writings.

I'm here to cure you of drill mania. This is a book of ideas that will give you *knowledge* and *confidence* in the unique vision of classic Taiji. With those two attributes, you can create any number of drills for yourself. But though I call them *ideas* rather than *drills*, they're as specific as they need to be. They're just right. If I got any more specific, this would turn into a blathering personal memoir. If less specific, it would be desiccated philosophy. These *practice ideas* will deliver palpable energy for you. If you can see that they aren't exactly drills in your expected sense, yet treat them with the dedicated disciplined seriousness that you would accord to a 'real' drill (something elaborately psycho-visual or physical) you'll be amazed that such seemingly simple stuff yields such a rich harvest.

The ideas in this book are way more powerful for generating and amplifying your internal power than any physical drill – except the form itself, correctly executed. The Taiji form has a built-in organic brilliance that no repetitive, formulaic drill could ever match. Not only do you need nothing else for internal power training, the constant drill chase will actually slow down your progress. Drills for other athletic purposes are fine. But the endless quest for that next, better internal power method is just keeping you bound in the shallows. *Let the form be your drill.* For internal energy work, you don't even need things like *shenfa*, the loosening and stretching exercises sometimes tacked on to the Taiji curriculum. All are distractions from the main idea.

Taiji trains you to *use your mind to convey spirit energy from your feet to your hands.* Taiji has additional effects and benefits, but that sentence rolls up the *defining feature* of radical energy-centric Taiji. The result should be a seamless unblocked torrent of effective spirit energy issued instantaneously on command. Since that's the goal, I don't care much about performance aesthetics or physical/structural trivia. There's nothing new about this concept. It's the central tenet of the Taiji classic writings. But we haven't been taking it seriously enough. We are distracted by external and superficial stuff, such as the aesthetics of form theatrics.

Consider a live electric wire. As long as the current at both ends is balanced correctly, and the wire is made of a good conductive material, the juice is going to flow regardless of what *shape* that wire may happen to be bent or coiled into. If unshielded, that live wire will shock you wherever and however you touch it. So I look at the structural/postural/anatomical obsession that characterizes a lot of current Taiji teaching as something that doesn't matter. The one precondition of true Taiji is mindful relaxation. Any Taiji system that promotes relaxation will get you over.

People sometimes ask me why I fuss so much about relaxation: *What's the big deal? Why should that be the primary attribute?* They're right to question, because relaxation per se actually *doesn't* matter. Relaxation is a means, not an end. It's the way to access the cosmic energy – and that is an unbelievable, almost inhumanly powerful experience. But you won't get it for yourself until you understand and can demonstrate relaxation. By that I mean core relaxation, not surface looseness.

When it comes to energy, there are basically two topics: *cultivation* and *deployment*. Those correspond to the two main sections of this book: Chapter 3 (Form) and Chapter 4 (Push), respectively. Throughout the book, I'll have a lot more to say about the fundamentals of radical energy-centric Taiji. It may seem that I'm endlessly belaboring and repeating myself, or just splitting hairs, yet there's method to my repetitive madness. The book is structured in cycles; themes are introduced then revisited over and over, in greater detail or from another angle each time. I'm giving you ideas to optimize your practice and save you decades of groping in the dark.

Finally, my serving up pretty heavy and weird content (and all in my signature breezy tone) may get you wondering at some point: *Is this book for real?* Answer: *Yes, it is.* Everything in here is something you can experience personally with your body, mind, heart, and soul. And if the content of *this* book weirds you out, then I need to ask: *What do you think of the Taiji classic writings?* There's nothing here any stranger than what they served up. So if *this* book freaks you out, you'd have to conclude that those guys were seriously off their meds that day. This book is designed to water the desert of the real, remove a brick from the wall, and take you to a different space. Stick with me for a fun ride.

WHO?

When Edmond Halley, the discoverer of Halley's Comet, berated Isaac Newton for his work in astrology, the brilliant scientist replied, "Sir, I have studied the subject, you have not".

- Apocryphal

Yeah right, I'm Isaac Newton. But seriously, I've learned several styles of Taiji under a number of great masters over decades. My primary Taiji teacher is a supremely skilled Taiji master who drank directly from the last truly great wellspring. Additionally, I've done a lot of martial arts and physical training in addition to Taiji, including: Western boxing; Ashtanga yoga; Russian martial arts; Chinese Bagua, Xingyi, Yiquan, and Northern Shaolin; and dozens of Qigong and other Daoist internal cultivation systems; as well as Japanese weapons arts, and so on. But Taiji is the queen of the inner disciplines. Therefore in this work I unapologetically elevate it above all others. (That said, I will occasionally offer insights from some of the other practices I've worked, wherever they can shed useful light onto Taiji – or vice-versa.)

It isn't that I dislike the blood, sweat, and dirt of ordinary physical and combative disciplines. It's just that I have bigger fish to fry. From the first I heard and read about Professor Zheng Manqing (鄭曼青1902 – 1975), he struck me as an embodiment of the entire *point* of martial arts in the *first* place. That's the idea that somebody who appears weaker and smaller (or at whatever physical disadvantage) might conclusively mop the floor with a stronger and bigger opponent. That appealed to me on a practical level because I'm not especially strong, heavy, or physically gifted. I was seeking something that promised to *transcend* rather than *leverage* and *reinforce* all the usual human obsessions - size, weight, muscles,

14

speed, gender, killer attitude, and so on. Taiji seemed to offer an Owner's Manual for the enlightened body and mind, geared to realizing the Dao De Jing's famous theoretical point:

Nothing in the world is softer than water,
Yet nothing is better at overcoming the hard and strong.
This is because nothing can alter it.

That the soft conquers the hard
And the gentle overwhelms the aggressive
Is something that everybody knows
But none can accomplish.

Since then I've found that the material scene doesn't yield so easily to airy philosophy. But I'm still in love with the *idea* of Taiji. How cool would it be to demonstrate graphically that gentleness can prevail over the brutality of this world? I've always felt that an attainment like Prof. Zheng's was (at least symbolically) the best real-world expression of the comic book superhero *Silver Surfer's* warning to the human race:

From cradle to grave –
Your lives are rooted in senseless violence!
Since power is your god –
I'll show you power –
Such as you have never known!!
If ever you are to come of age –
You must be taught to reason!
You must be shown that force can never be the answer!

But philosophy aside, I've done plenty of sweaty, bloody, gritty physical martial arts training in my time, including wrestling; boxing, *san da / san shou* (before people in the USA even knew those words); lots of edged weapons training; not to mention exotic stuff like Russian Systema's underwater fight training, whip/stick/punch pain endurance regimen, mass attack survival work,

15

and much besides. As a result, though I'm certainly no Rambo, I have just enough background to be slightly dangerous, in a dinky kind of way. I'm like a cornered squirrel in your living room. You aren't *afraid* of it exactly, but you don't especially look forward to having to *deal* with it either. Speaking of four-legged friends, at a center for stray animal adoptions I once saw a wall poster listing the *Ten Commandments of Pet Ownership*, intended to teach newbie pet owners how to treat their fresh adoptees right. One struck me:

The 7th Commandment of Pet Ownership:
7. Remember before you hit me that I have teeth that could easily crush the bones of your hand but that I choose not to bite you.

That's how you should feel about me. Come to think of it though, that's how you should feel about *anybody.* Because even if your *helicopter arm bar* or *slingshot suplex* are absolutely *nonpareil,* a knife-wielding or crowbar-swinging assailant sneaking up from behind could still drop you cold.

I'm not a master of Taiji. If I'm honest I should say I'll never learn it. I'll be a beginner all my life. But I've been dunked into the cosmic ecstasy of the art and I'm willing to drop these bread crumbs on the path behind. All I've done is merely collate my own energy experiences against the huge repository of theory and practical guidance produced by the universally acknowledged masters and wizards of the art. Those works span eons, from the Yellow Emperor's time down to about Professor Zheng Manqing's mid-20th century writings. This book is no more than the compilation of personal practice against theory that any veteran Taiji student might produce – just a bit clearer, more comprehensive, less timid, and more entertaining than many modern treatments I've seen. Ecclesiastes has taught that there's nothing new under the sun, and that goes double or triple for Taiji. All we can do is endlessly re-package stuff, making it approachable again for a new time and a new audience.

WHY?

The defining purpose of Taiji as energy connection from feet to hands doesn't specifically answer the question: *why learn Taiji?* More broadly, why learn (or do) *anything*? Historically, there seem to be two main motivations for human action: pleasure and power.

The centrality of *pleasure* is obvious from the relentless human craving for the Big Three:

1.   *Wine*
2.   *Opposite (or Same) Gender*
3.   *Song*

As for *power*, well, what conclusion do *you* draw from the insane popularity of guns, and the endless pursuit of bigger, smarter bombs and nukes, and the fact that the arms trade (legal and black market) is the biggest business in the world? So, *pleasure* and *power* are the first two candidates for answering 'why'. When it comes to Taiji, I should tip my hat to common practice by also mentioning the prospect of improved *health*. Illness prevention and cure are usually cited as a prime if not *the* prime rationale for taking up Taiji (and since I've mentioned pleasure here, obviously good health is a kind of pleasure too). Thus we have three distinct candidates (pleasure, power, and health). Any or all of these could serve as the prime motivator of your Taiji practice. Which of these do I hold with? Let's step through the list, in reverse order.

HEALTH?

First up – *health*. There must be *something* to the idea of Taiji as a cure-all and supreme health maintenance method. After all, we have dramatic testimony from some of the greatest 20th century Taiji masters, such as Professor Zheng Manqing:

> *In my childhood I was weak and sickly and should have died forty years ago, but later I practiced Taiji, and my health improved. Now I am seventy, and my eyes and teeth are like a young man's. This I owe to Taiji.*

> *Based on my personal experience I believe that Taiji is superior to any health or recreational activity. As a young man, my health was terrible, really unspeakably terrible, and no medicine was able to cure me. However, after practicing Taiji, and without taking drugs or injections, I naturally improved day by day. I had contracted tuberculosis, which at that time was a very serious, very frightening disease, and I myself felt that my fate was sealed. I had already reached the stage where both Western and Chinese medicine had no effect. Practicing Taiji saved my life. Taiji truly has unexpected power.*

> *Later I concluded that Taiji was very beneficial and began to teach students. I discovered that students who practiced Taiji saw their stomach ailments and other internal disorders improve. If Taiji is practiced faithfully, cancer will never develop, and I have never seen a single case among my students.*

That's a very strong vote for Taiji as a cure-all and a health promotion practice. It's a voice I'd very much like to agree with. But from a skeptical Western perspective we don't really know for sure. Maybe some other form of activity or exercise, or just time passing, would have resulted in equal or better outcomes. The link between cause and presumed effect is always weak in these anecdotes. The

National Center for Complementary and Alternative Medicine (NCCAM) has this to say about Taiji and health:

> *Scientific research on the health benefits of tai chi is ongoing. Several studies have focused on the elderly, including tai chi's potential for preventing falls and improving cardiovascular fitness and overall well-being. A 2007 NCCAM-funded study on the immune response to varicella-zoster virus (the virus that causes shingles) suggested that tai chi may enhance the immune system and improve overall well-being in older adults. Tai chi has also been studied for improving functional capacity in breast cancer patients and quality of life in people with HIV infection. Studies have also looked at tai chi's possible benefits for a variety of other conditions, including cardiovascular disease, hypertension, and osteoarthritis. In 2008, a review of published research, also funded by NCCAM, found that tai chi reduced participants' blood pressure in 22 (of 26) studies. [But] in general, studies of tai chi have been small, or they have had design limitations that may limit their conclusions. The cumulative evidence suggests that additional research is warranted and needed before tai chi can be widely recommended as an effective therapy.*

To my ears that's not exactly a hearty ringing endorsement. I don't doubt that doing Taiji is superior to doing nothing at all. But most of these research studies don't consider the question of Taiji's presumptive marginal benefit over a baseline comparison to dog-walking or shuffleboard or anything else that just gets people moving gently every day for a reasonable chunk of time. It's possible the putative health benefits of Taiji are analogous to the claims for acupuncture and traditional Chinese medicine in general - intriguing but largely unproven.

With the current focus on "Evidence-Based Medicine", scientific skepticism has motivated creative research with stuff like "placebo acupuncture" (real acu-needles, inserted by correct method, into theoretically "wrong" or random body spots) systematically evaluated against real acupuncture and against no treatment at all. These kinds of studies tend to conclude that acupuncture is a very sophisticated form of placebo treatment. That isn't necessarily a bad thing, but in general, the whole area is extremely murky and in any case beyond the scope of my limited focus in this book. (However, you will occasionally catch me mining the abstruse classics of traditional Chinese medicine for the imaginative ideas and inspiring images and vocabulary they offer, wherever those can illuminate our Taiji practice.)

The factual track record of medical outcomes in the lives of the great masters is also mixed. If we assume that the primary function of Taiji is to cultivate and refine the internal power, then we might consider internal power masters from a variety of training venues other than Taiji. For example, Aikido founder Morihei Ueshiba (1883 – 1969) lived to a ripe old age and continued practicing, teaching, and farming during all that time. He died of stomach cancer at age 86. Not bad, and I guess people have to die no matter what, but definitely not a superhuman outcome. Sword master Yamaoka Tesshu (1836 - 1888), who was by all contemporary accounts an internal energy wizard, died in his fifties, also of stomach cancer. Professor Zheng Manqing died in his mid-seventies, though apparently that was an accidental poisoning. Even Yang Chengfu, one of the truly greatest of all time, didn't exactly live to a ripe old age. The record is muddy and mixed. It was a different time. Rationalizations are plentiful. But despite the varying ages of death, it must be said that the great masters stayed strong, tough, and active right up to their last breath.

Whatever the case, this book does not harp on the health benefits of the art, mainly because I don't know what they are. I'm not going to wave my hands over such an important topic. You'd need to crank out decades worth of meticulous, painstaking science to get at the real answer. This book deals only with my personal energetic experiences, which are available to anybody, as confirmed through the Taiji classic writings. For all I know, just walking your dog daily could keep you hale and hearty til your last breath. That may be just as good as any exotic yoga or martial arts regimen. If you have health concerns, consult your physician.

POWER?

The next candidate motivator of your Taiji practice is *power*. This is even trickier than health, for several reasons. First, Taiji as a combative system is, like most so-called self-defense training, almost irrelevant for practical use. That's because of what I call the *Goldilocks Attack Paradox*. According to the Goldilocks Attack Paradox, martial arts training may be fairly worthless for actual self-defense. It may be that most actual "situations" are either too trivial to really make much demand on your decades of hard training, or too intense to handle however you've trained.

On the milder end, when threatened you could run away, scream for help, hurl an ashtray, etc. On the really savage end of the curve, if syndicate drug lords dispatch a goon squad of DEA-trained Federales to kidnap, torture, and necklace you with a gasoline-soaked tire, it's questionable whether your unarmed combat skills, no matter how awesome, would suffice to extract you alive. So in the real world, most attack situations are liable to be either *too small* or *too big* to fit what you can do. The probability of facing a Goldilocks situation that's *just right* is vanishingly small. I suppose if you get into something with a belligerent drunk at a club your training might stand you in good stead - but you'll still be left with a nightmarish legal hangover.

No matter how far you take your Taiji (or any other) unarmed combative development, you can always be mowed down by a machine gun at close quarters. A knife will always be able to cut you. It's unlikely you'll ever achieve true invulnerability – what the Chinese call: 刀枪不入 - the legendary condition of un-cutability and un-stabability (if that's humanly possible at all). No matter how high and far your Taiji achievements may eventually go, a bowling ball dropped on your bare foot is always going to hurt like hell. So even though Taiji is translated as *Grand Ultimate Boxing*, I don't believe it can spark enough real-world power to justify a superhero fantasy. (But I will have more to say on fighting and self-defense later in the book, just because it's fun to talk about).

SURVIVAL SENSITIVITY?

You are a fair viol, and your sense the strings.

- Shakespeare (Pericles, Prince of Tyre)

I do believe that Taiji can enhance your *survival* power, which is not quite the same thing as *combative* power, by making you more sensitive to energy flow and dynamics in your environment. Of course, the energy from long-term Taiji practice is not the ordinary sort described by conventional physics - kinetics, heat, sound, etc. If it can be likened to anything physical, the energy of Taiji may be most closely analogized to electricity or hydraulics. I'll use those metaphors frequently throughout this book. The Taiji energy is not *any* of the physical forces of daily life. But somehow the practice of Taiji sensitizes you to those physical forms of energy, and to the energetic interplay all around you at every moment. And that can enhance your survivability.

When I'm on a plane, my body often registers impending physical movements of my seatmate(s). For example, I'll be dozing, eyes shut, with no physical contact with my adjacent seat-mate. Then I'll feel either a kinetic type of jolt (like a physical bump) or alternatively, I'll feel a rip-through electric type of shock (not painful) through a certain body part, typically leg, arm, hand, or neck. These will occur simultaneously with, or pre-figure slightly, my seatmate's corresponding physical movement. It isn't a visual cue, as my eyes are shut, nor is it aural. It's unconscious energy sensing. This works well on airplanes because they're fairly stable, apart from occasional turbulence. To check yourself, you need close seated proximity to others, but no physical contact or direct pressure. Buses can work, but movie theaters are better, because on a bus you may be jammed so closely that physical detection of your fellow passengers' movements is possible, or even unavoidable. You need a place where:

1. You are seated closely but not in actual contact.
2. The setting calls for physical restraint and quietude, but allows for occasional shifting or small arm motions.
3. You can close your eyes to avoid distractions. It's also good if there's ambient noise (as in a jet plane or movie theater) to mask overt aural cues.

This isn't something I've set out to do consciously. It just happens. To distinguish this natural phenomenon from Taiji's trained, quasi-combative 'listening energy' skill, I call this seatmate thing the MIRR (Mimicked Internal Reflective Receptor) effect. What you're really catching in the higher end of this (mostly unconscious) 'practice' is the spark of your seatmate's *neural intent* at its source. As soon as you feel it, glance (unobtrusively) sideways to confirm. The MIRR precedes the physical gesture by a half-beat or so. The MIRR is also co-located in your body with the relevant area in the source. For example, if s/he's about to move shift his/her right leg a little, you'll get the immediately prior MIRR in your own right leg.

Recently I was in a movie theater before the show started. I was at the far end of a row and my nearest neighbor was eight seats from me, down along the row. I was resting with eyes lightly shut, when I suddenly felt an electric jolt along my right arm, shoulder to fingers. It bumped me 'awake' so I shifted a look to the side and after the slightest pause, my nearest neighbor, the man eight seats away, lifted his right arm to adjust his carry bag. I knew it before it happened because my own energy system pre-emptively picked up the energetic signature of his intent. This kind of thing happens all the time.

The MIRR, while not a direct power source *per se,* can be leveraged to create a safer daily existence through enhanced sensitivity. It can also be integrated into any kind of martial art or combative training such as boxing or Jiu-Jitsu. This kind of attribute development for enhanced survivability is probably the best protection we can realistically hope for in a world full of napalm, Tasers, Patriot missiles, Claymore mines, Daisy Cutter bombs, and VX nerve gas – or plain old broken beer bottles and pool cues.

But you'd still like to ask: *is Taiji a fighting art or not*? I can't say it is. How could I, a man who hasn't worked the door in some tough club for a year (or even a day), a man who's never had a UFC cage fight (or even an undercard match at the local Indian gambling casino) possibly assert such a thing? I can't. But I will have a bit more to say about Taiji for self-defense in the chapter on Push Hands. I should note that Taiji can definitely make you *feel* a great deal more powerful, both internally and externally, as you amuse yourself tossing people around in Taiji practice sessions (once you've patted them down to ensure they aren't packing).

PLEASURE!

One good thing about music - when it hits, you feel no pain.

- Bob Marley

The most surprising and outstanding feature of Taiji is the payload of sheer *pleasure* it delivers. This is the one true enduring motivation for practicing the art. I've already noted the various pleasure paths humans can pursue, basically: sex, drugs, and rock 'n roll. But two out of three have serious downsides. They're all expensive in the long run. The longer you go on with them, the more expensive they get. And each involves external dependencies – a substance, another person, money, etc. Of course, merely living on earth as an ordinary human being implies a heap of addiction-like external dependencies on material stuff, such as food, clothing, and shelter. But there's no need to pour gas on the flames.

The absolute ecstasy of the internal power cultivated in correct Taiji practice is totally mind-shredding - far surpassing any legal or illegal meds on the market. So if you're going to get addicted to anything, make it Taiji, which, once you've learned it, demands no further material input. And though the learning curve is long, and the return-on-investment is seriously delayed, the pleasure of the internal energy, once you really get it sparked up compares favorably with … how can I phrase this delicately – the perennially highest-ranked human pleasure experience, often surpassing it. In fact, if you subtract all the hassles that come along with sex, I'd say Taiji energy, net-net, is probably the top feeling you can have in a human body. In other words, Taiji, done right, feels so good the Feds should make it illegal.

I'm sure there'd be a lot less depression, addiction, and aggression in the world if more people had the direct experience of their own

25

energetic super-structure. The ultimate motivation and main focus of this book is simply the pure pleasure of Taiji energetics. The internal energy is the point. Cultivate the energy via Taiji and see where it leads - possibly to health, maybe to power, probably to pleasure - maybe to all those or something else entirely. Maybe you'll become a great calligrapher or painter, like some of the ancient masters. But no matter how it grows out for you, the energy is the root of everything. The absolute comedy of the whole legal/illegal drug scene is that if you do Taiji correctly, you get a charge of pure internal energy dopamine that'll totally rock your soul better than any drug. But there are two practical problems with the Taiji path to drug-like ecstasy:

1.   *Nobody really believes in it.*
2.   *It's too hard.*

Let's take up point (1) *Nobody believes in it.* After all, how could it possibly be the case that just by practicing a daily knee-bending and arm flapping regimen you could awaken an energy that will totally blow your mind, body, heart and soul to the infinite cosmos and beyond? It's absurd on the face of it. Nonetheless, if you really understand it, if you really do it right, you suddenly jack in to an overwhelming energy and pure bliss that blows the doors off any substance the drug lords can crank out, whether from corporate research parks or deep-woods meth shacks. But you know humans... you can lead them to water, but. Even when people *do* begin to feel a little buzz – well, that's fine, but then to convince them that a dinky little hand or spine tingle can be amped up a billion times til you experience, as the Bhagavad Gita put it: *a thousand suns rising together in the sky*? That's like telling a country boy who's never seen the ocean that the substance of morning dewdrops on the leaves can mass into a tsunami that scrapes a city off the earth. But Taiji isn't a religion, so why the need to convince anybody of anything? In the beginning a kind of faith *is* required, to jump-start your motivation and persistent practice.

26

That brings us to point (2) *It's too hard.* This one I too can feel, up close and personal. It really *is* too hard. The physical practice is fairly simple to pick up, but it has to be learned and practiced precisely and people have trouble understanding that. I know, because I had trouble with the fundamentals at first also. Then, there's a bigger issue: it takes both *calendar* time (though if you're taught correctly not nearly the decades many teachers cite) and *clock* time, hours each day. You need that daily discipline.

So, even though Taiji is the ultimate pleasure drug, it's rather impractical as such. God knows no teenager would put up with a reputed mind blowing substance that takes bare minimum a few months (or years) of boring, awkward-looking *practice* to kick in, when you could just scarf a pill or snort a powder. If Taiji weren't so hard to practice correctly, it would bankrupt the psycho-pharmaceutical Goliaths, wipe out their Prozac and Effexor. It would also put the illegal drug pushers out of business, end all the wars, and choke off the whole human spitstorm right at the source. But what fun would *that* be? So, after all maybe it's good that Taiji is so fiendishly difficult, lest we should grow too fond of it.

Anyway, it will ultimately be up to you, not any teacher or expert, to decide why you pursue Taiji. Carlos Castaneda quoted his teacher Don Juan: *All paths are the same - they lead nowhere.* Meaning we're all going to die, and lose our physical body and everything else. All we can do is enjoy the scenery along the way. In this book I want to convince you that when you understand what Taiji really is, you'll be amazed and enthralled by the landscape this path cuts across. Then you'll be like Don Genaro in Castaneda's story of the eternal *Journey to Ixtlan,* where he says of his path:

> *There I travel, and the only worthwhile challenge for me is to traverse its full length. There I travel - looking, looking, breathlessly.*

27

CHAPTER 2:
THEORY & PRACTICE

THEORY

At age thirteen, I attended my first Taiji class - an early morning freebie at the local Y. I was dragged there by my junior high school Tae Kwan Do classmate. How he'd heard of Taiji back in those Dark Ages, and why he wanted to explore it, I never figured out. Of course, everybody there knew more than we did. For our sake, the teacher (martial arts author Robert W. Smith) began with a detailed review of the opening move, *Raise Hands*. This is common to most styles of Taiji. You slowly lift your arms to shoulder height and lower them again. He began talking us through it, and we raised our arms softly as instructed. Then, as we began to lower them, he said: *Imagine you're moving your arms downward through some slight gentle resistance, like water or cotton candy…* just then, I felt a tremendous rush of energy through both arms, like a jolt of (painless) electricity zapping across my skin and through my tissue.

I was amazed. I'd heard of the Chinese concept of internal energy or *qi* from the few books on Kung Fu available back then, but it hadn't occurred to me that *qi* could be a personally accessible thing. I'd assumed that *qi* was the exclusive province of the white-bearded masters in their mountain monasteries and secret caves. Turns out I was half-right, because total mastery of internal energy is found only among the very few truly great historical adepts. Even a slight functional command of internal energy takes decades of hard training. And yet, the immediate experience of its undeniable reality turned out to be instantly available to me, and, I assumed, to anybody. That's what I was amazed to discover.

31

After class I turned to my friend:

Me: *"Hey! Wasn't that incredible? Wasn't it just freaking amazing?"*
Classmate: *"Huh? Was what amazing?"*
Me: *"I mean the qi buzz, that electrical thing in our arms!"*
Classmate: *"What the hell are you talking about?"*

That's when it hit me that not everybody feels their *qi* immediately or in quite the same way. Some people may practice for years without having the least sensation. But no matter, from that day on I was hooked. I've done lots of other stuff over the ensuing four decades, but since that Saturday I've never missed even a single day of energy practice. William Blake nailed it: *Energy is eternal delight.*

PURE THEORETICS

Turns out, that electro-hydraulic arm rush not only wasn't the whole iceberg, it was barely the iceberg's tip. As I later learned, there's a mountain of well-pedigreed theory and speculation on the human body's mysterious energy workings. The theoretical substrate ranges from ancient classics such as the Chinese medical classic *Huangdi Neijing* (黃帝內經) of about 2,500 years ago to the modern textbooks used today in acupuncture training institutes. There's a ton of this stuff. And the theoretical picture that emerges from it is an absolute hairball of overwhelming complexity. Furthermore, you find a lot of Daoist internal energy cultivation theory, and spiritual vocabulary, bolted over the basic medical framework. It seems that only when you've digested all that are you qualified to tackle the trickle-down application to your martial arts practice and personal development.

I know something about the above from my background study (Daoist and medical theory books, in the original ancient Chinese), and from having intensively practiced a variety of Daoist meditation systems for a long time. I know about meridians and points and internal organ energy spirits and the inner pathways linking them all. But none of that theory is going to make much difference if you can't sense, guide, and cultivate the live energy directly within yourself. *If you can't feel it, you can't feed it.*

Don't be conned that somebody out there knows it all. No matter how many exotic words they toss around, nobody knows the final truth of human body energetics. Over time, sensitive people experience things, notice things in themselves, write up some notes, somebody else picks that up, puzzles over it, tweaks it, the beat goes on. That's what I've done here. Nobody has the final word. Often the greatest experts disagree on the most fundamental points.

For example, classical Chinese energy theory posits an important circulation of internal energy up the spine, through the head, and then descending down the front to rise in back again, forming the main vertical energy circle of the body. Yet even this most basic concept is disputed by reputable experts such as Dr. Zhi Chen Guo, who claims in his book *Body Space Medicine* that the primary direction of circulation is actually the *reverse* – it's *down* the spine, *up* the front. I'm not taking a position on this particular technical point. I'm merely asking you to understand that all this stuff is still up for grabs and nobody has a final monopoly on truth. Another interesting phenomenon along these lines is so-called *empirical acupoints*, the term for therapeutically effective places to needle the body, which can be found by expert palpitation – but which do not exist as such on the standard acupuncture charts. In other words, making it up - and making it *work* - as you go along.

I'm emphasizing this because we're still at the shallow end of this book. At some point, as the chapters roll on, you're going to hit an epistemological wall. Maybe not on this page, maybe not the next, but soon, and for the rest of the book. You're going to sit back and ask yourself: *How in hell can this guy claim to know this stuff?* That's understandable. After all, I don't cite scientific research papers, I don't point to URL's and web links, I don't directly quote my teacher, and I'm not the head of a big powerful Taiji organization, school, or lineage. So I have no good answer except: *I'm writing what I feel.* The whole book is based on my personal experience with the energy. It's what I've felt. But unlike most people, I really *trust* what I feel, not blindly but fiercely. I pursue any small interesting inkling like an overly-caffeinated pit bull. Eventually, I either confirm it as the manifestation in my own body-mind of something the old masters covered in the Taiji classic writings, or else I identify it as unproductive and toss it overboard. Everything I write about has been vetted through that process.

Of course, *trust me* is how every religious nut job justifies himself. But in the case of the practices I describe in this book, *you can verify it all on your own.* You just need to be taught what to try. Many of my students, some of them serious veterans of decades of martial arts training, have been amazed to finally experience for themselves pieces of what this book covers. But now for the first time I'm laying out the whole thing in one big feast. When you read one of my pointers, suspend disbelief long enough to check it out for yourself. Believe *lightly,* and take it for a road test. (The only issue is that in Taiji, sometimes that test drive could turn out to be 100,000+ miles because even correct teaching may take a long time to pay off. What can I say? Taiji is a tough field of study.) Anyway, though I'm not religious, I've always admired this beautiful description of Jesus' ministry:

> *For he taught them as one having authority, and not as the scribes.*

> - Matthew 7:29

No, I'm not comparing myself to Jesus. I'm not even comparing myself to John Lennon. But I admire the badass spirit of that line. That's the kind of kick-butt, reality-based attitude to which all authors and teachers, and their students, should aspire. So you can use this book as a random idea generator and then, as Siddhartha Gautama said: *Be a lamp to light your own way.* By far the best way to judge this book is not to look at me at all, but rather take a glance in your own mirror. Here's an infalliable guide to the quality of this book, self-checkable against your own reaction to it:

> *When a superior man hears of the Way,*
> *he immediately begins to embody it.*
> *When an average man hears of the Way,*
> *he half believes and half doubts.*
> *When a foolish man hears of the Way,*
> *he laughs at it long and loud.*
> *If he doesn't laugh at it, it can't be the true Way.*

> - Dao De Jing: 41

We've moved well beyond the ignorant Dark Ages of my Taiji beginnings. Now, most newbies would show up at a YMCA Qigong or Taiji class expecting to feel at least *something* right out of the starting gate, first hour of the first day. And typically they can, if the instructor introduces some classic workhorse drills, such as the 'palms-feel-doughiness' *qi* experience. In the 'feel-doughiness' *qi* drill, students are told to imagine gently compressing and expanding a rubbery soft ball between their hands. Almost everybody attempting this immediately feels some kind of tingly pressure between their hands. That's a very basic manifestation of the internal energy. The exercise per se isn't all that useful, so I won't make a big deal out of it in this book. Compared to the energy experiences induced by serious long-term Taiji practice, the dinky little palm-tingle sensations from this drill are as a dewdrop to a tsunami.

But that simple exercise illustrates my point: you don't need to know every meridian and channel, every point and cross-organ linkage chain, to get your juice on. So I'm going to take a machete to the overgrown weed patch of Taiji and internal energy theory, and cut it down to what actually matters.

WHAT ACTUALLY MATTERS

Mama may have,
Papa may have,
But God bless the child
That's got his own

- Billie Holiday

The *locations* of special energy areas, and the correlation of those abstract zones and points with specific body parts is one huge preoccupation of traditional internal energy theory. The other big theoretical thing is different *types* of internal energy.

ENERGY HOT SPOTS

First, I'll lay out the relatively few basic anatomical concepts/ structures you'll need from the Chinese medical canon and Daoist theory. There are hundreds of named acupuncture points in the human body, but you need fewer than a dozen to work your Taiji energetics. The significant areas are listed below. (I'm not sure you need to know even these, but it won't kill you to read it).

- **Feet** (湧泉 *yongquan*) Sometimes you'll need to focus awareness on the soles of the feet.
- **Perineum** (會陰 *huiyin*) Sometimes the energy will

seem to rise to, or concentrate, here.

- **Sacrum, coccyx to lower back** (尾閭 *weilu*, to 命門 *mingmen*) Sometimes the energy will seem to rise along here.
- **Mid-back** (靈台 *lingtai*) Key concentration point for the upward energy flow powering the arms.
- **Crown of head** (百會 *baihui*) Sometimes the energy will seem to concentrate or terminate here.
- **Heart** (膻中 *shanzhong*) Sometimes the energy will seem to concentrate here.
- **Inner wrist** (大陵 *daling*) Key concentration point for arm/hand projection.
- **Center of palms** (勞宮 *laogong*) Secondary extension point for hand projection.
- **Lower abdomen** (氣海 *qihai*, and 丹田 *dantian*) The energy will seem to concentrate or originate here.

(…and there's one additional absolutely crucial point that I'll cover separately, in due course.)

Many people are a bit too grabby, even anal-compulsive, about finding the perfect exact "locations" of these things. Myself, I'm not a big point fetishist. I'm not going to try to zero you in on the precise micrometer "location" of each of these, as though they were pinpoint physical spots in your body. They aren't physical. They are *emergent energy foci*. Emergent means you don't call them, they'll call you. As you begin to relax and settle into your Taiji form work, these points will begin to announce themselves naturally. As they do, you should take a mental snapshot of the sensation, and store that away. Some later processes will require a more pro-active mustering of your points. But in the beginning give them some breathing room, let them raise their hands before you call on them. Key thing for now is: don't overlook the forest for the trees. That stuff above is a list of the *trees*. The *forest* is your entire body-mind complex. When you really get your juice on, the energy will permeate you entirely, without any differentiation, instantly available anywhere - from toenail to eyebrow and beyond. *That state of total permeation is the real goal.* Then you can forget about any particular point or local area.

All that said, here are a few very rough guidelines of where to locate some of the points listed above. If you really think you need it, you can find more fetishistic micromanagement guidelines anywhere on the web, just search it.

- *yongquan* – along the centerline of foot sole, bit frontward of middle
- *huiyin* – between anus and genitals
- *weilu* – coccyx
- *mingmen* – lower back, bit above sacrum, along spine
- *lingtai* – mid/upper-back, along spine just below or between bottom edges of shoulder blades
- *baihui* – crown of head
- *shanzhong* – between eyebrows
- *daling* – center line of inner wrist just below base of palm
- *laogong* – center of palm
- *qihai* – lower abdomen
- *dantian* – within lower abdomen, about 2 inches below naval, 3 inches inward

ENERGETIC TYPOLOGY

The best workaday parsing of the energy types and states that matter for real-world training was created by internal grandmaster Guo Yunshen (郭雲深 1829 – 1898). The original text of Master Guo's concise and logical theoretical framework is published on the web, just enter his name into any Chinese search site. He covered everything we regular people (as opposed to you Daoist saints out there) really need to know on this topic. I advise, in the interest of time and sanity, that you limit your foundation of internal energy theory to pretty much what Guo has provided. In case you don't read semi-classical Chinese well enough, I'll summarize the gist of it here. This will serve as my starting energy taxonomy for the book. With this as a baseline, I'll be adding my own augmentations and annotations, based on stuff experienced in my own intensive Taiji practice.

Now another little disclaimer. I understand that some of you out there consider yourselves Daoist warrior adepts or saints or scholar monks or whatever. You guys aren't going to take such a simple-minded, and, in your eyes, plain *wrong* taxonomy lying down. You're going to want to nitpick and henpeck the thing to death, saying: *no way, this word isn't concept X, as you've written, it's concept Y* or *the whole framework is missing critical element Z,* and so on.

My advice is, give it a rest. This taxonomy is practical and functional. Of course, I'm cutting up a natural zone here, a spectrum where there are no posted boundaries. But I can make "good enough" functional distinctions – categories like 'day' and 'night', that have no absolute borderline but which do some work for us. If you just roll with the practices in the book, each of the elements will come to life in its own time and style. It's true that especially with the highest-end energies and states, everything gets a little fuzzy, very psycho-spiritual. There's a lot of wiggle room for religious discussion in that zone. And after all, Daoism *is* a religion. Problem is, whatever corrections *you* know are mandatory, the *other* guy next block over (who's *also* figured out the meaning of life) would laugh off the stage. So for now, I'd advise that you just accept the old saying: *two of a trade never agree.* Leave it at that for now. Roll with the practical stuff I'll be offering, take what you need, and leave the rest.

For the rest of you, if you aren't a scholarly researcher, once you're familiar with my skeletal outline you can leave it at that. To get your juice on, you don't need many more words and concepts. *Practice* is the thing, and that's the focus of this book. Obsessing over the details of the theoretical framework risks missing the moon while fussing over the finger. You need just enough theory so that when you spontaneously begin to feel the next energetic experience you can say to yourself: "Ah, so *that's* what they meant!" – and then move on.

Many energy types and states are said to exist. A partial list of the broadest categories would include:

- **jing** (精) Natural function of biological and sexual substances
- **qi** (气) Breath-linked, quasi-electrical current powering all life
- **shen** (神) Intangible spirit of mind-emanation, intent and attention
- **xu** (虚) Unification with the Dao, formless omnipresence

That's pure Daoism in its 'alchemical' (body substance transformation) mode. Complicating matters is the *martial arts overlay* that crosscuts these, and the numerous internal power subtypes conjectured to exist within each of these major categories. So before I continue with my minimal summary of master Guo's theoretical treatise, I need to clarify a point of terminology. Confusingly, there are two different Chinese characters popping up in this discussion that sound similar and are sometimes transliterated identically in the Pinyin system. They are, first, *jing* (精) which is a medical term referring to biological secretions or sexual essence (e.g. semen and sperm in the male), and which also sometimes occurs in discussion of the nervous system or psychological phenomena. This is the first line in the list above. There's also a similar-sounding but distinct word, *jing* (勁) that has variant pronunciation *jin*. That second one is a cover term for functional energies in the body, and is often applied to martial arts combative energies. Try not to mix them up.

In their martial arts modality, the four energy types or states listed above are said to engender various kinds of functional powers, which are considered to be (the second type of) *jing* (勁) which in turn is an umbrella category that's subtyped into combative gestures such as pushing, drilling, splitting, sticking, and many others. Viewed abstractly, these *jing* powers range from the lowest 'obvious energy' *mingjing* (明勁), through 'secret energy' *anjing* (暗勁), and culminate with the supreme 'mysterious energy' (化勁). In traditional philosophy, these three *jing* powers are often said to correspond to the first three lines of energy states listed above, the so-called 'Three Treasures' of Daoism: *jing-qi-shen* respectively. The common association is to equate *mingjing* (obvious energy) with ordinary physical kinetics, and then assume that any kind of *qi* experience (such as described in the previous section above) must be the subsequent stage, that of *anjing* (secret energy).

But in my experience, *mingjing* corresponds to the electrical/ hydraulic experience of *qi*. So my personal experience with these states has led me to posit the following correlation, with the matching bumped up by one position in the list:

- *mingjing* (obvious energy: electro/hydraulic sharp resonance experience) => *qi*
- *anjing* (secret energy: soft resonance experience) => *shen*
- *huajing* (mysterious energy: instantaneous identification with the universe) => *xu*

Mingjing is experienced as an electric-feeling flow in a body area, or localized pulsations of sparky/spike-y energy. But the *mingjing* represents a *range*. It's a spectrum, not a point. At the lowest end of the *mingjing* range are the little tinglings, heat flashes, and skin-brushing type of energy sensations that any beginner will feel from even five minutes or so of Qigong instruction. These first *mingjing* sensations are brushes, rushes, and tingles of energy that most people can feel easily, even without any training, for example, when startled or when very happy or intensely afraid. Any powerful emotional experience can bring them on. Qigong practice intensifies awareness of these simple energy sensations. This lowest form of the scattered, superficial *qi* I will call the BRUTE (Brushes-RUshes-Tingles-Energy) experience level. That's what happened in my first Taiji class described above. The BRUTE sensations should probably be thought of as straddling the border between the biological substrate of *jing* (the bio-secretion kind) and *qi*.

The next higher experience of the *mingjing* is a sunburst or starburst of electrical-thermal-hydraulic (feeling) radiation, seemingly centered from the *qihai* in the abdomen, and then further concentrated in the *dantian*, the smaller point within the lower abdomen. This is sometimes the result of long-term sedentary meditation, but can be achieved through Taiji form work just as well. The *mingjing* energy concentrates in the abdominal area, but the abdomen is also a way station on the body's most important energy route. The continuous vertical loop of energy up the spine, through the head, and down through the neck, chest, and belly is called the *microcosmic orbit* (小周天 *xiaozhoutian*). This circulation of energy runs all the time in all living people. With Taiji or Daoist meditation, you can intensify the microcosmic current to the point that it evokes things you'll never actually feel (or not for long) but these weird images just spring to mind: *sluice flow at Hoover dam… internal plutonium bomb… radioactive beehive.* It's very obvious. You can't mistake or overlook it unless you've never really turned up the volume.

So the *mingjing* can be experienced as the BRUTE sensations, and also as the power running through the microcosmic orbit. Now let's take a quick break from the theoretical discussion to play with yet a third manifestation of the *mingjing*.

THE EDWARDIAN FOP POWER CHECK

In addition to what we've already discussed, the *mingjing* can be experienced as continuous vibrations or waves. Here's an exercise that gives you an immediate baby lick of the *mingjing* energy (the concentrated or functional *qi*) in that guise. In acknowledgement of the distinctive physical gesture involved, I call this the *Edwardian Fop Power Check*. It's a small exercise that'll give you a taste of bigger things to come.

Set your forearm upright on a table of comfortable height, as though you were going to arm-wrestle. Keeping your forearm straight up at 90 degrees to the table, stretch your fingers upright and point to the ceiling, so that your whole arm from elbow to fingertips is straight, kind of like a karate-chop pose. Relax as much as possible with this configuration. Now, bend back your hand at the wrist, maintaining your upright forearm. Imagine you are reaching back only your hand toward the rear wall. Make a definite movement of it without straining too much physically.

Now gently, relaxing as much as possible while still keeping the same extended hand shape and upright forearm, bring your hand slowly forward, through the initial straight up phase and further forward, until its almost 90 degrees bent forward at the wrist. As you do so, imagine your fingertips are gently extending upward, even brushing the ceiling as you cross over. If you can relax enough, yet keep the idea of extending and projecting your fingers (not collapsing or slumping), after a few repetitions you'll feel a kind of chunky power wave, extending in pulses from the base of your forearm on the table up through the fingertips. Move slowly, take it easy, don't rush it.

Now reverse it back the way you came, and you'll again feel the vibrations in the other direction too. That's your first taste of the surging or wave form of the *mingjing*. It's a very trivial, very babyish degree of the energy that will later manifest as the full-body internal power.

43

Figure 1 The Edwardian Fop Power Check, a very simple way to experience a crude and limited form of *mingjing* energy.

Your first reaction (once you can feel it at all) will be to dismiss this as some kind of natural muscle effect, merely due to the mechanics and kinetics of the move. That's wrong. Later you'll understand that this same effect can be felt with the entire body (rather than merely the forearm) as the axis. The more sensitive reader will pose a deeper challenge – that this kind of vibration or pulsing must be due to an (undesirable) energy blockage. That's basically correct. At this early stage, the energy is being forced out along a partially blocked channel with a narrowed outlet, an outlet narrowed by *physical tension*. The tension in this case is bunched in your wrist. That's a local example of the problem that Taiji was created to fix – *overall body tension*. Nevertheless, what you just felt is the internal energy of *mingjing*. As you learn to relax more and more, the sharpness of the waves will decrease and their rate will slow. The power will manifest differently. For now though, this exercise is a small-scale local introduction to the '*yang* resonance' or the first of the various wave phenomena covered in the next chapter. It helps convince some people that there's something going on here.

So, we've seen that the *mingjing* manifestation of the *qi* level of energy can be experienced in a number of ways. It can be felt via Qigong, via meditation, and via the Edwardian Fop check, respectively (although there are many other routes to all three of these low-level manifestations). Here's that summary again:

- *mingjing* as: the BRUTE sensations anywhere in the body (often near the skin)
- *mingjing* as: a continuous flow, looped through hot spots in the microcosmic orbit
- *mingjing* as: a wave of pulsing energy though one or more joints

Some people would classify the first two lines as pure *qi* manifestations, and reserve the term *mingjing* for the bottom line, the more functional wave energy alone. But to me they're all points in the *mingjing* obvious energy spectrum. They are all manifested forms of the body's latent *qi* energy which is always present whether you feel it (as *mingjing*) or not, and they can all coalesce into higher forms of *jing* which I'll cover in the next section, Practice.

Now, what's the *anjing* secret energy? That's a horse of another color and even harder to verbalize. It's a much quieter, more subtle, and yet far deeper feeling experience. It's a soft resonance. The energy pulses inside your body as multiple, thick layers of some hard-yet-soft element. It's not the baby bubbling-well type of mini-pulses you may sometimes feel at any energy hotspot in the BRUTE stage of *mingjing*. These are long, slow and seismic-feeling. You feel your tissues are changed into something like a police baton's rubber - incredibly hard and yet with some 'give'. And in fact, secret energy is correlated in the classical Chinese texts with changing the sinews (this doesn't mean grab your *Gray's Anatomy* and start memorizing the muscle and tendon structure of the human body. We aren't getting physical in this book, remember? It merely refers to a comprehensive energetic process).

I'm mainly interested in the actual *feeling* of it, the personal experience. It's soft and slow, also silky and strong. This is a broader feeling than the microcosmic orbit. At the lower end of the *anjing* mode, the energy permeates and pulses continuously from the bottom of the feet to the top of the head. At the higher end, instead of being experienced as distinct parts, all your limbs and joints and tissues are experienced as a single chunk of unified substance. Instead of the hydraulic/electrical/flow type of sparky-current feeling of the obvious energy, this is a feeling of almost uniform static intensity like a truck tire at maximum pressure - super hard but with a slight wave of elasticity.

The *mingjing* obvious energy pulsations are like the large waves which crest and actually *break* on the shore, but the *anjing* secret energy is like the huge ocean swells far out at sea, which don't break but just *roll* - long, deep, and slow. It's an incredible, unearthly feeling – a very different kind of wave experience than the *mingjing* shocker type of vibrations. And that's only the lower-end experience of *anjing*. The higher-end experience of the *anjing* is a mind-blowing state of absolute permeation, which I'll cover in detail in the next section. The *mingjing* obvious energy is fundamentally experienced as *hydraulic* or *electric*, while the *anjing* secret energy in motion is more *seismic* somehow, and in stasis more a *pneumatic* feeling. I will zoom-in to discuss the different energy qualities and strata in greater detail in the next section (Practice), and also correlate their various sub-categories with the classical *yin-yang* concept (two powers philosophy of ancient China).

Finally, we arrive at the *huajing* or mysterious energy, emerging from the state of emptiness (*xu*). That's even harder to talk about. The state of *xu* is a loss of body differentiation altogether. Your body merges with its environment completely. But the ability to *use* the *huajing* that emerges from this state depends on lots of practical experience. You don't get magic omnipotence just from understanding the theory or even achieving the state itself. And even if you get it a little, or make it work sometimes, you've only caught the tiger's tail because it's infinite. I'll have more to say about the functional distinctions of the applied energies in the chapter Push.

Confused yet? I fully get that the words I'm using so far don't do anything for your concrete training progress. And I haven't said much about Taiji in relation to all this yet. There's more specific material in later sections and chapters. But this discussion of basic theory gives us the words to begin to talk about all this. All you need to believe for now is that there may be something here worth working toward - even if blindly at first. The key point is that for Taiji practice you need only the most elementary subset of the acupuncture school theoretics.

Here is our first summary of the types of energy experience covered so far:

Summary Table of Traditional Terms

Level	Functional Category	Energetic Experience
精 *jing*	*systemic*	Chemical: biological, sexual, neural.

气 *qi*	obvious *mingjing*	Electric - sparky, spiky, electric, hydraulic, concentrated:
		
		   i. BRUTE scattered
		
		   ii. microcosmic orbit
		
		   iii. Power waves

神 *shen*	secret *anjing*	Pneumatic - seismic, subtle, soft:
		
		   i. Seismic long waves
		
		   ii. Unitary substance permeation

虚 *xu*	mysterious *huajing*	Absolute non-differentiation

I'll be adding more meat to this skeleton in later sections and in the following chapter. But apart from the skeletal set of theoretical terms listed above, for the remainder of this book I'm mostly going to use specific descriptions and more concrete vocabulary. I'll try to describe energy effects in terms of their mobility, intensity, location, and so on.

PRACTICE

Looking for your light,
I went out:
it was like the sudden dawn
of a million million suns,
a ganglion of lightnings
for my wonder.
O Lord of Caves,
if you are light,
there can be no metaphor.

- Allama Prabhu

THE ENERGETIC EXPERIENCE

First, let's be careful not to throw out the baby with the bath. I mostly avoid the traditional terminology and try not to get quicksanded in the full theoretical jungle. But that doesn't mean I'm going to shred the internal energy thing down into *physical* concepts. That kind of revisionism is popular these days. A lot of teachers and authors seem uncomfortable with the traditional foundation of internal arts in the spooky energies laid out by Guo Yunshen and traditional Daoism. There's a current trend to redefine internal power effects as something anatomically rigorous and structurally correct. It's becoming a matter of mechanical muscular-skeletal alignment engineering. You'll be taught to seek just that correct angle of cant in your *acetabulum* socket, just the precise degree of physiologically perfect pressure on your *iliopsoas* and presto - you're good. That kind of naïve materialist reductionism leads into a dead-end. The old masters said what they meant and meant what they said. People are easily dazzled by externalities such as the exotic spectacle of the Taiji form theatrics, or the martial art techniques they imagine are coded within it. That kind of superficial focus is misguided and actually tragic, when it leads to a distraction from the unique jewel that is the true Taiji.

Chronicler Howard Pyle re-tells the story, from the Arthurian cycle, of how the young King mistook the relative worth of his new sword vs. its scabbard:

> *Now as they rode thus through the forest together, Merlin said to the King: "Lord, which wouldst thou rather have, Excalibur, or the sheath that holds him?" To which King Arthur replied, "Ten thousand times would I rather have Excalibur than his sheath." "In that thou art wrong, my Lord," said Merlin, "for let me tell thee, that though Excalibur is of so great a temper that he may cut in twain either a feather or a bar of iron, yet is his sheath of such a sort that he who wears it can suffer no wound in battle, neither may he lose a single drop of blood."*

The workaday sheath, not the gleaming sword, was the priceless thing. That's what it is with Taiji's true substance vs. its visible postures and techniques. People love to focus on overt movements, physical structure, and body mechanics but those things are not the art. Isn't it sad that many Western students and teachers of Taiji have given up on the essence of the art and turned into structure geeks and posture nazis? They're firm believers in bones, muscles, tendons, and ligaments as the source of Taiji power. (But I'm no better, right? I'm a *juice* nazi…)

The way some people interpret Taiji in physical terms reminds me of the foolish man who saw a chess tournament. He fell in love with the solemn atmosphere, the fierce concentration of the bearded Russian players slamming their time clocks, and the exotic shapes of the game pieces. But when somebody explained the game itself to him, he responded: *My god, all the different moves for every piece… strategies, openings, endgames … Sicilian Defense and castled kings…*

it's all too much for me. Can't handle that. But I adore these game pieces, knight, bishop, rook, queen ... Hey, let's use this chess set to play checkers!

You can do whatever you want – but it isn't Taiji. Nature's true Way is beyond the physical. *The real purpose and result of Taiji have as much to do with human anatomy, physical structure, and body mechanics as the location and trajectory of the full moon have to do with the metacarpophalangeal, interphalangeal, and pisiform joints and ligaments of the hand that points it out in the night sky.* The true situation is exactly the opposite of what the mechanically-minded assume. That is, instead of needing to create the perfect alignment within your body to attract the higher energies, the *energies sculpt your body to suit themselves.* The alignment doesn't create the energy - *the energy creates the alignment.*

Of course, you *could* try to interpret Taiji as a mechanical system of torque and leverage and momentum and so on. But why bother? It's a completely meaningless discussion. Don't be like the imposter pauper boy in Mark Twain's story, who was found cracking walnuts with the Great Seal of England – mis-using something in a way far removed from its highest intended purpose. Why use a horse to pull a car (unless you've got no gas in the tank)?

More than anything, Taiji is an *idea* – a really radical idea. Taiji, at the bone, is no more than a few dozen lines of Wang Zongyue's text in the Taiji classic writings. As long as you focus on any aspect of the physical - even if it's to obsess over the physical aspects of relaxation itself - you'll have no idea just how radical Taiji really is and how deep the rabbit hole goes. To think otherwise, to try to understand this radical art as movements, techniques, anatomy or any kind of physical principle is like assuming there are little shrunken people inside your TV set, singing and dancing and acting for you. Maybe they sleep when you turn off the set? It just isn't so. Though it seems to explain the facts, it's completely off-base and totally irrelevant. The idea that the sun circles the earth

51

might, for some purposes, be an adequate assumption. Farming was carried on with that understanding for millennia. But for going to the moon, that framework needs to be, not tweaked, but entirely tossed out.

To do Taiji under the assumption that it is a mechanical system (sure, one of sublime subtleness, delicacy, sensitivity etc.) is to completely miss the point and no amount of tweaking or rewording of this mistake will salvage it. Of course, it can be done as a physical practice - you can have a little fun, and stretch your joints a bit. You *can* practice Taiji under this totally wrong idea - just as you can use a USB flash memory stick to stir a cocktail - but it isn't the point at all. The test of a correct Taiji method is not whether it enhances and displays your physical torque or leverage or momentum, whether it's large or small 'frame', or how high or low the postures are, but rather the following checkpoints:

> *Does it foster the total elimination of all physical tension whatsoever, consistent with the requirement to remain upright?*
>
> *Does it promote the absolute permeation and projection of relaxed aware mind into every single cell of the body?*
>
> *Does it shun attention to itself as a theatrical display?*

These things are the main criteria for the "physical" part of the art. *The visible and physical part of the art is not the art.* That's just a finger pointing to the moon. The moon is the *energy itself*, which first seeps in and then roars up like a mighty wave when you've cleared yourself out for it. For now, before you've got your juice turned on, the 'moon' is the *idea* of the energy, which should be your polestar - no matter how tempting it is to slip back into a mechanical mindset. And beware, because the physicality wolf often sneaks back over the fence in sheep drag. For example, I've seen Taiji writings that say things such as:

It is totally wrong to move using the arm muscles … Don't ever do that.

So far so good, right? Sounds like a properly non-physical emphasis. The writer continues:

Instead you must engage the core abdomen and back muscles, only then is it really internal practice…

Awk! There it is again. All this talk of 'core muscles' or any talk of which muscles to use and how, that's not the game of true Taiji at all. Forget all that stuff. It's a bottomless pit of body obsession. I'm not posing a dichotomy here between mechanically structured Taiji vs. some kind of airy-fairy, roll-your-own, free-form, flower-child *dance* Taiji. That's a false dichotomy. I am merely rejecting the current *obsession* with physical structure as the be-all-end-all of Taiji practice. The real energy-centric Taiji method is an absolutely specific mode of practice. It's quite rigorous. In fact, it's a crucible. You start with a firm foundation of basic classical posture practice. Yes, those rudiments are physical. But with that once in place, the rest of the work and the results are purely energetic.

The ongoing attempt to reduce Taiji to this or that joint section, or tissue type, or large or small muscles or some kind of structural torque is misguided. It's all based on the same fundamentally mistaken mechanical assumption. There *are* a few physical foundation points for beginners, simple things like keeping your body upright. But to fuss obsessively with that anatomical and postural stuff is to take the finger for the moon. It's as if you went for pilot flight training and they gave you a six-month course on how to fasten your seatbelt in the aesthetically optimal way, or how to sit just so in the pilot's chair (so your butt looks cute from behind). That's not doing what you came in the door for.

I've made the point repeatedly. I realize I've totally beaten this horse to death and stomped its carcass into hamburger. But getting you to renounce the physical is the main purpose of this book. Deprogramming your mind, body and soul away from their decades of physical conditioning (engendered by all the hard knocks of this material plane) is a taller order than you may now appreciate.

THE ARC

曲中求直 (*Find the straight in the arc*)

- The Taiji classic writings

Within the umbrella idea of Taiji as absolute command of internal power, there are three subcomponents we need to work. I'll use the mnemonic ARC: Accumulate, Rebound, Catch. These are the three things you must do to get the most intense output from Taiji form practice, and it's the core teaching of this book.

1. *Accumulate* (use your mind to) link to the universal energy and allow it to concentrate in the *dantian*.
2. *Rebound* (use your mind to) drop the energy to your feet so it can rebound back up.
3. *Catch* (use your mind to) bring the energy up from feet to the hands when needed

When you've understood all of these and can trigger the feet-to-hands chain instantaneously under any conditions, you've reached the watershed stage of *Fully Activated Body* or FAB. This is the first coherent energy state. What complicates the discussion is that these three tasks could be partially mis-understood as *levels of progression* – i.e. first you learn to accumulate, then rebound, then catch. That isn't totally wrong, but it's also a simultaneous and continuous process, from the very beginning. Even without any formal practice, you're always engaged in some small degree of accumulation and rebound, just because you're alive. The internal power is always accumulating and circulating throughout your body, humming mildly along the weed-choked byways, loose, leaky and sputtery like a 40-watt light bulb halfway screwed in. (Yes, you're going to see quite a few mixed metaphors in this book. Keeps you on your toes.)

But in Taiji we're going to take things radically further in those first two natural areas (accumulate and rebound), and add in our third process - catch. I mentioned earlier that Taiji practice boils down to two things: *cultivation* and *deployment*. The accumulate aspect is the beginning of cultivation. The rebound and catch aspects are part of cultivation and also the beginning of deployment. Together, they result in an unobstructed integration of the massed energy from the downward rebound in your feet up through catching it with your hands – and projecting it beyond, as we'll see later. I call this unobstructed integration the Fully Activated Body or FAB.

Accumulate: Before you can accumulate anything you need to be aware of its source, or point of origin. You always have immediate and full access to the universal energy through an intake point in your head near the *baihui* (crown). I'll have a lot more to say about details of the intake point in a separate section below. From the input jack, energy is constantly being circulated via natural, unconscious mechanisms throughout your body. Eventually you'll be able to consciously perceive and control the continuous circulation of obvious energy from your perineum (*huiyin*), up your spine, through your head (where it can be amplified via the universal intake on every loop) and down your front to your lower abdomen (*dantian*). This is the Taiji way to achieve the classical microcosmic orbit, which was introduced in the previous section. The microcosmic orbit was associated there with sedentary Daoist meditation. Taiji form and posture-holding practice can accomplish the same thing, in a gentle, natural fashion.

While there are many traditional Qigong and Daoist meditation methods that aim specifically at kick-starting the microcosmic orbit, Taiji works along a more organic game plan. In Taiji, *the orbit opens itself* naturally over time. We don't pull a sapling up by its branches, we just nurture its natural growth. This gives the Taiji energy its uniquely powerful signature when it's later put into deployment. As the flow along the microcosmic orbit strengthens, you'll perceive a natural filling of your *dantian* with a strange kind of power. It's as though the *dantian* is a lake that is fed by a large river and drained by a smaller one. The water level rises naturally. This is the work of accumulation.

Rebound: To rebound your energy refers to *dropping* the natural accumulation at the *dantian* further down, into the soles of your feet. This can be confusing, because the energy is already flowing throughout your body at all times anyway. But in Taiji work, you use your mind to sink the feeling of energy, gently, with a very light mental touch, down to the soles of the feet. I use the word 'rebounding' for this process within the ARC, where others might talk about 'grounding' or 'rooting'. The problem with those latter terms is that they lend themselves too easily to a mechanical interpretation. Too many students think of Taiji in terms befitting an NFL linebacker – a man who's trained to brace himself structurally, to make himself immoveable by physical principles alone. Becoming such a mountain of meat has no relevance what I'm getting at with the idea of dropping the energy and bouncing it from the feet. The accumulate aspect is largely passive and unconscious (at first), but at some point you must begin to work consciously on the drop and rebound aspects as you do your Taiji form.

Catch: The integration of energy from feet to hands is something unique to Taiji as a martial art. It could also be called projection. All energetic components of the body are finally fully coordinated, resulting in a fundamentally different quality from the concentration of energy in discrete body parts. In Taiji, you eventually learn to instantaneously 'rebound' or bounce the internal power up from the soles of your feet to your fingertips. This is the final piece of the ARC.

In summary, the full ARC of Taiji runs as follows: the energy is absorbed via a point in your head. The absorbed energy is combined with scattered life force energies freed up by relaxation and it all drops down the front to your *dantian*, then to your feet. It then rebounds from your feet back to your *dantian* (filling it from below this time), then crosses to the backside to begin its ascent from the weilu point at the base of the sacrum, rising up the lower and mid spine to the *lingtai*, where it will seem to particularly concentrate. From the lingtai, it will ascend through the cervical spine in the back of the neck and re-enter the origination point in the head. From there, it can be flashed out instantaneously to the hands as required for deployment.

The ARC cycle doesn't happen only once, nor is it limited to a single level. You continually revisit the process along a spiral of infinite ability levels. The ARC concept and training is fundamental to Taiji, in fact it is the defining process of Taiji as opposed to related practices such as Qigong and zazen meditation. You should now have an idea of the basic concept, but obviously the sketch you've just read isn't sufficient for you to begin working the ARC for real, in practice. No worries though - I'll cover all the crucial details in a separate expanded discussion, The ARC of STEEL.

THE ENERGY EXPERIENCE

Now I need to tweak the terminology again. The microcosmic orbit was presented in the Theory section above as one manifestation of *mingjing* (obvious energy), strongly associated with sedentary meditation. When you have fully accomplished the entire ARC process introduced here, working the energy from head to feet to hands, you will have expanded your natural microcosmic orbit to include the limbs, and achieved the Fully Activated Body (FAB). This is one of the Taiji manifestations of the *mingjing*, but Daoists have noticed it too. Since it's beyond the microcosmic orbit, Daoists have traditionally called this full body linkage (inclusion of limbs) the *macrocosmic* orbit (*dazhoutian*). When applied to Taiji however, there's a bit of ambiguity, because just like the microcosmic orbit, the macrocosmic orbit is really just a pathway, through which energy continually circulates at different strength levels in any human being – even without any special training. So from now on, I'll reserve the term 'Fully Activated Body' (FAB) to differentiate the result of Taiji's ARC work from both the microcosmic orbit and the macrocosmic orbit. But the macrocosmic orbit and the FAB are closely related ideas - the linking of all body sections into one energetic component – both power generation station and hi-voltage transmission line, all in one.

I can now refine my breakdown of *mingjing* (functional *qi*) manifestations as shown below:

Mingjing manifestations:

- As BRUTE superficial sensations
- As the Fully Activated Body (FAB) - result of the ARC process
- As power waves (listed in the earlier classification)

All these are palpable, fully distinct conditions that you can learn to recognize and trigger through consistent practice of the Taiji form. However, as far as I can tell, many Taiji practitioners never get close to serious ARC work, beyond the natural, unconscious mechanisms that operate anyway. Most practitioners, including theatrical (dance) oriented Taiji players, as well as the structure geeks, are unconsciously tense – which blocks the ARC. So who can blame them for giving up on the real Taiji practice (in all but name)? It's hard to work in the dark. It's easier to substitute plausible physical simulations for each of A, R, and C components, like margarine for butter. It's always much easier to get physical, and lecture people about how their *kua* is messed up, misaligned with their gluteal torque or mandibular ratchet. All that joint, bone, muscle, and structure talk has no connection to real Taiji energetics. Receiving Taiji instruction from a mechanical perspective is like hiring All-Star pitcher Pedro Martinez to coach you to accurately and powerfully throw bullets. Entirely beside the point.

Everything you need in terms of basic physicality is already written up clearly in the Taiji classic writings, and expressed straight-forwardly in the more principled Taiji form sequences. After that, it's all mental. I believe that many long-time practitioners never complete all three components (accumulate, rebound, catch) listed above. Only a minority ever begins to understand even one of them. And sometimes, if they start to understand one process, they often over-emphasize that one at the expense of the others. Even ZMQ37 practitioners, for instance, often mistake their physical "rooting" and "grounding" practices as the true rebound step discussed above. It's a natural mistake because I've talked in terms of 'dropping' the energy. But the real work is non-physical, and can't be understood as a literal expression of anchoring your feet physically, like a linebacker.

Likewise, some modern schools of Taiji thought emphasize the "groundpath" structural support concept. The 'groundpath' is a notion of structural projection of the physical base (the ground) via strong-standing postures. But at the upper Taiji levels, you'll be able to achieve the full internal power deployment (feet to fingers) whether you are slumping, kneeling, sitting, or even lying down - with your feet entirely off the ground. There is no particular structural or postural requirement at all, except as a 'training wheels' mode, which may help a beginner's imagery.

Or, sometimes people talk about "moving from the *dantian*" as though that's the essence of an *internal* art like Taiji. But that's again the wrong way to think of it, because that's largely a physical concept. Like some kind of Pilates 'powerhouse' thing, involving muscles, tendons, joints and physical dynamics. The energy may originate in the *dantian*, may move through the *dantian* - but it's not a matter of moving your body *from* anywhere, in a physical sense. In fact, your body per se hardly needs to move at all.

It's a matter of issuing energy, which is sucked from the universe by your mind through your head centers, dropped to your feet, and then deployed from the feet upward along the spine, back through the head center and on to the hands. The mind triggers your energy like a spark of fire on a pile of gunpowder. The difference between energetic vs. physical manifestation is like the difference between old-school electronics with tubes and mechanical switches, as opposed to modern solid state electronics which have no moving parts (other than the electrons themselves). Too many practitioners reduce Taiji to a physicalized dance or mechanized calisthenics – I'm suggesting you resist that temptation.

If you can maintain your commitment to internal energy connected by mind alone, you'll achieve the FAB Fully Activated Body that triggers *pure pleasure* like you would not believe. It's such a blast - and it's infinite. Then, for the real Taiji moon launch, you've still got the further levels of *mingjing*, and then the entire *anjing* spectrum to explore. But in the beginning, just work on activating the pieces of the ARC, and then their integration. It's like the ingredients for gunpowder or an atomic bomb - in isolation they are fairly useless. It's the combination that really rocks your world. At the ice cream parlor, they have dinky spoons dipped in a tub, to give you a morsel of taste sample. If that could be done with the Taiji full-body energy activation, if you could have people sample for just two minutes the results of seriously getting that, people would flock in their billions to the Taiji parlors of the world and forget everything else. Real Taiji is the stuff of Schedule One listing.

This has been just a quick sketch of the ARC concept, which is the key process of beginner Taiji. It's not quite complete, so I'll be revisiting it in much greater detail in a later section. But before we can go deeper into the ARC process, you need to understand something else that's so big I call it *The Missing Basic* of Taiji training. And before we get to *that*, we must first ponder the Prime Directive of Taiji – *relax*.

RELAX

A day will dawn when you will yourself laugh at your effort.
That which is on the day of laughter is also now.

- Ramana Maharishi

THE PRIME DIRECTIVE

Relaxation is the razor's edge between *tensing* (into even an ounce more muscular force than needed to achieve the one correct soft line of a given Taiji posture) on the one hand, and *collapsing* (below that line, by even half a centimeter) on the other.

You must be consciously and entirely dedicated to achieving maximum relaxation in every moment of your Taiji practice. Don't ever get swayed or sucked into the idea that there's some *special* or *scientific* type of tension, some nuanced redefinition of the concept, some *correct* way to use it, that's the "real meaning" of the Taiji energy. Not so. The Taiji energy depends on getting physical tension out of the way - out the door and down the stairs. Taiji is something special - something different - above and beyond the material world (though its principles have some application to daily life). If something billed as Taiji or internal practice involves any kind of physical tension - whether in postures, drills, partner practice or anything else - abandon that system immediately. Or, at least don't fool yourself that you'll ever manifest the true Taiji energetics that way.

People these days expend a lot of effort re-interpreting Taiji. There's a lot of revisionism, mostly centered on dodging or finessing the basic point that you've got to relax to the max. This isn't relaxation for its own sake. Nor does it derive from some doctrinal commitment. It's simply the practical pre-requisite to kick-starting the layers of internal energy in the body. If you don't understand this yet, if you still believe there can be such a thing as scientifically, anatomically, or structurally correct use of any kind of tension whatsoever in Taiji, then you are very far from the true art. Possibly, later on, you'll understand this, suddenly give up all tension, and be ecstatically swept away by the energy flood. Then you'll think: *Darn. Why didn't I just get that point when I read it in that stupid JUICE book in the first place?* Or else you'll continue forever as you are now, happy to imagine you've tapped into the real Taiji though missing it by a country mile. But if you drop your materialistic pride and give maximal relaxation a chance, then as you really begin to climb the energy ladder, you'll be blown away better than your first LSD trip.

Muscular force and tension can be useful in daily life tasks. You need muscular force to move a piano. The point is not that tension and the ordinary use of muscles are somehow evil. The problem is that for most people, mind and muscular tension are inextricably bound together. Closer than a dog and a flea. The broadest lesson of Taiji for daily life is learning to use tension only and exactly when you *need* it – for moving the piano – but being quick to drop it (the tension not the piano) at will. When it comes to Taiji, whether doing the form or push hands, *you never need it.*

The work of Taiji is not so much to *eliminate* tension completely from your life as it is to help you *understand* it. We must learn to *stop it and drop it* whenever we need to tap into the universal energy flow. When I teach the form, I sometimes model a hand shape for a particular posture and ask the student to do likewise. Then I feel his/her hand and arm in the requested configuration. Invariably they've tensed it up, way beyond the mild dynamic called for by the pose. It's perfectly natural that their mind had to go to their hands - to make the unfamiliar shape. That's fine. But for almost all of us, where the mind goes, the *physical tension* comes along too, as a stowaway. There's no need for that. I didn't instruct the student to tense up, I merely requested the hand shape. As you advance in Taiji work, the internal power will be connected and directed by the mind alone, not the muscular force.

The work of Taiji is to separate mind from physical tension, so that the internal power has a fighting chance to creep in. Certain conditions are naturally physically relaxed, such as being asleep, unconscious, or drunk. That's genuine physical relaxation, but we could also use the word *collapsed* – with its negative connotation – for those kinds of states. The difference between relaxed and collapsed is that in collapse the mind is missing. For most people, as soon as the mind is re-introduced, physical tension comes along for the ride. So we bounce between two undesirable poles: *collapsed* vs. *tensed*, blasting straight past the ideal state of *relaxed* every time.

Don't accept any so-called Taiji method that requires or fosters tension. Notice I'm talking only about Taiji practice. There's absolutely nothing wrong with doing all kinds of physical, athletic stuff - just so long as you don't confuse athletics with your internal development. Despite what you really may want to believe, they aren't the same thing. Yoga, dance, martial sports, running, weightlifting – all these kinds of exercises are great for your physical body. But people doing these activities naively, without understanding Taiji principles, are all unconsciously very tense in my experience, no matter how flexible, fast, strong, coordinated

63

etc. they may become. Thus, they can easily be made to stumble all over themselves in unbalancing practice (see Chapter 4, Push). Let Taiji be the unique tool for you that it can be - when you don't try to overload it with all kinds of pseudo-scientific "structural", "anatomical", and "physics-based" baggage. (That said, whether you develop internally or not, you do need to keep your body in good physical shape.)

If you want a quick check on your degree of superficial tension, get hold of a speed jump rope, the real lightweight kind, and try it out. If you're maintaining any excess tension in your hands, arms, shoulders, neck, face, jaw, chest or related areas, you won't be able to jump fast and furious yet simultaneously light and cool. This is a minimal diagnostic tool for beginners working on surface tension. Although this jump rope diagnostic is a boxing thing, and not sufficient for making serious Taiji progress, it has some carryover to checking Taiji's beginning stages. When you can do continuous crossovers with double-under, or when you can jump as shown in the Floyd Mayweather training videos, you'll know you've understood something. In fact, boxing is good for a variety of work on superficial tension. If you're tense in the ring, your stamina won't last even a single three-minute round. And boxing teaches you to stay relaxed even while being hit hard. But all that's still only superficial relaxation. There's a yet deeper form of tension inside almost everyone that a Taiji master can easily detect.

There are thousands of Qigong training programs, all over the USA, Europe and Asia. They're all similar: very easy arm extensions and swings, moderately controlled breath, and a bit of stretching and bending to evoke the superficial type of tingly-warmish *qi* feeling (the lowest level of *qi* experience, what I call the BRUTE level of *mingjing*). A raw beginner can learn to accomplish that in about five minutes. The rest is a bit of mild anaerobics, to make people feel they've done something. The same evocation of BRUTE energy sensations can be achieved by playing any retro rock song, like Jerry Lee Lewis or Little Richard, and having everybody clap along and dance wildly with total abandon for a few minutes, then suddenly stop stock-still for a moment and feel the buzz. (The guy who pioneered that simple way to feel a small bite of live BRUTE energy, was Osho, with his Dynamic Meditation based on alternating frenetic motion with stillness).

If you do any of these programs enough, eventually the BRUTE *anjing* experience will deepen and full body vibration will start to spasmodically kick in. But even that is low level. As long as you're feeling all kinds of ripples and tingles and little shocks, the old Chinese saying applies: When shaken, the half-full vinegar bottle (半瓶醋) makes the most noise. The full bottle is silent. These kinds of superficial *qi* experiences won't do much for your long-term development. They're just fun and games. But mild *qi* teachings do have some value, as a kind of bridge between being absolutely sedentary vs. having a committed athletic practice. The selling points of these light *qi* methods are:

a. the inspiration and amazement people feel when they get that first touch of BRUTE *qi*
b. the physical simplicity of learning and performing them.

But *qi* per se isn't the tough nut. It doesn't take much to get some *qi* on. *Relaxation* is the key to the deeper work. Most people, even after they begin feel and control their *qi*, carry just as much unconscious tension as before. That's the real challenge. I've pushed hands with many supposed *qi* masters – people with decades of experience - who are easy to toss around the room. Even though they can feel their *qi* as *anjing*, it's a null operator in deployment mode, because they aren't *relaxed*. They hold so much unconscious tension you can move them around at will. Locking onto their tension is like grabbing the handle of a teapot to move it. Qigong masters often can't mobilize their energy functionally because they aren't relaxed

– even though, to themselves, they feel relaxed inside. But not to a sensitive Taiji touch. Qigong alone won't relax you – only correct practice of Taiji will take you all the way down the rabbit hole.

The cornerstone of Taiji is, in a word, *relax*. Yang Chengfu said it. The Taiji classic writings say it. But relaxation can be boring and difficult. Therefore many people ignore it. Even hardcore Taiji specialists are sometimes more into "proper structure" and "alignment" and other mechanical stuff – anything rather than address the basic issue: the need to relax. Therefore many Taiji players are actually doing something else, something I'd call 'slow Shaolin' or 'slow karate'. Many who think they are relaxed aren't. Often a simple visual check suffices to tell you whether or not a Taiji practitioner is relaxed. Of course, somebody who appears tense may be internally relaxed and vice-versa. But nine times out of ten, a simple visual assessment turns out to be correct. You just need to use the right criteria (Hint: it's not based on how theatrically appealing their Taiji dance performance appears).

Sometimes Taiji people look at my definition of relaxation (at the top of this section) and explain that postures in their form are *supposed* to have some tension. *It's built-in for functional reasons*, they'll say. *But... well, that's how we do the pose*. That kind of thing. Those people need to find a new form. Any randomly chosen posture gives it away. You can usually see the tension right on the surface. For example, Single Whip tends to be an especially good diagnostic pose. If you see any of the following features, the practitioner likely carries a lot of internal tension no matter how pretty his/her form may appear:

- step too long, wide, or low (unable to sit 100% of all weight onto back leg and raise the front foot in-situ with no upper-body adjustment)
- back leg straight or knee locked
- arm(s) straight or elbow locked

- one shoulder higher than the other
- open hand straight upright and/or wrist bent and/or fingers rigid
- upper body leans forward or sideways

All those things require excess tension, beyond what real Taiji and the classic writings call for. The standards I'm using to judge may seem structural or mechanical. And isn't that the very thing I'm railing against? True, I'm using a minimal dash of structural criteria as a diagnostic, to make unconscious tension more visible. It's like using just a bit of poison as a protection against a big fatal dose.

Taiji does have an inventory of distinctive postures, structures if you will. But there's a certain knack to doing them without overdoing them. The postures should be recognizable and have a bit of spirit to them. But fundamentally the goal really isn't to achieve any particular structure beyond minimally keeping the body upright. Doing much more than that is *adding* stuff, *building up* something. The goal is more to *strip away all the tension*, which would leave you without structure, like water. But how can you really make money *taking away* something? That's one reason there are so few good books on Taiji. It can be hard to write about *not* doing stuff, as opposed to piling more things on. Like most of Daoism, real Taiji goes against our simpleminded human nature. We humans are grinchy-grabby animals, we want to *get* something, *do* something, *build* something, *have* something, *show* something. Not *give something up*. That's no fun. You can't build a decent marketing program around *that* message.

It's a difficult point to appreciate, because people *love* tension, structure, and forward-focused aggression. Anything else feels weak and unsafe – even psychologically threatening. It's a human thing. Taiji is rowing against the genetic tide on this point. Real Taiji is energetic, not physical, structural, postural, or anatomical. Forget about whole body (physical) power, alignment, torque, bone and tendon positioning, structural-spinal twiddling. None of that matters. The only thing you need from physical structure and posture is something negative: at the very least, it must not inherently *engender* tension. You need a posture set that at least doesn't *require* or *encourage* you to be tense just for show (while fantasizing that you're relaxed). Unfortunately, that criterion disqualifies a lot of the so-called Taiji taught around the world.

Taiji's power delivery is no more physically structured than is electricity. Once you plug one end of an extension cord into your wall outlet and the other to your electric chainsaw, it doesn't matter whether that orange extension cord is coiled or straight. Your saw will grind just as well either way, because electrical power, for practical purposes, isn't structural or material. It's energetic, and it flows fine regardless of the wire's shape, as long as there's no impedance or short circuit. (Those would be analogous to physical tension in the Taiji space.)

The energy is actually pooled in the legs and feet. Nothing functional in the hands til it's called out. The relaxed hands are merely used to maintain sensitive contact. This is why when you work with a real Taiji master you feel the power is coming from far away, yet you can't get out from under it. You think his power must somehow be in his arms and hands, but it isn't - it's in his feet and legs. I don't mean strong legs like a linebacker. I mean literally the legs are the intermediate energetic storage. They're like a gun magazine, chambering the round (energetic, not physical). The little hand movement at the end is just the muzzle flash. This all comes from correct form practice. So you need a form that not so much fusses about 'correct' structure the way most do, but rather one that gets out of your way. One that at the very least doesn't actually require and encourage you tense up, the way many of them do.

Some readers may feel I'm reinforcing the obsolete concept of Cartesian duality, of mind-body split, with this emphasis on Taiji as

99% mental and only a little physical. Some may feel that modern research has established that mind and body are inextricably interwoven and thus there's no point in talking the way I do anymore. Mind is like a pint of sugar dissolved in a bathtub of milk - you can't tell where one leaves off and the other begins.

This is absolutely correct in a logical sense, but I'm not dealing with abstract logic. I'm always and only talking about the level of individual experience. But though it's individual, it's not completely subjective - with the right work everybody will get consistent results. The main point is, at the level of your own work, right now, who you are and where you are, there's a gigantic difference between working to get the next move just right, get your sacroiliac positioned just so, or wanting to look good as an athlete or dancer, vs. the real mental work of genuine energetic Taiji. They are absolutely distinct practice experiences and the two paths lead to entirely different ends. Nor is Taiji equivalent to static meditation. Taiji is Taiji. That's why we have a name for it.

Taiji is energy art for energy art's sake. The real, energy-centric Taiji delivers freakish power from quiet, relaxed practice. There's a great line in Chinese poetry: *light wind and fine rain* (輕風細雨 *qingfengxiyu*) - that gentle phrase has the feeling-quality of the strange Taiji power. But few people in this mechanical age of transformer bots and performance-enhancing drugs want to hear it. I'm on the path and can usually demonstrate the art effectively. Yet I too haven't yet fully mastered this amazing power (Obviously! Because I haven't yet entered the UFC to walk the talk). So even as Taiji becomes a worldwide phenomenon, the point of it as expressed by Wang Zongyue and Zheng Manqing is being obscured as the practice degenerates into either tepid theatrics, or mechanistic antagonism. Is Taiji too subtle for us modern-day 'roided-up beasts? Sometimes I feel that even as the shell or corpse of this art straddles the whole world, it's become zombie Taiji, with its secret heart sucked out and spit into the trash.

People sometimes carp to me that I keep harping on them to relax, but never tell them exactly *how* to do it. It's mental, that's all. It's not that hard, but you have to take it seriously. Most students don't. Try starting your Taiji form and then stopping a few moves into it. Now check yourself. Are you really relaxed? Is every part, every muscle and tissue, that isn't *essential* to holding you upright soft as tofu? Thought not. At that point, students make excuses: *Well, this tension is needed to make the move look right* or *This tension is special, it's tactical tension* or *I'm not tense, I'm moving from my core* or *This isn't tension, this is projection* or *I'm balancing hard and soft* or whatever. No. If you let yourself off the hook like that, you're no longer doing Taiji, you're just dancing. There's no royal road to relaxation. But it isn't *that* complicated a thing. You just need to pay continual attention to it until it becomes second nature.

TEN BLOCKS TO TAIJI DEVELOPMENT

Listed below are some reasons why you may fail to get much beyond the superficial BRUTE stage of random sensations:

1. You aren't relaxed and don't even know or care that you aren't.
2. You aren't working at the relaxation aspect of your Taiji form, so you're doing slow motion karate instead of Taiji.
3. You feel an irresistible urge to redefine relaxation idiosyncratically as "proper structure" or "correct alignment" or "appropriately timed sequential entrainment of facile force" or any other weasel phrase.
4. You care too much how you look while doing the form (distraction).
5. You don't care enough how you look while doing the form (loss of mind).
6. You don't practice push hands.
7. You practice too much push hands.

8. You scoff at the notion of internal energy, or you acknowledge it but doubt that it could ever be functional for anything.

9. You're a New Age bunny who is blissed out on meditative energy - but you *still* aren't relaxed.

10. You believe about the *dantian* what legendary physical culturist Feldenkrais said: *It's a point that is full of shit, literally. That point is full of shit. And this is the point of qi.*

Many approaches to "internal" training at present are missing the boat. Qigong, Taiji, Baguazhang, Xingyiquan, White Crane, Yiquan - pretty much all of them introduce *physical tension* into their modern forms of practice. Whether tension is smuggled in under the guise of structuralism, whether it's the by-product of the Theatric Fallacy (covered in Chapter 3, Form), whether it's simple machismo, or whether it's just plain ignorance - it's all wrong. You'll miss the point. Always remember great Taiji master Yang Chengfu's Prime Directive: *relax*.

STRUCTURE MANIA

Let's put it out there again - *structure*. There's a word everybody loves. And although teachers apply a fig leaf of high-falutin' energy talk, these days they're mostly all about *physical* structure – how to efficiently deploy your fascia, tendons, ligaments, muscles, bone, etc. Let's see how that applies to real Taiji. Water has molecular structure, and spontaneous kinetic structure, but it isn't a Lego set. It has no *mechanical* structure. Water is a heap of molecular looseness that transmits energy flow. And for Taiji purposes, that's all the human body is. Understand that your body is just a pile of cells, no one type better than another. It's the same as a water-filled heavy bag in a boxing gym. What matters for Taiji is not the cells' functional arrangement but their energy conduction properties. Always think water. Don't be a structure geek. Of course, I can't expect educated citizens of the 21st century to lightly toss aside their mechanistic blinders. And despite the recent surge of structure geeks, I shouldn't paint everybody with the same brush. There are lots of New Age bunnies out there who *do* feel the energy, and who are totally unstructured. And they don't know an *iliotibial band* from a *trochanteric crest*. Far from being structure geeks, they're inherently aligned with The Force, by mere assertion alone. Yet these types can also be tossed around easily, by the slightest soft touch on their unconscious tension. Because they too aren't relaxed.

The beginning student of Taiji needs a dose of physical structure teaching to get him/her going. That is provided by proper Taiji form practice. But that isn't at all comparable to the mechanical alignment fetishism that pervades Taiji teaching now. That's just tensing you up. The great Hindu sage Ramana Maharishi said: *If the traveler in a train car which can carry any weight does not lay his luggage down, but bears it painfully on his head, whose is the fault?* So put it down. The train carries all.

But why have any structure in the first place? The one bit of physical structure that I allow on the game board is what's found in the postures of a relaxation-centric Taiji form, such as ZMQ37. The postures are a bit of structure that serves only one purpose – to keep your mind on a dog chain so it doesn't go wandering off down the street. That's all. A posture is just a place-holder, to keep your mind on the playing field. In real Taiji the postures have no further inherent function – neither combative nor calisthenic nor therapeutic nor decorative. The postures are essential though because our target is relaxation *with mind*. If we relax by sitting or lying down, our mind will quickly go AWOL on us. That little bit of Taiji standing structure helps nail the mind's feet to the floor (you think *that's* an appalling mixed metaphor? You ain't seen *nothing* yet).

It's ironic that many of the big-name Taiji and inner martial arts teachers of the present emphasize a sophisticated, but ultimately

72

physical, linking up – i.e. structuring - of fascia or small muscles or whatever inside the body as their internal power basis. That's completely wrong. The more you link up and entrain physical stuff of any kind, even if you use your mind to do it, the tenser you become. In fact, structural linking is the very *definition* of tension. In real Taiji, we do use our mind, but we use it to *de-link everything physical inside ourselves*. We use our mind to *soften everything inside*. Softening is de-structuring and de-linking all those physical innards so they are left connected by energy alone. Strangely, *the more softened and de-linked physically* you get, *the more hardened and connected energetically* you'll be. It's ironic, it's weird, it's counter-intuitive, but that's just how it is. Only physical softening and de-linking can produce the ultimate badass Taiji power stream.

Ramana was asked why he taught the method of self-inquiry (to continually self-question: 'Who am I?') for obliterating the small egoic self, and all its suffering. He answered that his inquiry method is like a man who gets a thorn in his foot, then uses another thorn to dig it out, then throws both away. The consciously applied thorn of minimal Taiji form *structure* (yes, *any* structure implies *some* degree of tension) helps us become aware, by contrast, of the offending thorn of overall *unconscious tension* (which is a bigger, nastier mass of uncontrolled structure). Once we identify and remove the deep tension from the body we can throw both kinds of structure away and be free.

There is only one goal: to relax with mind. The minimal structure of a good Taiji posture is solely geared to that end. Once you've relaxed enough to trigger the internal power flow-through, you're good to go. Then your energy can take on any shape at will, like water, and physical structure won't matter in the least. When a sponge is fully soaked, it's equally wet all over no matter what shape you push it into. To get the maximum benefit from the fun stuff in the remaining chapters, you'll need a quality Taiji practice that puts relaxation first. If you even need to ask "Hmm *does* my style put relaxation first?" then there's your answer – it doesn't. Find something better.

THE MISSING BASIC

Feed your head.

- Grace Slick

In the earlier discussion, I listed the *baihui* (crown of the head) as a focal point for the Taiji energy in the microcosmic orbit. That common idea should help guide your practice, but there's something crucial left unsaid. The *baihui* point isn't a concrete physical location. All these points are abstractions that need to be located anew for each patient (acupuncture) or practitioner (Taiji). So with what body area should we identify the *baihui*? And is it really the most useful intake point for the raw universal energy?

Here's where we run into, not exactly secrets, but confusion. Confusion and distraction can turn open knowledge into a kind of secret – something *hidden in plain sight*. So it is with the Missing Basic. Before I get to it, you need some background. I'm going to nit-pick some classical energy theory and terminology here, which may seem to contradict my practical focus, but all in a good cause. This is an exceptionally important concept. I want you to be confusion-proofed on this fundamental point forever. I want you to understand not just what I'm saying but why.

As I've already mentioned, literally hundreds of energy focal points have been identified in traditional Chinese medical theory. Professor Zheng in his writings called attention to one of these in particular, as a fundamental key to internal energy work. This special point he referred to as the *niwan* (泥丸). It is associated with the head and is identified as a terminus or pole of the microcosmic orbit. We see this in statements such as:

越過尾閭，復衝開夾脊，度玉枕，達泥丸，亦若是，此為入門

This line describes the energy passing through a portion of the microcosmic orbit (which is always circulating in any living person). It is said to rise up from the coccyx and sacrum, and then open the points along the spine, to the neck and head. The line above lists the points along the spinal section from the sacrum to the *niwan* in the head, and states that when the circulation to the *niwan* is strongly established, you've 'entered the gate' of serious Taiji achievement. This is a very well-known description, and fine as far as it goes.

The confusion comes up when we zero in on the working "location" of that *niwan* point. I put "location" in quotes because we aren't dealing with a purely physical or anatomical location or organ of the body. The *niwan* needs to be understood as a point in an energy double of the physical body that is co-present with it, but not identical to it. For convenience I'll often talk about the "location" of a point as if it were a physical spot. But don't forget that what we're really after is an abstract energy focal point – whatever brings on the most powerful or therapeutic energetic experience. In most commentaries and even translations of traditional writings on these spinal and cranial points, the *niwan* is either left as transliterated Chinese (carried over as plain '*niwan*'), or else it's translated as "the crown of the head". In the latter case, it's often then mistakenly identified with the *baihui* point which was listed earlier as 'crown of the head'. The *baihui* is by far the more frequent word in these kinds of discussions. So by default and mistake the *niwan* has become an uneasy synonym for the more common term *baihui*, and left at that.

Normally I try not to split terminological hairs. Words don't matter – only reality matters. But here's a case where getting the words wrong can seriously delay your progress, for years or decades. Because the *niwan* is the most essential energy focal point of them all, and, crucially – the *niwan* isn't the *baihui*. They are two separate points. The *niwan* is not at the crown of the head. The *niwan*, the key point that you need to catch and hold, is actually *inside* the brain, deep in the center. It's experienced a couple of inches directly below the crown. Draw a straight vertical line through the *baihui*, and then draw a straight horizontal line back into the brain from another classical point, the *yintang* (印堂, sometimes called the Brow Chakra or 'Third Eye'). The place in the center of the brain where those two lines intersect is the *true inlet point for the universal energy*. This is the *niwan* location that Professor Zheng was talking about.

The confusion has arisen partly due to translation confusion. Even within classical Chinese theory, the term *niwan* for this location is not uniform. Sometimes the term *songguoti* (松果體 pineal gland, an endocrine gland located near the upper part of the thalamus) is freely substituted. And there are other, vaguer terms associated with this area, such as *shangdantian* (上丹田 upper dantian). These pseudo-synonyms are in their turn dragged in yet other directions. But the Pineal Gland is a physical, anatomical entity, and not specifically suited to serve as a point of internal energy work per se. Meanwhile, the 'upper dantian' concept is most often associated with the brow point that I've listed (in the Theory section) as the *yintang*. And the crown of the head (*baihui*) confusion mentioned earlier also persists.

All this mess has arisen because humans have trouble with things that aren't palpable or visible. The crown and brow points map to areas that are easily accessible to acupuncture needles. You can see them. They're a lot easier to wrap your mind around (so to speak). But they aren't what concern us for serious Taiji development. What we care about is the true *niwan* – in the center of the brain. It has a radically different feel from any other energy point in the body. So I've re-named the *niwan* as the 'Neural EXchange Universal-to-Somatic' Point (NEXUS Point). This is your connection to the energy of creation. When you've sensitized yourself, you'll feel that universal power streaming in through the NEXUS and spreading through your body.

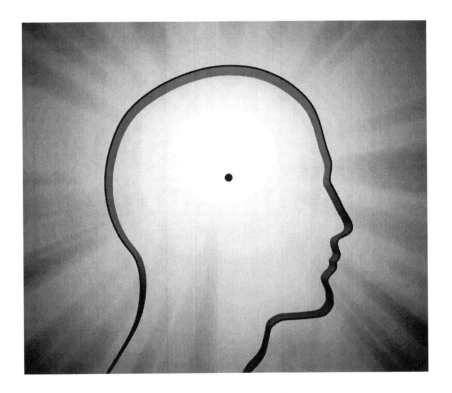

Figure 2 The *niwan* or NEXUS Point is the Missing Basic, the cornerstone of universal energy access.

You need to focus on it at certain times in your practice, especially at the start of a session, in order to prime it or warm it up, and also at the end as I'll discuss further on. But don't heavily or obsessively concentrate on it. Don't give yourself a headache. Just be aware that it's there. *Lightly* place your mind there. Feel it absorbing the cosmic energies for circulation (initially via the microcosmic orbit, later via the Full Body Activation) throughout the body. I realize that locating this point is a tricky, subtle job. In the beginning you can't really feel it as your primary energy inlet. Though I've used physical descriptions to help you find it, in practice it's better not to think of it as a particular area of the physical brain or any kind of actual anatomical structure in your head. It's an *energetic focus point* that happens to overlap, or be co-located, with some physical brain stuff in there.

This isn't exactly a secret, in the sense of never having been discussed. Professor Zheng's writings on Taiji have been widely distributed for over 50 years, and they're based on a medical and meditative lineage going back thousands of years. In addition, the *niwan*, or NEXUS Point, has been known to other traditions as well. In the classical Indian meditative tradition, the *niwan* is the *ajna* point, at the same center brain spot already described. The effect of concentration on the *ajna* in yoga is described in literally glowing terms. When the meditator hits that spot just right, dig *this*:

> *He then also sees the Light which is in the form of a flaming lamp. It is lustrous like the clearly shining morning sun, and glows between the Sky and the Earth. It is here that the Bhagavan manifests Himself in the fullness of His might. He knows no decay, and witnesseth all, and is here as He is in the region of Fire, Moon, and Sun. This is the incomparable and delightful abode of Vishnu. The excellent Yogi at the time of death joyfully places his vital breath (Prana) here and enters (after death) that Supreme, Eternal, Birthless, Primeval Deva,*

the Purusa, who was before the three worlds, and who is known
by the Vedanta.

(from *The Ajna Cakra according to the Satcakra-Narupana of Purnananda*
Swami, translated by Arthur Avalon in: *The Serpent Power*)

It's interesting that, just as in the Chinese case, in the Indian
tradition there is similar confusion with other nearby points. The
ajna chakra (a *chakra* is an energy hot spot in the body) is sometimes
cited in Tantric doctrine as being located in the brow region – the
same confusion we saw above with the Chinese *yintang*. But the
actual position of the *ajna* point is in the middle of the brain, well
behind the brows – it's the *niwan* in Sanskrit drag. Some Tantric
texts do attempt to maintain a distinction between the brow point
and the true internal *ajna* by positing two *ajna* points - 'external' and
'internal'. It's confusing, but for your Taiji all you need to know is
the NEXUS Point concept explained here.

Whether working with the energy in solo cultivation mode, or
partnered deployment mode, it's important to keep a cold mind. That
doesn't mean cruel or unsympathetic. It's more like... *uninvolved*,
keeping yourself mentally just slightly at a distance from whatever
is happening in and around your body. Paradoxically this increases
your functional awareness, but more importantly, keeping cold
and calm like that seems to greatly increase the energy absorption
capacity of the NEXUS Point. The NEXUS Point differs from the
baihui crown point by more than a few inches of location. It's also
different in being fundamentally aligned and magnetized to the
earth, while the *baihui* is the link to heaven, in classical symbology.
I know all this stuff seems very subtle, pedantic, and abstract. But
it's not in the least. The effects *start* small but when you get cooking
it all comes together and rocks you like a tsunami that takes out a
coastline. The NEXUS Point is the essential taproot for everything
that follows in this book.

I refer to the NEXUS Point as the Missing Basic not because the point itself is a new discovery or top secret, but because, while widely known, it hasn't been a very important part of the Taiji discussion, especially in the West. And when it is emphasized, it's usually wrongly identified with the *baihui* crown point. But the NEXUS Point is the key to all the Art because that's where your energy intake is sourced. I'm not gilding the lily here. I don't introduce theory for its own sake, or to dazzle you with exotic lore. I care only about what matters for your personal practice, what pays cash for you. The NEXUS Point pays cold, hard cash. Take note.

THE ARC OF STEEL

I defined the ARC of Taiji earlier as: accumulate, rebound, and catch. This ARC concept is as important as the Missing Basic. Just like the *niwan* / NEXUS Point, it's not actually *missing* either, in the sense of never having been offered. In fact, the ARC process is the central idea of the Taiji classic writings. The most important line in the Taiji classic writings is the following:

其根在腳。發於腿。主宰於腰。形於手指。由腳而腿而腰。

The power is rooted in the feet, issued from the legs. It is commanded by the waist, and is functionally manifested in the fingers. It goes from feet to legs to waist.

To the extent people consider this line at all these days, they re-interpret it to suit current prejudices in terms of physical structure, anatomy, posture, the mechanics of leverage, kinetic force vectors, muscle-fascia integration and so on. Unfortunately that interpretation is completely wrong. The Chinese line above is a description of an *internal energy* process. And I don't mean by that the propagation of *kinetic* energy through the relaxed body frame – another popular modern mistake. The misunderstanding has arisen because the concept hasn't been worked through at a sufficient level of detail before. Existing explanations are too sketchy or too elaborate – impractical and overblown. So though I introduced highlights of the ARC process in the section on Theory above, here I'll dive into each of these three subcomponents (accumulate, rebound, and catch) more deeply. Generally, the key thing to understand is that this feet-to-hands power transmission isn't limited to a single energy phenomenon, a single type of energy experience. There's a whole inventory of energy types and experiences, both meditative/ecstatic and more functional types, that all manifest within that same fundamental linkage. Once you marshal your mind to work along that path, all kinds of interesting stuff pops up. Nor do I mean merely the psycho-visual imagery of a pathway, waveform, or other imaginary construct. Those things are just the finger, but I'm talking about the moon - a genuine, specific energetic state which emerges spontaneously from the correct training configuration. All these misunderstandings have arisen because the concept hasn't been worked through at a sufficient level of detail before. So let's get to it.

ACCUMULATE

First, as discussed above, you feel in yourself how to light up the NEXUS Point. If you work with it you'll naturally start to feel it. That's the 'Start Me Up' moment. Pressing the NEXUS starter also accelerates the microcosmic orbit and hugely strengthens the volume of natural energy flow throughout the body. That allows for a surplus. Thereafter, the work of accumulation (the gradual sinking and concentration of the surplus orbit energy into the *dantian*) happens largely (but not entirely, as we'll see) unconsciously and naturally through persistent correct practice of a good Taiji form.

The key point here is that you don't need to continuously concentrate on the NEXUS for the accumulation to happen. Perhaps in some forms of seated meditation you'd need to keep pushing the button, so to speak. But in Taiji, you can just touch it mentally, then trust that it's working optimally for you thereafter. You mainly need awareness of the NEXUS Point at two stages in a practice session – the start and the end. The NEXUS Point is the alpha and omega of the ARC training. Even though the final power is manifested in the hands (the 'catch' component of the ARC), you must first work the power through the entire ARC, which begins and ends with the NEXUS Point. At the start though, flicking the NEXUS Point on is like turning an automobile ignition key – after you turn the key once in the starter and get the engine cranked, you don't keep grinding the key in the starter. You just let it be.

Taiji practice works similarly. With the NEXUS activated, regular practice of a correct Taiji form will naturally foster the accumulation process. Though it's happening naturally, without any special meditative attention to particular acupoints of the abdomen (such as *qihai* or *dantian*, etc.), you still need to engage your mind and attention sufficiently to keep the whole abdominal area *relaxed* during practice. If you can do that much, you'll start directly and consciously feeling the amassing of energy much more quickly than you would otherwise. You'll often feel warmth, buzzing, and the other superficial BRUTE sensations in the *qihai* and *dantian* areas. Then, as you keep putting in your hours of practice, suddenly one day your *qi* will finally drop into the *qihai*. That's an amazing moment. It must be purely energetic, meaning spontaneously generated and mentally guided always.

Have you seen those video clips of Manhattan-size glaciers calving off Antarctica and Greenland, due to climate change or whatever? You know the awed impression of unleashed power you get watching that? The moment your *qi* finally drops to the *dantian* is somehow similar, only far more intimately felt, of course. It seems to happen in a moment, but the process has been working all along, covertly, through your correct, relaxed form practice. It's been happening but you haven't noticed it. It's as though you had to drill from a dark room through a concrete wall 3 meters thick to get at the sunlight. For the first 2.99999 meters you wouldn't notice any change in illumination from your starting condition. Then at the end - *blammo* – breakthrough to a flood of sunbeams. But while you were drilling you'd been progressing all along. It's just that the progress didn't make any visible difference.

I've said that accumulation happens as a natural process as long as you work your Taiji form correctly (in accordance with the Taiji classic writings). While that's absolutely true, there are some additional considerations in how you visualize relaxing your body and leading the energy that can greatly accelerate your development of the goal state of Fully Activated Body (FAB). These 'accelerant' methods manifest some of the more specific teachings of the Taiji classic writings. Some accelerants apply specifically to the accumulate phase, while others are targeted to the rebound and/or catch. The accelerants will be covered in the next chapter, Form.

REBOUND

First things first: understand that 'rebound' describes a process. The rebound in my terms is dropping the amassed energy from the *qihai* to the soles of the feet. It's possible to work with the idea that the rebound consists of both the 'drop' and the 'pop' back up, like a basketball dribble action. But in practice, I restrict the rebound to the 'drop' of energy to the feet. The 'pop' back up is part of the Catch aspect of the ARC.

I say the soles of the feet. Many teachers, however, prefer to emphasize the 'point' concept, which would be the *yongquan* introduced earlier. The *yongquan* lies on the sole of each foot, along the center line but a bit forward, just beyond the midpoint toward the toes. The *yongquan* is the classical location for foot-based energy projection or rooting energy. However, I've found that in practice you don't need to fixate on that particular point. For rebounding, it's actually better and less of a mental distraction simply to remain gently mindful of the full sole of each foot.

The rebound subcomponent is the simplest of the ARC elements. You just need to relax and keep a small part of your mind gently on the soles at all times as you do your Taiji form. That is sufficient to lead the amassed energy in the *dantian* down to the feet, and ready it to pop back up to be caught by your hands. However, there is an accelerant that applies to the rebound aspect of the ARC process, just as there is for the accumulate phase. That accelerant will be covered in the next chapter, Form. For now, just keep in mind that the drop of energy to the feet is the true – the *energetic* – source of a Taiji adept's outlandish rooted stability, rather than any kind of physical or structural vectoring and support. That's how the Taiji adage *stand like a tree* is cashed out. Your legs will start to feel incredibly good. But if, in pursuit of 'root', you physically dig in or clench your toes or anything overt like that you'll never experience this amazing ability. Again, it must be purely energetic, meaning mentally engendered.

CATCH

Catch means to convey or conduct the energy from its rebound in the feet up to the hands. It's the final move of the basketball dribble – and the point at which you'd actually issue functional energy, like a basketball shot for the hoop, if you were in partner practice mode. (Mind you, basketball energy is physical and in Taiji we don't work with physical energy – it's just another analogy.) The optimal route when you start is to mentally work the energy current up from the backs of your legs. The rise begins with the back of the heels, and then up along the inside or backside of the legs to the perineum. Later, the rise from the feet is not limited to the rear contour. The energy will encompass the entire muscle, tissue, and bone mass of both legs without differentiation, There's more on how to run energy up the backs of the legs in Chapter Three, Form.

Between the rebound and catch phases, you'll feel something particularly interesting. I'm sure you've heard the common Taiji adage: *the qi sinks to the dantian* (气沉丹田). That's one way of describing the accumulate phase already discussed. That's the *dantian* filling from above as you relax your shoulders, etc. In the rebound and catch phase though, as the energy comes up from the feet, you'll feel the amazing sensation of *the dantian filling from below*. After the rise from the legs, and before switching rearwards to the *weilu* point at the base of the spine, the *dantian* swells with energy. It's freakishly weird but fun.

Now's a good time to re-hammer the difference between psycho-visual *imagery designed to encourage an effect* vs. *the actual effect itself* happening in you. They aren't the same thing. This book has some psycho-visual training suggestions that may help set the stage for the energy's grand entrance. But the energy happens as an actual experiential phenomenon – it is emphatically distinct from the *training imagery* you may use to evoke it. It becomes the real thing. *Fantasizing* about having sex with Mr. or Ms. X is a completely distinct experience from *actually doing so*. Please bear this important difference in mind as you read on. These psycho-visualization games are the *finger*. But this book is more about describing the *moon* – the electrifying energy experience in and of itself. If you still think in terms of training imagery, you don't yet know it at all.

After refilling the *dantian* from below, the energy starts up again, this time running along the inner backside and spine (as opposed to the inner front path on the way down). The *qihai* is full all over, like a volley ball inside, so it's already in contact with both front and back sides, and the *huiyin* at the bottom. It will begin the upward circulation from the *weilu* point at the base of the sacrum and you'll feel it rise straight along the spine from there, through the lower spine up to the *lingtai* in the upper midback.

It continues its rise from there of course, but I single out the *lingtai* because the concentration there is most easily felt. It offers a good checkpoint for sensing whether anything's actually happening. The *lingtai* should feel as though its concentrating and radiating huge amounts of pure energy. I'm not asking you to *imagine*, this isn't a psycho-visual imagery exercise. Just objectively check if you actually feel what I'm saying. A current of pure power from your feet to your massively radiating *lingtai* – is it happening for you, in every pose of your form, or not? If not, you still aren't relaxed enough, so things aren't perking yet. Keep practicing.

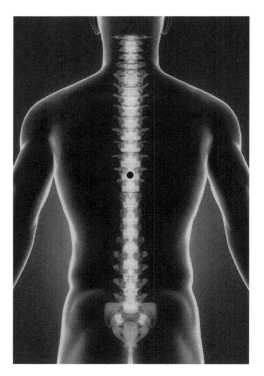

Figure 3 The *lingtai* point, an important intermediate concentration spot in the ARC feet-to-hands energy linkage. In some people, the *lingtai* may be felt a notch higher than the point depicted.

From the *lingtai* the rising circulation continues upward to the head. It will pass some traditionally named points in the cervical spine and lower skull that we don't need to worry about now. The main thing is to keep your head upright and your neck, shoulders and jaw soft and relaxed. The key thing is that *the energy needs to get back to where we kicked off the ARC process – the NEXUS Point.* This is the most crucial teaching in this book. If you don't *start and end* the energy circuit with the NEXUS Point, you'll never get near real Taiji. You may be confused by my talking about the NEXUS Point as the "end" when we haven't reached the hands yet, as the hands were part of the definition of the ARC process to begin with, so let me explain the astonishing details.

One of the most famously weird and incomprehensible lines in the Taiji classic writings is the teaching有气者无力，无气者纯钢. It's usually translated: *Where there is qi, there is no power. Where there is no qi, there is (the power of) pure steel.* This line has been freaking out translators and practitioners alike for decades. First of all, everybody thought *qi* was the whole point of Taiji in the first place, so what gives with this sudden suggestion that it's somehow weak? Second, the use of the term "steel" seems to suggest some kind of rigidity - which everybody thought was to be avoided. So people have gone round and round, some saying that *qi* here (unlike everywhere else in the classic writings) doesn't actually refer to the internal energy, that what they're telling us here is that if you focus on your *breath* (a variant translation of the same word *qi*) you won't get the real (non-breath) *qi* internal energy. There are many other such vague, hand-waving types of interpretations.

So what's really going on here? There are two feedstock sources of unorganized energy available inside and outside the body. One we've already discussed – the semi-random patches and flashes of BRUTE *qi* bursts that everybody has all over their body, but which the insensitive person rarely feels. The other feedstock type of energy is external to the body, it's the *qi* of the air and water and land and so on, all around us. I will call this type of feedstock energy the Original Raw Energy (ORE). So we have ORE and BRUTE energies as raw material. They are real but unrefined. Good enough to keep us alive but not good enough for high-quality Taiji.

The accumulate phase of the ARC training is dealing with these two feedstock energies - taking in (which applies to the ORE) and organizing (which applies to the BRUTE). The ARC process overall is kneading them into your body, putting them under the control of your mind, and gradually refining, strengthening, *tempering* them... see where we're going with this?

The Japanese Sword Museum in Tokyo describes the forging of a samurai sword from two grades of metal thusly:

> *The actual forging of the blade was a complex process. Strips of two different grades of iron were welded together by the smith's hammer. The resulting billet of metal was then folded upon itself and hammered out again to its original length and thickness. This process was repeated many times, until the final blade consisted of many thin, tightly welded layers of the original metal.*

> - Nippon Bijutsu Token Hozon Kyokai (N.B.T.H.K.)

This is what the ARC process, cycling down to the feet and back up, over and over, is doing to the ORE and BRUTE energies. *It's forging a new form of refined internal energy that manifests from the NEXUS Point.* Now we see that the NEXUS Point is an intake valve but also an emanation point. What accumulates in the *dantian* in the first phase is intake universal energy (ORE) from the NEXUS Point, as well as scattered disorganized BRUTE *qi*, which theoretically comes from all over the body but in practice results largely from the release of tension in the upper body. What is available at the NEXUS Point as a result of the ARC tempering is something so awesome I'll just

88

this once forgo the pleasure of acronymizing it. I'm just going to call it STEEL (all caps to remind you it's a technical term of art, not the common noun), same concept used in the Taiji classic writings. STEEL is my word for the final, fully refined, absolutely awesome and pure 24K Taiji energy.

But what about the final stage of the catch, which I defined as 'energy reaching the hands'? The final stage is actually the instantaneous jump of the energy from the NEXUS Point (return base) to *anywhere in the body*. It doesn't have to be the hands, but I use the hands as a stand-in for everything else just because they are the most natural area for functional use in Taiji or anything else. The last stage of the catch component is complete when the STEEL energy flashes out directly from the NEXUS Point to the hands. That is what I've meant when I've talked about the 'spirit power' of real Taiji.

In fact, the STEEL energy is following some specific pathway in the body to reach the hands, much as the energy traveled within specific body parts in the earlier parts of the ARC. But in deployment it sure doesn't feel that way. In deployment it must be instantaneous. You couldn't deploy the energy meaningfully for martial arts if you had to consciously lead it down and around all kinds of body byways with complex fragile imagery and all that. So the ARC training primes the pump and readies the NEXUS Point to deliver this STEEL instantly on demand.

That final jump, from the NEXUS Point to the hands, I will call the FLASHOUT. That's what a real Taiji master can do, and it's the source of their freakish oddball power. In deployment (for example, in Taiji push hands practice) you won't feel that you're leading all your energy through the entire ARC and then out. That's too slow and too distracting. In deployment, *you merely relax absolutely* and then the FLASHOUT can be triggered by your mind in an instantaneous-feeling leap from NEXUS Point to your hands. However, in energy *cultivation* through your form practice, and in some special types of Taiji deployment of energy, there's no need to do the instantaneous FLASHOUT thing. In training or cultivation mode, you want to feel the continuous unbroken linkage of the ARC at all times, from the NEXUS Point down to the feet, from the feet back to the NEXUS Point, and from there to the hands. The only adjustment needed is to mentally decelerate the FLASHOUT - to the point that it becomes an even unbroken stream of the STEEL energy from NEXUS Point to hands, which I'll call the STREAMOUT. Here's the maxim you need to enshrine:

Your hands are not entitled to express any energy of any kind that you didn't feel originating in your feet.

A person who is capable of deploying the STEEL from the NEXUS Point via FLASHOUT and STREAMOUT has achieved the Fully Activated Body (FAB) mentioned earlier. But here's a key caveat: there are two conditions under which the FLASHOUT and STREAMOUT won't work, even if you do the right kind of mental command to trigger them. Remember that the ARC, STEEL, FLASHOUT, and STREAMOUT are not mere imaginary imagery exercises. They are subtle realities of your energy body. They can be honed and trained somewhat by imagery exercises, but they aren't the same thing. Therefore the two failure conditions for the FLASHOUT and STREAMOUT are:

i. You haven't got enough *energy* to play the game. You need more basic ARC work.

ii. You have the STEEL but your body isn't *relaxed in deployment* (from the NEXUS Point to the hands)

The first condition is self-explanatory but the second is a reminder that relaxation is *still* the paramount consideration. All the spirit energy in the world won't help you if at the time of deployment you aren't relaxed, due to over-involvement in the situation, habit, ego, fear, or any other reason. Taiji is relaxation - first, last, and always.

There are three ways that students typically hope to shortcut the ARC and the FLASHOUT cultivation/deployment model.

    i.   Simulation: Try to simulate the effect by psycho-visualization and imagery rather than working with the actual, tangible energy.

    ii.   Attempting to FLASHOUT or STREAMOUT directly from the NEXUS Point without going through the full ARC tempering cycle described.

    iii.   Attempting to deploy the energy from the *lingtai* instead of going through the entire return to the NEXUS Point and relaxation into FLASHOUT or STREAMOUT.

The first two are plain wrong. In *simulation,* you merely imagine a wave of energy coming up your body from your feet. That barely works at all against a good push hands player (push hands can be one of your diagnostic tools). It's true that some imagery is used for long-term training of the ARC, but that beginning phase soon gives way to actual mental control of the real, felt energy. And, more than imagination, relaxation of various body parts is always the lion's share of ARC training anyway, since the result mostly occurs naturally. If you haven't got the money you can't sit down at the table, that's all. Work more on the ARC before re-attempting.

The *direct* attempt to FLASHOUT or STREAMOUT mental energy to your hands without tempering it through the full ARC at all is doomed to total failure. While imagination has a role in training the energy, particularly in the beginning, this kind of fantasizing will get you nowhere. The raw energy must be concentrated and tempered and returned via the full body path to the NEXUS Point as STEEL before it can be of any use whatsoever. The Taiji classic writings themselves say so, as we've seen. Trying to use the spirit energy directly without ARC-tempering it is like standing a telephone pole on the ground instead of staking it in – doomed to crash uselessly. This is why no amount of purely mental work, such as *zazen* or sedentary Taoist mediation, can ever yield Taiji-like results. Forget this idea.

The *lingtai* deployment is altogether different from the other two shortcuts, and it has some validity. Once the ARC energy has reached the *lingtai*, it becomes available for direct deployment from the *lingtai* up through the backs of the shoulders, down the arms and into the hands. This is a way of using the *yang* (choppier element of the energy) before it's fully tempered into STEEL (which can only happen at the return to, and FLASHOUT/STREAMOUT from, the NEXUS Point). I will not disparage this mode, because even though it's inferior to the NEXUS Point FLASHOUT/STREAMOUT of pure STEEL, it can be used in deployment (e.g. push hands) to some extent. And more importantly for this book's stated purpose, it can feel simply ecstatic. That said, compared to the full STEEL energy, deployment of *yang* power from the *lingtai* through the arms directly is like loading a fine Remington model 870 12-gauge shotgun with birdshot or beans. It would be a shame if you got habituated to that lazy style of deployment as 'real Taiji' and never learn the higher stuff that you're so close to. Nevertheless, the *lingtai* is such an important point of concentration and feels so good to play with that I suggest a way to enjoy incorporating it into sword training (Chapter 5).

But I need to tell you a little more about the target terminal point for the ARC. To do that, I need to back up and talk about energy point theory, just one more time. As I've said, according to classical Chinese medical doctrine, there are hundreds of named points in the body, each with its associated meridians, indications for medical use, and so on. In every book on Taiji or Qigong, including this one, you'll find the author parroting the standard points we all know and love, such as the *dantian* (inner lower abdomen) and *baihui* (crown of head) and so on. Additionally, every author needs to make his or her own 'market differentiation' cherry-pick of one or two uncommon points to play up big.

Some people like the 'Bubbling Well' (*yongquan*), others the 'Jade Pillow' (*yuzhen*), still others groove on wilder stuff like the 'Armpit Abyss' (*yuanye*) and so forth. My lack of special focus on any of these doesn't mean I deny their existence or consider them useless or have never experienced their effects. But I'm here to teach you the Taiji ARC of STEEL. Once you get the ARC running and you have got your body full activated (FAB condition) all points of the entire body's energy structure are gonna light up like a Christmas tree. Every single point is on the circuit of the ARC.

But - practice time is limited. Our minds, bodies, and attention spans are also limited. There's only so much complexity we can effectively handle. My job is to give you, not 'all you can carry' but the absolute minimum effective outfitting so you can spend your resources where it's going to matter the most. Minimalism and simplicity are the keys to success. It's no good for me to emphasize 25 different points and 10 special breathing techniques and 15 inner linking protocols – because you aren't going to practice those. Those kinds of systems are just too much and most people will end up dropping their practice.

This is a book on Taiji. I've said it already: Let your Taiji form be your drill. A good Taiji form is all you need once you understand the ARC process. And to understand the ARC, apart from the *dantian* which is discussed in all Taiji materials, you only need to work with three key points.

Here are the Big Three:

- *niwan*: the NEXUS source point in the head
- *lingtai*: the concentration point in the upper mid-back
- *daling*: the concentration point at the inner wrist

I've already covered the first two. The final point you need for the ARC is the *daling*, located at the inner wrist, as shown in the illustration. When I talk about FLASHOUT or STREAMOUT as the final stage of the ARC (the final stage of energy projection either from the NEXUS Point in the full ARC, or direct from the *lingtai* in the 'shortcut' ARC, as discussed above), the *daling* is the main target point.

Of course, ultimately the energy needs to reach, and will reach, all the way out to your fingertips and beyond. That goes without saying. But the *daling* is the essential concentration point along the way. It's like a boosting or relay station for that final long stretch. Some Yang style Taiji teachers emphasize a concept called 'setting the wrists'. What this actually means, and how it's really done, has long been a mystery to many Taiji students, so they usually just end up concluding that it's a code phrase for the standard teachings, such as 'relax' or 'keep Beautiful Lady's Hand' (for ZMQ37 style). Those are great general injunctions, to be sure, but in this case there's a bit more technical detail to add to the 'set the wrists' teaching.

That technical detail is using the *daling* point as a booster station. The hand point that you'll normally hear about in standard Qigong is the *laogong* point in the center of the palm. This is certainly an energy hot spot and it will of course be included in the final ARC linkage and projection. But it's not the most effective target point if you really want to get your juice on through this ARC process. When doing the STREAMOUT from the NEXUS Point (or the shortcut projection from the *lingtai*), keep your forearms, wrists, and hands completely relaxed (without losing the spirit of the given Taiji pose). Feel the energy come alive in the *daling* before expanding it into your hands (palms, *laogong*, inner surface of the fingers, fingertips, entire hand). That is 'setting the wrists' – it boils down to feeling the energy activate itself at the *daling* via extreme and uncompromising forearm and hand relaxation before the final extension and activation into the hands per se.)

Figure 4 The *daling* point is the concentration booster station for the final leg of ARC energy projection. It will be activated as soon as you maximally relax your forearms, inner wrists and hands while doing your form.

For the ARC you need to work mainly with the Big Three points I've already listed. Notice that each one of the Big Three points for the ARC roughly corresponds in location and function to a more commonly emphasized point nearby. In my terms, the *niwan* is doing what in other books is covered by the *baihui* (crown point), the *lingtai* is doing what in other books is covered by the *mingmen* (lower mid-back), and the *daling* is doing what in other books is covered by the *laogong* (center palms). This does not mean I deny the existence or utility of any points. They're all in there, doing their thing or you'd be dead meat right now as we speak.

But I'm presenting the optimally efficient ARC process for Taiji power training. You can't handle too much complexity (if you try, it'll just tense you up, and no matter how many points we pile up, relax is still, first, last, and always our Prime Directive.) Choices have to be made. I have found in four decades of practice and teaching that working the ARC with these Big Three, in conjunction with absolute dedication to utter relaxation at all times, gives, I estimate, approximately a *hundredfold amplification of energy* over working with any alternate set of points you might more commonly hear of. Furthermore, these Big Three are mentally and physically the most compatible with the bedrock Prime Directive of Taiji, which is … ? Care to guess? Enough said.

SEVEN STAGES OF ARC TRAINING

Achieving the Fully Activated Body state (FAB) via the ARC process is not all that hard. It's one of those 'knack' things, like riding a bicycle. At some point it just clicks in and from then on your mind/body knows on its own how to replicate the right conditions. To get started, first choose a restricted experimental framework. This should probably be a subset of your preferred Taiji form. If you have learned a very long form, e.g. 50 postures or more that require 20 minutes or longer to finish, you'll want to begin the ARC training using a subset that takes about 10 to 12 minutes to finish at normal Taiji slow-motion speed.

First, mentally activate the NEXUS Point (location as described above). That must be done by a very light focus, just relaxed and calm awareness of the *niwan*. Don't over concentrate or heavily meditate on it. Mentally find it, just touch-and-go. After doing that once for a given session, you don't need to explicitly activate it again (except in the final two stages below). Then, repeat your chosen sequence (whole form or subset) seven times, with your mind fixed and focused as follows, changing on each rep. Your mind's shadow, just a touch of awareness, stays with the parenthesized element but primarily you focus on the bolded component:

1. (NEXUS Point to) **qihai and dantian**
2. (*qihai* and *dantian* to) **soles of feet**
3. (feet to) **qihai (the re-filling from below)**
4. (*qihai* to) **weilu**
5. (*weilu* to) **lingtai**
6. (*lingtai* to) **NEXUS Point (the return)**
7. (NEXUS Point to) **daling and hands (the STREAMOUT)**

Now you see why I suggested a shorter subset of your form, optimally about 10 minutes or less for a single rep. Even with a short subset, the above practice session will take over an hour. At every step of your form (or the mini-form subset you've selected for this), you should strive to fulfill the minimal correct posture requirements. That means, even if I've written that you concentrate on your feet or your *dantian* or wherever at a certain point, you don't just let everything else go. Keep the minimally correct posture at every stage.

Once you're very familiar with all the endpoints and linkages in the above partial paths, you can return to your normal full form practice on a regular basis. You should perform your whole form in a single 'long take' as they say in Hollywood. You never stop and never speed up. Keep the rate absolutely even, and focus on streaming the energy up from your feet to the NEXUS Point and from there keeping your arms and hands entirely suffused with the energy supplied by the continuous unbroken STREAMOUT (the FLASHOUT is more appropriate for deployment than for cultivation). The common Taiji term 'unbroken' has two meanings: first, that your physical motions of the form have no stoppage or speedup, and second, that the absolute fullness and energy permeation of your arms and hands is never interrupted. As soon as it's kicked off, the STREAMOUT energy condition never stops and is never re-started in a given round of the form. As long as the mind maintains the invariant target zone (arms and hands), the STREAMOUT, once begun, will continue uninterrupted for the duration of your full set, keeping your arms and hands fully soaked with energy.

At first, you're going to be tempted to try running the ARC either as a physical process or as an imaginary psycho-visualization. If you incline to the physical, you're going to want to shiver your legs, shake your butt, wriggle your spine, and flap your arms to get a pseudo-propagation of force up your body. That's very tempting. Don't do that. The ARC, just like the spontaneous wave energetics covered later in this chapter, has nothing to do with that kind of physicality. The ARC process is purely energetic. Don't try to game it with a physical simulacrum.

If you're more of a psycho-visual person, you'll be tempted to just keep on imagining this process. That seems closer to the mark, but ultimately that's also a red herring and taking the finger for the moon. It may seem strange that in this book which after all presents a number of psycho-visualization exercises I should sound this note of skepticism about them. They certainly have their place as training wheels. But that's all they are. They aren't the end goal or state, which seems like an obvious point but people very easily get wedded to trivialities. It's the difference between *instruct* and *notify*. Imagine I were your Taijij teacher (God forbid, eh?) I could instruct you with very specific imagery guidance: *imagine your arms are balloons*, or *picture yourself with all the muscles melting off your bones*, or much wilder stuff.

That's all fine as a startup idea. But still, that's *instruction* and you might get stuck right there. It's much better if instead I teach you just a few energy fundamentals of your inner makeup and then get out of the way by telling you: *relax*. The more you work on relaxing, the more likely it is that at some point the direction will reverse. Instead of *instruction* it will become *notification*, meaning *you* will come to *me*, and tell me: *Hey, that's amazing! I just felt it for real!*. And at that point, it won't be just a trickle of BRUTE *qi* leaking here and there, now and then in your arms as you're lost in your imagery effort, it will be a torrent of energy like a fire hose in your arms - from the real ARC activation.

So even though this book teaches some visualization and imagery exercises, it's always best to focus on real energetic experience, not yet another imagery drill. You'll get farthest fastest if you concern yourself mainly with relaxing all mental, physical and energetic components of the ARC. Then the transmission will happen for real, all on its own, and you'll be astonished simply to notice it, rather than always merely imagining you have it. Noticing and later manipulating real energetic phenomena, no matter how subtly they begin, is always preferable to imaginary drills. The energetics will emerge spontaneously once you relax everything.

FULLY ACTIVATED BODY

When your arms – shoulder to fingertips – feel like a single unit of pure molten steel, and your feet begin to feel hot like you're standing on a lava bed, congrats – you have fully activated the ARC integration. That is the Taiji Fully Activated Body (FAB) state.

In Chinese: *quanshentong* (全身通). When that happens, remember that this ARC thing is a level of internal achievement, but most of all it's a training *process*. The Fully Activated Body is a state that can take on an infinite variety of flavors as you develop. It is the end of the beginning of your Taiji training, not the ultimate end or the final goal. Sometimes people ask me whether there are special tests or self-checks to verify that this Fully Activated Body has been achieved. There's really no need for any special drill or rote to check whether you've at least got to the first level of body energy activation. Once you have it, you'll know it. You'll just feel that million volts of radioactive beehive buzz.

When people start to learn public speaking, their first big question is: *What do I do with my hands?* In beginning Taiji practice, you have plenty to do with your hands, but over time, Taiji students start to ask 'What do I do with my *mind*?' As a beginner it's easy to engage the mind in trying to get your body looking just right in a new posture, or trying to remember what pose is next in the sequence. But when you've become thoroughly familiar with the physical framework, the question really starts to gnaw: *What do I do with my mind?*

There are many arbitrary answers depending whom you ask… mind in your hands, mind in your feet, mind in your *dantian*, try to relax, feel your whole body, mind on [*fill in some acupoint*], feel the threat of an opponent in front of you, visualize the reality of each posture's combative application, gently sense your surroundings – the list of possible mental preoccupations as you go through the form is endless. What most people end up with is a jumble of 10% switching randomly among everything listed above, and 90% daydreaming and distraction around daily life (health, finances, and personal relationships).

The ARC process puts all that to rest once and for all. The accumulate part of the ARC is handled automatically via just relaxing and doing the form. So when you're doing the form, your mind's big job (after gently activating the NEXUS Point in your head at the start of practice) is working consciously with the rebound and catch parts of the ARC – trying to maintain the feet-to-arms connection, via full body relaxation and directed imagery. Gently maintain that mental connection. The accelerants presented in the next Chapter, Form, will greatly assist in this. When you feel you're standing on a surface made of the purest, softest, warmest cotton – I mean, really have that physical feeling in your feet, even when training in thin soles on cold, hard concrete – then you're getting very close to the FAB Fully Activated Body state which is the goal of the ARC.

Once you have enabled the basic flow-through by the ARC training process, the types of energy phenomena you'll begin to experience are potentially infinite. But for exposition I'll be grouping the various phenomena into major subtypes, which I'll call the Four Facets of internal energy. For now, just take away that this ARC process underlies and frames your experience of all the Four Facets of Energy, which are covered in greater detail in the next chapter.

This section on the ARC process is the working heart of this book. I don't want to hear anyone saying: *That book didn't give me anything to actually* do *as a practice, it was all verbiage - no photos!* Listen up: this ARC thing *is* what you do. But since it's done with your mind and your energy, not by putting your hands and feet just so, I can't lard this chapter up with lots of photos. That's why we call Taiji an *internal* discipline. The ARC process is the most important thing you can do in your practice. Connect the energy from feet to hands. But you need to do it with your mind, not your body. Your body's job is to relax, soften, de-link internally, and just get out of the way. Whatever style you play, unless you engage your *mind* in this particular way you aren't going to harvest what Taiji has to offer.

HEADSTAND ENERGY CHECK

If you're an adventurous soul, and you've got the FAB going, there are a few fun things you can do in this general space. I'll give one example here but I'm sure you'll come up with many others on your own. If you know yoga, pop into yoga *shirsasana* or headstand pose (Note: this paragraph applies only to experienced yoga practitioners under the supervision of a qualified yoga instructor. Do not attempt it otherwise. Please re-read the Disclaimer before proceeding.) Your feet are pointed straight up. Then you'll feel a tremendous buzz-saw type of energy effect in your feet, assuming your *mingjing* energy is fully activated. It's really a blast. It doesn't matter much in the big picture, because if your *mingjing* is activated (through the ARC training process) then your feet are continually buzzing pleasantly like a background coffee grinder no matter how you stand, even in daily life. But experiencing it in *shirsasana* is a real trip.

MORE MENTAL STUFF

BELIEVE

I mentioned above that while Taiji is not a religion, still a kind of faith is needed to get started with it. I know this *believe* thing is a tough one. The prevalence of New Age scams, creeps, and cults has motivated people to deconstruct Taiji into physics, structures, and angles - things they think they can get a grip on, jettisoning the medieval baggage. All well and good except - the Daoist energy ladder is for real. If you deny that in yourself, and always try to force-fit your initial baby BRUTE energy experiences (which everybody can quickly feel) into the Procrustean bed of scientific angles and joints and tendons and torque and all that, you'll never get beyond those baby steps and launched into the real stuff.

You don't have to believe like a fervent religious nutcase, but you need to have absolute unshakable *confidence* that when the great masters like Zheng Manqing, Li Yaxuan, Yang Chengfu, Morihei Ueshiba, Tesshu Yamaoka, and many others talked about *qi* as well as other, higher forms of energy and spirit, they meant it. They weren't idiot savants miraculously functioning at genius level, who need to have their words force-fit into a smug little anatomically or kinesthetically correct playpen. They had the real stuff and they're trying to give it to you even now, but you have to step up and meet them halfway. This emphasis on faith and belief only applies at the beginning. After a while you'll be so radioactively throbbing with your own energy permeation that questions of belief, doubt, and credibility won't even come up for you anymore. You'll just be looking forward to your next practice session.

It's not a religion or cult. It's like unicycle riding, is that a religion? But imagine if you'd never seen a unicycle and somebody told you that yes, you can stay upright and ride all over on just one wheel, *it is possible*. But if you'd reacted: *Nah that just can't be, I'd fall over for sure* – in that case, you probably would never even attempt it. But even if you fell over the first thousand times, you'd eventually get the knack of it, if you tried hard enough. I'd have had a lot more internal power a lot earlier in my life if I could've just straightforwardly accepted the total relaxation approach that I was taught the first day. People often write in to me from my blog site, asking questions like: *You talk a lot about relaxation, but you don't say* how *we're supposed to actually do* that, drop our tension and so on. How are we supposed to accomplish the stuff you write about? Well, this is it. The reason you're tense is that you don't really believe in relaxation. If you did you could drop that tension in a nano-second. You have the ability. We know that much, because you're relaxed every night in your sleep. The reason you're tensed up now is only that on some level you have a fear-based or habit-based belief that you can't let down your guard.

NOTICE

Eventually you need to be able to feel the energy running inside yourself. *If you can't feel it, you can't feed it.* And though you can find all kinds of wonderfully complicated meridian charts on the net, that stuff is only the roughest starting point. You need to learn to feel and focus within yourself. It's like the kids game of *cold, cold, warm, warmer, hot!* You're continually either focusing more precisely and thereby strengthening the energy run, or else you're moving away from it. Just as in the game, you need to seize on even small sensations, not to fool yourself but to check them out. Pursue them awhile. Some sensations are dead ends or self-delusion. But sometimes very minor sensations are the camel's nose beneath the tent, the first indication of a big new development. Those small sensations are the equivalent of the other kids shouting "Warmer!"

PERSIST

Never ever miss a daily practice. NEVER! I've been in horrific car accidents, been assaulted by maniacs, been laid out on emergency room gurneys, been stuck in police holding cells, and all kinds of other stuff - but by close of every day for over forty years I've *always* found some quiet corner where I can do some kind of Taiji practice. I never miss.

If you aren't doing a good Taiji system like ZMQ37 every single day of your life, it's going to be hard to forge ahead along the lines of this chapter. In that case, you aren't really on the game board. And even if you're fairly persistent in your practice, still the old adage applies, at least in the first few years: *If you miss a day, you're starting over.* So if you take nothing else from this section, brand the following on your butt: *Never miss a day.* If the sky that we look upon should tumble and fall, and the mountains should crumble to the sea, still, still, STILL - never *miss a day of practice.* When strongman bodybuilder Mariusz Pudzianowski was asked in early 2004 when he'd last taken steroids, he answered: *What time is it now?* That's the spirit! If anybody wonders how long it's been since you last did your Taiji form, your answer should be the same.

CHAPTER 3:
FORM

POSTURES

I got it. Just stay close enough to get it.

- Lady Gaga

All styles of Taiji are built around a set sequence of linked movements. That's the form, which may be anywhere from a dozen common postures to well over a hundred exotic specimens. A good Taiji form is your workbench, your playpen, and your crucible for cultivating and beginning to deploy your internal power. It is both anvil and hammer at once. But be careful, because teachers like to make much of the supposed distinction and superiority of their form (with, say, 24 movements) vs. Brand X (with 86 movements). None of that matters in the least. A given form may be vastly superior to another for the real purpose (energy cultivation) but that has nothing to do with its length or number of movements.

If a given form is too short to fill the time available for practice, just repeat as needed. If it's too long to get through in one session, do part of it. This isn't rocket science. None of these surface differences in the number or sequencing of postures matters at all. All Taiji forms should be thought of as circular and therefore infinite. They're designed to be seamlessly repeatable any number of times. Obsessing about the particular sequence of postures in Style X vs. Style Y, or getting fetishistic about the overall length is just another example of the Theatric Fallacy – the belief that the *appearance* of the physical practice is the key thing (see next chapter's section on 'The Fallacies').

Backing up a little, we need to preface this whole discussion on form with a re-statement of the mechanism of true Taiji: it functions to get your *mind fully and pervasively interpenetrating your body –*

exclusive of any blocking physical tension or muscularity - so that spirit energy is connected seamlessly from feet to hands. (We could also play word games and turn that around, saying: put your body in your mind). Most people when they read/hear the above sort of statement have one of two more or less opposite reactions:

1. They assume that they've already *got* their mind fully into their body, either through training done to-date or just from the mere fact of being alive. After all, aren't we all functionally aware of our own bodies? If you drop a brick on your foot, it hurts. If tickled, you laugh. If you want to move your little finger, you have merely to think of doing so and lo, it has been done. But this kind of ordinary mind/body synthesis is not what I'm getting at here.

2. They assume that the "mind into body" instruction is just some kind of high falutin' philosophical or metaphorical BS, the kind of teaching toward which you genuflect and then get on with real life. To be respected, maybe, but basically ignored in practice because it seems abstract and useless.

Both reactions (1) and (2) above are totally wrong interpretations of what I'm saying here. When I say mind pervades body I'm talking about an absolutely real, concrete, self-checkable state that may not be scientifically verifiable (yet), but which feels as real as sex or dental drilling - an absolutely concrete, unambiguously intense personal experience. If you haven't yet been totally consumed by the ecstatic energy of your Taiji practice, you shouldn't necessarily blame yourself. As I've stated repeatedly, the one essential prerequisite of Taiji is relaxation. Strangely though, many widely practiced forms (specific sequences) of Taiji movements not only don't especially foster the practitioner's relaxation, they may actually hinder it. That's usually because either (a) the form was designed to look cool on stage, or (b) the form was tensed up a little to make it feel combatively real.

110

SELF-CHECKING

This book has an energetic, non-physical focus. I've said that it doesn't matter what flavor of Taiji you practice. All forms and styles are equal. But of course some are more equal than others. We have to remove prejudice based on lineage, accidental personal connection, economic considerations, history, habit, and so on. Fortunately we have a Gold Standard for evaluating the physical aspect of a Taiji form. The Gold Standard is the question: *Does this form optimally promote relaxation?* Relaxation is the immediate physical goal because it enables the energetic connection.

So you can do any form, but check yourself as you do it. There are many easy diagnostics. For example, ask yourself whether your form requires you to lean your upper body forward. Even slightly? If so, experiment for a moment with a variation – keeping your body upright. Now ask yourself, objectively, which way requires a bit more muscular tension to maintain? If you honestly think leaning is more relaxed, then that's the way for you. Many other people will find that keeping the body upright is more relaxed. Either way, the point is that we have an impartial standard – the degree to which a given practice fosters or hinders relaxation.

Or consider the typical Taiji "bow posture" where you have a bent front knee with more weight on the front than the back. You may have been taught to do this with a straightened rear leg. If so test again, as above. Try that same posture: once as you've been taught with a straight back leg, and now again with a gently bent knee in the rear leg. In which version is your leg, in fact your whole body, more relaxed? If the straightened-leg version, then that's your truth. You can be confident that you're in line with the Taiji classic writing's admonition to relax, because you've tested yourself and you know the truth through personal experience, not because somebody said so. Many other people will find that the bent rear leg calls for a bit less tension and is more conducive to Taiji's Prime Directive of relaxation.

Another example might be your hand position. Execute your style's version of a typical Taiji pose such as 'Single Whip' or any other pose with a frontward palm orientation, such as 'Press' or 'Push'. Notice your wrist and hand position. Is there any tension? Do you see tendons or bones bulging out of the backs of your hands? That could indicate tension. If you do notice that, and you've been taught to bend your wrist in these poses, try another version where you don't bend the wrist, but keep your wrist and hands gently straightened in a soft line with the forearm. Does that feel more relaxed or not? Just go with what you honestly feel.

Basically any form that deviates from the Taiji classic writings is cutting across the grain of our one true goal – to foster relaxation. However beautiful it may look (see next chapter's section on 'The Fallacies', specifically the Theatric Fallacy) it isn't Taiji, it's something else (maybe a lame type of folk dance). Don't get posture-fixated. Don't fall in love with the physical postures themselves, maybe because they feel good physically, or they have nice exotic names, or you think you look cool doing them. That will only distract you. The form is a finely honed machine with only one purpose – to help you understand relaxation and thereby establish the energy path.

Always remember that real Taiji is the art of *energy cultivation and deployment*. Though the physical body is employed, the true skill is not mechanical, not structural, not anatomical, not angular or momentum-based or any of that crude physical/structural stuff. To think otherwise is to be like the primitive tribesmen who took the tiger mouth painted on a fighter plane's nose as a real animal and ascribed the power of the airplane to the animal.

THE RAZOR'S EDGE

For convenience, we can define three states of the body-mind. For now, these body-mind states are applied to Taiji posture work, but they actually manifest in anything you could ever possibly do.

Relaxed: In the relaxed state you're using no more physical force or muscular tension than is required to correctly maintain a given body configuration.

Tensed: In the tense state you're using either using more physical force or muscular tension than is required to maintain the desired body configuration, or else, even worse, you're attempting a configuration which actually *requires* tension for its "correct" execution.

Collapsed: In a state of collapse you've eliminated all physical force, but you've thrown out the baby with the bath, meaning that your mind is unable to effectively engage your body to accomplish anything (e.g. sleep, unconsciousness, and drunkenness).

Figure 5 The Razor's Edge - Collapsed (left side), ideally Relaxed (middle), Tensed (right side). The sample pose is Yang/ZMQ37 'Single Whip'.

Taiji's ultimate paradox and point of power is its insistence that you maintain yourself on the razor's edge: *just enough physical support* to achieve the posture – not even four ounces more. You need to stand right on the line between collapsed and tensed. That is the position of ultimate power. And, speaking of standing, let's go a little deeper on that subject.

STANDING WORK

Taiji normally consists of slowly flowing movements. But before we talk about movement we need to talk about static practice. Energy (mind into body state) can be cultivated via purely static work, the body remaining immobile for long stretches of time. This is well known in Daoist meditation as well as in Zen sitting (*zazen*) and some martial arts practices.

Standing work in Taiji has two main functions:

1. The requirement to maintain an awkward physically demanding posture over an extended period teaches you to drop all excess effort (because you can't afford to waste energy) – the precondition for true relaxation.

2. Static postures are the stable launch pad on which the first stirrings of true internal energy will be felt. This is the beginning of the paradoxical Taiji feature known as 'movement within stillness'. You may have regarded that as just another drive-by Taiji truism, but this phenomenon is actually a centrally important aspect of Taiji. The body is still, while the energy moves. Static practice is the setting within which this can first be noticed.

The posture you use doesn't matter much. Some postures such as the shoulder-width straight up 'Preparation Posture' of traditional Yang style and also ZMQ37 are physically undemanding and can be held for an hour or more with ease. Others such as 'Play Guitar', which require a low sit on a single leg become excruciating for most people after only a few minutes of correct holding. This type of posture is the best crucible for function (1) above. It's exacting mental training takes your endurance to the edge. You learn to relax because if you engage even a single fiber of muscle beyond what's needed to hold the correct shape, you'll quickly burn out. This type of work highlights the ultimate paradox of Taiji, which is that you're told to relax entirely yet you must keep a particular shape, formed accurately in every detail – hand shape and position, back upright, feet correctly aligned, etc. The details of structure don't matter much (as long as it's maximally relaxed). But the requirement to hold to a particular standard focuses concentration.

It seems like a contradiction and it probably is, but a productive one. This is the fundamental paradox of Taiji. The energy begins to boil right at that razor's edge between *ice* (need to keep perfect form) and *fire* (your endurance pushed beyond its limit). The main thing to emphasize in this work is relaxation of everything. In particular, there's no point in priding yourself on a long hold of, say, an hour or two during which your shoulders were stiff and your elbows held rigidly high. The function of static work is to facilitate the ARC process leading to the Fully Activated Body condition described in the previous chapter.

THE FALLACIES

There are many conceptual fallacies you could fall into. These Fallacies may cause you to layer other kinds of movement over your fundamental ARC. Any of the fallacies listed below can delay or destroy your chances of ever experiencing the truly ecstatic energy.

By the way, some common (but mistaken) Taiji practices exemplify more than one Fallacy type. But the Fallacies are all similar anyway, in that they all superficially enact a kind of pseudo-vibratory effect that mimics the resonance of the true internal energy. So, watch out for the Fallacies listed below.

THE KRIYA FALLACY (*Get a Grip on Yourself*)

As your energy develops, take care not to fall into a typical movement mistake that I call the *Kriya fallacy*. *Kriya* are the strange movements you sometimes see Qigong students getting into – uncontrolled physical contortions such as writhing, jumping, twisting like redneck snake handlers – because, it seems, their big *qi* energy is jacking them around. This uncontrollable shaking and body and limb distortion is supposedly brought on by the extreme power of the internal energy rampaging through their bodies.

Although this can sometimes be a true energy phenomenon, most often it's an extremely hammed-up, low-level thing that leads nowhere. It's another dead end. Because, although the real internal energy feels incredibly powerful on the inside, and though that energy can have real-world external effects in some restricted martial arts practices, the waves of the real energy are nevertheless *truly internal* as far as I'm concerned. I discuss various types of wave-like internal effects in the following sections, but even they result in only barely perceptible outer vibration, if any at all. I've touched hands with many yoga types who can express *Kriya* beautifully, squirming like Elvis on a hot tin roof, but I instantly know, with a single touch, that they haven't even begun to shed their deepest physical tension. With the internal energy running, even at full buzz, onlookers should emphatically *not* see you spazzing, thrashing, and generally freaking out. If they do, you haven't tapped into the true power at all - you're just putting on a show, which leads into the next (in fact, overlapping) mistake – the Theatric Fallacy.

116

In Taiji, movement originates only from the Taiji form, shaped by the mind alone, or else from the spontaneous emergence of the sharp or soft waves described in a following section ('The Four Facets of Energy'). No other kind of movement means anything. The *Kriya* movement is totally the wrong track. It's all tension, ego, and theatrics. If you're truly relaxed that kind of nonsense won't happen. The spontaneous movement of the 'real *yang* power' (introduced in a following section, 'The Four Facets of Energy') is invisible and subtle - but much more powerful in its eventual applications than *Kriya* energy, which is essentially just physical.

THE THEATRIC FALLACY (*Just Throw Money*)

Some Taiji styles exhibit flourishes of the palms, flapping the hands dramatically back and forth as though energy too great to contain is being spewed all over the awed spectators. That flapping stuff is a strictly physical vibration. It's done as pure showmanship, which gives the crowd a good time, but has nothing to do with real internal power.

There's an inherent conflict between aesthetic appeal and functional training. They cannot both be simultaneously optimized for maximal quality. Ask yourself a basic question from engineering: Is it possible to *jointly maximize* two or more truly orthogonal variables, such as time and space, in a software program? Theatric focus includes stuff like foot-stomping and body-shivering intended to showcase your awesome energetic intensity. That kind of silliness is no different in principle from the Lotus-seated butt-bouncing (aka "levitation") that certain meditation schools seem to enjoy publicly embarrassing themselves with. A sub-type of the Theatric Fallacy is the pole-shaking craze (which can also be cited as an example of the Structural Fallacy just below).

Russian Systema master Vladimir Vasiliev (not a Taiji player but a kickass guy) has put it very well with his classic line: *Don't care how you look.* This is an extremely important point if you're ever going to get beyond the shallow end, because the theatric mindset, caring how you look to others, introduces psychological, and thus physical, tension. Part of the problem is that everybody wants to look good. That desire induces tension. Good Taiji doesn't look like much. (Problem is, *bad* Taiji often doesn't look like much either. And bad Taiji can also look stupendously great.)

THE STRUCTURAL FALLACY (*Got the words but not the music*)

This Fallacy is special in that the other two (above) at least pay lip service to the *idea* of internal power, whereas under *The Structural Fallacy* we find the emphasis is entirely on physical concepts from mechanical engineering and physics. The falseness of that kind of approach to Taiji has been exhaustively covered throughout this book. There are more subtle forms of this Fallacy however, including practices such as pole-shaking. In pole-shaking, all parts of the practitioner's body - joints, mass, and muscles - have to be manipulated *just so*, with precise timing and coordination, to transmit a wave of kinetic power from the lower body out through the arms to the pole (or palm in the empty hand version, see the *Theatric Fallacy* above). This too makes for great demo performances, but it's a primitive thing that has nothing to do with serious internal development.

It's a very attractive mistake because it's fun. And it seems to incorporate at least some semblance of the teaching on "relaxation" – after all, you do need to relax somewhat to propagate that physical snap (kinetic impulse) up and out through your arms. So it's a subtle mistake but still a mistake. Nowadays there are lots of teachers who like to waggle the ends of poles to show their "internal" power (usually best demonstrated by very large guys, but sometimes little guys perform this also). This is very fun to do. You feel really badass, and the resulting physical impact could indeed do some damage to a passive target.

But if you take this kind of practice as "what the old masters were really talking about" you are way off track. Real Taiji power is invisible. It's essentially non-physical or at least non-muscular in origin (and not originating from tendons, ligaments, fascia, or any of that popular stuff either). It isn't physically originated in any obvious normal sense of the body, or anatomy, or of grounding as engineering. It's an invisible, non-physical, formless, almost bodiless power. If you are shaking and shimmying up a wave of snappy muscular jolts through your body, you may be having fun but you aren't touching the real thing. The real power *does* come up from below, just as the Classics state, but *not* as that physical shaky-snaky wavelet of serial mechanically propagated tension. That's far too crude - the real Taiji power is something else altogether.

Needless to say, flailing yourself around like that is, health-wise, pretty much contrary to the gentle, quiet spirit of Taiji. A rousing shake (like a dog) now and then is fine, but otherwise it's merely self-flagellation (literally turning yourself into a whip). Real Taiji power is completely invisible and is triggered and propagated by the mind alone, not by any kind of physical snap whatsoever.

THE CALISTHENIC FALLACY (*Let It Be*)

Examples of the *Calisthenic Fallacy* would include typical Aikido drills such as *tekubi-furi* and *furitama*. These involve shaking either the hands or the entire body in conjunction with controlled breath patterns. The Calisthenic Fallacy differs from the Structural Fallacy in that the results of the Calisthenic Fallacy are mistaken by its practitioners for true internal energy, which they do seek, while the Structural Fallacy denies the entire idea of internal energy altogether. But in both types the resonance is consciously created by physical manipulation. The key point that distinguishes the true internal resonances from this kind of deliberate shaking exercise is that the true energy vibrations arise *spontaneously* (at first) as a result of your prior internal development, openness to universal energy flow, and degree of relaxation. Later they can be controlled at will, but without any physical trigger or correlate. Bottom line, the initial internal resonance is not a consciously applied training mechanism. So these kinds of drills won't get you there.

If you get caught up in any of these Fallacies, or any of their dozens of sub-types and close kin, you're toast. So don't do that.

THE ARC ACCELERANTS

Remember I said this book is a long spiral, looping back to revisit the same stuff over and again, from higher angles every time around? We're now going to step through the ARC process one more time, with some powerful augmentations in mind. The ARC is the core process, the main idea of Taiji, and the Taiji form is essentially just a framework for injecting the ARC accelerants. That is, it *can* be – if you know how to work it and what to emphasize.

Your Taiji form is the operating table. This book is the surgical kit. The universal energies are the lightning and thunder crackling and booming outside your mountain lair. Your mind is the mad scientist. Your body is the lab rat. Tinker til you get the connection, gather the energy harvest, and toss the carcass in the trash. It's headed there anyway. But wait – we have to fit your *teacher* into this metaphor somewhere, don't we? After all, somebody helped you pick up that form in the first place... ok, your teacher is Igor.

Just kidding! It's very important to respect your teacher. But do you get the message? You are the one responsible for putting it all together for yourself. This is where I'll again resist the potential charge (that some fool out there will bring) that this book is merely a sales job, pimping one parochial Taiji style (ZMQ37). You don't need to think that way. Any style is really ok; all you need to do is make sure it adheres to the Taiji classic writings, including of course Yang Chengfu's Ten Important Points (太極拳十要 *taijiquanshiyao*).

When it comes to form evaluation, there's one key thing to remember. your form must adhere to the Taiji classic writings. Here are my jury instructions for you:

> *If the form doesn't fit, you gotta lose it.*
> *If the form don't conform, you gotta move on.*

Chief among those essential conformances is the *primacy of relaxation*, as covered in the previous chapter.

The ARC accelerants generally fit the three basic categories of Chinese philosophy and martial arts: Earth, Man, and Heaven, which correspond to feet, body, and head, respectively. In each area, there is an imaginative process you can use to supercharge your experience of ARC in the form practice and eventually 24/7, whatever you're doing. These are the ARC accelerants. If you can do at least one accelerant in each area (head, body, feet) all at once, thoroughly and correctly, for the entire duration of your form practice, then it'll take a while but you're on track to become the next Yang Luchan.

The accelerants are mental settings rather than paint-by-numbers processes or drills, so this section is another one that'll bring out the usual: *But how in hell do I actually do this?* response. Or you'll be tempted to skim the descriptions, appreciate the pictures, and conclude: *Yeah, got it.* But even though these aren't exactly drills in the normal sense, if you don't work with them actively they won't do a thing for you. The accelerants offer the simplest and clearest way to actively and deeply knead the essential qualities into your form every time you practice. I admit it's kind of weird – how can something you merely *think* of or *visualize* as you practice trigger energetic amplification which in turn has a very tangible outcome (in your body experience and in push hands practice)? But if you take them seriously, as seriously as any *full physical drill* which you might pick up at that big seminar next weekend, you'll be blown away by the energy.

FEET (EARTH)

Everyone's heard the standard Taiji injunctions: *stand like a great tree or a mountain*, *set your root*, or maybe *sink both legs one meter into the ground* (两腿入地三尺), etc. Is there anything to add? When standing, we need to work with correct distribution of weight, energy, and mind. First, let's talk about *physical* weight distribution in any Taiji posture. For Taiji purposes, there are three basic ways your weight can be physically distributed: equal (50-50), unequal-relative (e.g. 70-30 or 80-20, etc.), and unequal-absolute (100-0). Of course, there's lots of room for variation in the unequal-relative category, but these three categories are adequate for this discussion. When doing the Taiji form practice, equal physical weighting (sometimes called 'double weighting') should never occur. Throughout the form, one foot is always more heavily weighted than the other, either absolutely or relatively, as above. This is the simplest expression of what Yang Chengfu called the first principle of Taiji:

太極拳術以分虛實為第一義，如全身皆坐在右腿，則右腿為實，左腿為虛；全身皆坐在左腿，則左腿為實，右腿為虛。

The first principle of Taiji is separation of substantial and insubstantial. If the weight of the entire body is on the right leg, then the right leg is considered substantial and the left is insubstantial, while if the weight of the body is entirely on the left leg, then the left is substantial, and the right is insubstantial.

We can take this as a simple physical instruction, meaning that we must avoid physical double-weighting. But we can also go beyond the physical, into the use of *energy* and *mind* to support the concept in a more unified way. You must ensure that in any posture, you maintain *in your mind* a clear distinction between the energetically 'major' leg vs. the energetically 'minor' one. We could call this a typical *yin-yang* distinction. For every posture, you should decide which will be the active/major/*yang* side, and then imagine that you're staking or sinking your foot into the ground, below the surface – but *only on that side*.

My teacher has often said: *you only have one leg*. And this applies to all postures of the form, regardless of the physical weight distribution. If you mentally visualize *both* feet sinking into the ground, as sometimes taught, you may be *physically* single-weighted but you are *energetically* double-weighted. Don't do that. One foot (the *yang* side) is always visualized as sinking, as though *staked into* the ground while the other (the *yin* side) is visualized as being simply lightly *placed on* the surface of the ground.

Figure 6 The weighted *(yang)* foot is STAKED INTO the ground; the unweighted or lesser weighted foot *(yin)* is PLACED ON the ground. The sample pose is Yang/ZMQ37 'Repulse Monkey'.

Note that according to deep Chinese medical theory, the foot itself (actually, any part of the body) is energetically complex. So we could endlessly elaborate the idea expressed so simply by Yang Chengfu above. We could really decorate the Christmas tree here, by talking about the *yin* and *yang* sides of each single foot, or the three super-special energy points within the foot that you need to pay attention to when standing, and so on. But I like to keep things simple. There's no need for all that complexity, and no way to practice effectively with all that in your mind. For this work, you don't even need to fret much over the primary foot point (the *yongquan* on the centerline of the sole, covered in the chapter on Theory). Believe me, when you do the simple *yin-yang* separation thing right for a while, that point will start to throb with power spontaneously, all on its own.

Crucially, this principle of *yin-yang* differentiation can operate independently of the *physical* weight distribution - in theory. In other words, the leg bearing *less* physical weight could be selected as the 'staked in' *yang* leg and the physically *heavier* leg could be visualized as the lightly 'placed' or *yin* leg. (To assume that there's a necessary correlation – direct or inverse - between the physical weighting of a leg and internal power generation is an example of …. what? Can you guess by now? It's the *Structural Fallacy*). So you could consistently do the energy staking through the physically less weighted foot just as well. In practice though, it would get confusing to identify the physically lighter leg with the *yang* power stake-in. So in practice it's usually best, for most postures, to tie the physical and the energetic together, so that the physically weight-bearing leg is energetically 'staked in' the ground, while the physically lesser weighted leg is the one just 'placed on' the ground. If you pay continual attention to this, your internal energy will be greatly amplified in a short time.

Even though the illustration shows the Yang/ZMQ37 style pose *Repulse Monkey*, which happens to have an unequal-absolute (100-

0) weight distribution, the exact same *yin-yang* visualization and mental projection can be used in *any other posture*. It's all the same idea. For example, the Yang/ZMQ37 pose *Single Whip* (unequal-relative, 70-30) is depicted in some of the other illustrations in this book. In that case, the *yang* energy projection, staking the foot through the floor, would happen in the front leg, which has the greater physical weight. In the one double-weighted Yang/ZMQ37 pose, *Preparation Posture,* you can arbitrarily choose left or right to be energetically heavy, but even in that pose, you should still maintain the staked vs. placed energetic distinction.

This is an example of the pure genius of the Taiji energy method. The constant alternation in physical weighting gives us an immediately graspable and usable guide to the abstract *yin-yang* principle. Often, the binary *yin-yang* philosophical concept seems overly abstract, remote from us, and hard to apply to real practice. But Taiji's brilliant idea of using simple weight distribution to guide the mind and energy visualization gives us a way to work with it directly. But be careful to coordinate your mental/energetic work with the physical weight alternation. They absolutely go together. Don't dumb down your form work to merely observing the rule on distinguishing the physical weight distribution, that's not enough.

BODY (MAN)

We've covered a simple and extremely effective accelerant for the *yin-yang* alternation in the root. Now what about the rest of the body? In this section, I'll discuss mainly the alternation of the *yin* and *yang* distinction from the feet through the *lingtai* to the hands, the primary ARC route already introduced. The head is something of a special case. It has its own accelerant which will be covered in the next section.

There are several ways to amplify the connection of energy via *yin-yang* power alternation through the body in the ARC process, as follows:

- *Let it Be*
- *Spotlight Illumination*
- *Contour Surfing*
- *Painted Legs*

They're all somewhat similar in basic idea and ultimate effect. They all serve to strengthen the overall current that courses through the body in the ARC activation, by emphasizing the current's constituent *yin* and *yang* elements.

LET IT BE

Moving up now from the feet, the first thing we notice is that every posture in the Taiji form has distinctive hand positions. One hand is usually forward of the other, or held higher, or seems to be in a more aggressive configuration and so on. Therefore traditionally it's been tempting to extend the *yin-yang* concept to the hands, as well as the legs. In the feet and legs, the physical correlate of the *yin-yang* distinction is the weight distribution (heavier correlates to *yang*, etc., as discussed above). Extending to the arms and hands, we could say the more forward hand, or the higher hand, or the 'attacking' hand is *yang* and the other one is *yin*. Many teachers also distinguish the hands' *yin-yang* polarity by the physical configuration of the arm and palm (inward curved or outward projected) in each Taiji posture. This kind of *yin-yang* distinction for the hands and arms is commonly taught and it's basically accurate. This teaching is also consistent with Taiji's philosophical underpinning, and you can really feel the contrastive energies of it.

So the arm distinction is true, it's present, but you need to be careful here. Because crucially, you may not need to control that so explicitly in your practice. If you focus mainly on achieving the correct *yin-yang* distinction in the feet and legs, the *yin-yang* energy balance in the arms and hands will emerge naturally. Whereas if you attempt to mentally visualize and control *both* proper feet and leg alternation *and* try mentally to achieve the explicit *yin-yang* hand distinction in every particular pose, you may end by tensing yourself up. Sometimes it's all just too much to deal with at once.

Even if you could maintain the proper explicit mental visualization or control of hand and arm *yin-yang* distinction in every pose, keep in mind that even a single arm, a single hand, even one finger – each of these have their own *micro* sort of *yin-yang* power alternation *within themselves*. It's impossible to explicitly visualize and control all that accurately all the time while practicing. Your mind will tire quickly and you'll end up practicing less overall. You don't need to do that. The genius of the Taiji form is that the weighting alternation sets up everything just right, so the perfect power balance emerges naturally – as long as you stay relaxed. Paradoxically, you'll start to feel the *yin-yang* power distinction in your arms and hands more quickly and more intensely if you work on getting the main foot alternation right than you will if you try to explicitly create the *yin-yang* balance in arms or hands for every pose. That attempt usually just creates additional tension – just what we don't want.

This practice is one of many great examples of what's so cool about Taiji as opposed to the various complex forms of *Qigong* out there. A simple principle and practice triggers a cascade of complex effects that would all have to be separately and tiresomely worked out individually in other systems. Be an easy rider on the Taiji train. Let the system do its thing for you; let it fulfill the purpose for which it was so brilliantly designed.

Spotlight Illumination

However… there are a few fairly 'natural' ways to pump-prime the *yin-yang* energy contrast within the body and arms. These methods have the advantage that they don't require you to think about or memorize any feature of any particular posture. They are consistent, principled methods derived from simple settings in your mind.

The first of these are the spotlight methods. Imagining a single source of light, in a fixed position, and being gently aware of where the highlights and shadows would fall, greatly strengthens the ARC connection. The spotlight process mentally engages the *yin-yang* contrast (which is the constituent structure of the energy) – but without the stress of thinking which part of which posture or hand position requires which phase of energy.

Suppose there were a spotlight overhead, shining down on you at all times, right over you as you do your form. The lit up areas on the topside can be thought of as *yang*, while shadowed underside areas are *yin*. As long as you can gently and lightly imagine the contrastive zebra stripes on your body, you're good. Note that this isn't a rigorous meditation of visualizing the exact optically correct zones, given your clothing and the angles and contours. That would be exhausting. It's more like glancing at an Impressionist painting. You lightly keep in mind, from time to time, that the illumination source is there, dappling your topside and underside with these contrasting streaks. Of course, you mentally ignore any actual illumination effects from the real lighting around you in your practice area.

The same thing can be done using an imaginary light from *below*, like an illuminated dance floor.

Figure 7 Overhead spotlight imaging for feeling *yin-yang* power alternation. The pose is Yang/ZMQ37 'Single Whip'.

Figure 8 Bottom light imaging for feeling *yin-yang* power alternation. The pose is Yang/ZMQ37 'Single Whip'.

Those methods work very well in practice for intensifying the ARC connection. They are a natural, consistent, low mental overhead approach. But some people will have theoretical quibbles with them, because the contrast zones created (mentally) via the illumination method will sometimes cut across the theoretically correct *yin-yang* properties of any given gesture or body part. Sometimes, in conforming to this straight-forward illumination protocol, you'll find that a convex body contour, normally thought of as inherently *yang*, would be shaded (by the imaginary light source), and vice-versa, that a concave body contour or Taiji form gesture may be "incorrectly" spotlighted. No biggie. The idea will do its work for you anyway.

Contour Surfing

There's another "body" method for propagating the powerful *yin-yang* distinction beyond the fundamental earth contrast (weighted vs. lighter leg). In this next method (another mental visualization thing), you take advantage of the natural body contours. With the contour-focused method, just as with the spotlight effect, you don't need to memorize anything about any particular Taiji posture. The distinction emerges naturally from a single uniform consideration, the lines formed by your natural body segment contours. The body contour can be used to guide a *yin-yang* alternation that super-charges your ARC connection.

You want to begin from the back heel. The energy is rising there along an *outward* curve, a convex shape, so you can mentally imagine/associate it with *yang* energy. Just above that is a small *inward* sweep for the back of the ankle. Visualize that area as a curve of contrasting *yin* energy. Continue rising along (actually, *within*) the rear edge line of the leg. You'll find the curves alternating perfectly. They can be used as a simple, natural, straightforward anchoring for your contrastive *yin-yang* mental construct. As you raise the energy, alternating at the curves, you want to stick along the rear contour of the body. That works more powerfully than the front edge. You can take this contrastive rising current all the way up your back to the *lingtai*. Beyond the *lingtai*, the energy completes the ARC and at that stage this contrastive imagery no longer applies. The rising energy from the *lingtai* to the NEXUS Point, which manifests as STEEL in the FLASHOUT, is primarily *yin* quality.

Figure 9 Mental following of body contours for feeling yin-yang power alternation. The most important contour is the bottom heel flow (lowest small arrow). Sometimes the arc of *yang* power will jump directly from the lower rear heel to the *lingtai* mid-back concentration point (large arrow).

You will probably feel this amazing connected current most strongly at that first convex curve, *along the back heel*. That small, lowest area is the key to the 'body' or 'man' aspect of the ARC connection (of course, you still need to do all the other stuff right too). Later you'll feel the energy leap almost directly from that area straight to your hands. It seems to amplify itself instantaneously from the small *yang* curve of the rear heel, directly to the large *yang* curve of the mid back (with the *lingtai* at its center) and from there, when deployed as 'shortcut' *yang* mode (not completing the full ARC back to the NEXUS Point), right to the hands. It's an amazing sensation.

PAINTED LEGS

Finally, you could take the direct route. At all times as you go through your form, while maintaining all the other Taiji principles and good quality postures, you imagine that one leg is white and the other black. Simple. But it works really well for making the *yin-yang* distinction energetically real – which is what the Taiji classic writings instruct us to do. You can think of it as either the fabric color of your pants legs, or as the actual color of your legs themselves, doesn't much matter. For me, consistently 'painting' the weighted leg black and the other white works best, but your mileage will vary so try both ways. You can also try setting the right leg to black (or white) and the left to white (or black) from the start, then stick to that all the way through, which delivers a similar effect on your energy. It's just a mental game but it has powerfully real energetic results.

HEAD (HEAVEN)

Many people have heard of Yang Chengfu's teaching: 滿身輕利頂頭懸, '*the entire body is filled with light, lively energy while the top of the head is suspended*'. This is an extremely important teaching, but often either glossed overly too shallowly or totally misunderstood. Let's focus

133

on the part about the head being suspended. Most commentators and translators seem to assume this is just a dramatic way of telling us to keep our head upright and straight. Keep some spirit there. But it's deeper than that. It's another master key to Taiji. Remember that the Taiji classic writings admonish in several places that the body must be upright, spine straight, etc. There's no need for Yang Chengfu to re-iterate this basic point in this strange way, unless he was getting at something a little different.

What he was getting at is that the head should feel actually separated from the body. I know that sounds weird. Of course it isn't truly separated, you have continuous feeling throughout the body including the head, and after all, the NEXUS Point that powers the whole ensemble is in the brain. So it isn't truly separate. But when you do Taiji standing or form work, you must *feel as though* your head is truly separate, that it floats just slightly above the rest of your body, not fully physically connected. That is the true meaning of 頂頭懸 – *head top suspended*.

Can you grasp this difference? The difference between the above way of practicing vs. assuming that it's another way of emphasizing that you need to straighten up your head and spine? This is something deeper and when you get it, when the understanding clicks in – *Ah! That's what they mean!* – you'll know. You'll feel a huge energy flood like you won't believe. As with everything in this book, it sounds abstract but it's absolutely concrete.

So, for your practice, try to feel your *entire head* suspended by a string from the ceiling. You aren't just feeling the little crown attachment point, you're feeling the entire head as one big suspended unit like a party balloon. Carrying the balloon image further, the basic point works just as well if, rather than think of your head as 'suspended from the ceiling', you think of it as a helium balloon, attached by a string at your neck. That will also nudge you toward the right effect. From the physical point of view, that's the opposite image from

Yang's idea of 'suspended', because in the helium balloon version, the head is 'attached' from *below* (by the string). But in practice, it achieves the same effect – the idea of the *head as a unit* - light and mostly *detached* (I realize this isn't a horror movie screenplay, but I gotta go with the most evocative images). Once you *get it*, you can dump all my crazy comparisons and work out the more subtle feelings and images directly on your own.) Or else imagine your head is suspended from above *and* below, like a boxing double-end bag.

Figure 10 Detach your head like a double-end bag. The posture is Yang/ZMQ37 'Single Whip'.

This feeling of head detachment greatly enhances your ability to complete the final stage of the full ARC - the FLASHOUT from the NEXUS Point to the hands. It will also help you to achieve absolute control over the distinction between using the STEEL energy of the full ARC vs. the shortcut mode of deploying simple *yang* energy from the *lingtai* directly to the hands.

I want to emphasize again – these methods aren't just pretty pictures in a book. They start as imagination, but they're fingers pointing to a real moon out there. The point is to leverage them to gain the concrete experience of the overwhelming rush of energy which they can kickstart. If you put these into your practice consistently, with a moderate amount of concentration and application, you'll be well rewarded.

MOVEMENT

PRINCIPLES

The static work prepares you superbly for further development. Your standing practice should be continued and renewed frequently. But to really get off the launch pad, you need movement. In seriously radical energy-centric Taiji, movement isn't done for its own sake, neither is it for exercise, nor done as theatrics. It's not done for any of those irrelevant reasons that trip up 99% of would-be internal practitioners. Nothing wrong with those other purposes per se, it's just that they should not be overlapped with serious Taiji internal training.

When you've stored up some energy connection (pervaded your body with mind) through your standing work, gentle, soft, and slow movement kneads in the energy, stapling it right into your tissues. The movement helps your mind permeate your body with internal energy. When you've established some basic connection with the energy through strictly static work (standing or seated meditation), you can then use gentle, relaxed movement - stripped of both physical intent and momentum, to set the stage for the spontaneous initiation of the real *yang* power, the resonant impulse introduced in the next section, which manifests on its own as a series of internal energy jolts. You then mentally unify, smooth, layer and temper this resonance until you achieve complete conscious control over both the amplitude and the location (hands, feet, etc.) of its manifestation.

The vibratory manifestation of the real internal *yang* power will be discussed in detail in the section 'The Four Facets of Energy' below. In this section, I'll go over some fundamental considerations of correct movement in the Taiji form work. There are two kinds of movement: spontaneous and controlled. Spontaneous internal movement of the energy is one of the emergent phenomena described in the section 'The Four Facets of Energy'. Controlled movement consists of both the externalities of your Taiji form practice, and also consciously directed movement of the internal energy. The initially spontaneous energy phenomena eventually move into the controlled category.

But even when I'm talking about consciously controlled movement, I am emphatically *not* talking about a *mechanical* system. The movement is directed and fueled by your mind alone. If you physically force the movement, even slightly, with intent to effect any external goal (hurt opponent, show off your skill, get some exercise) you are hopelessly barking up the wrong tree. Your movements cannot be forced or over-controlled in any way for any reason.

SLOSHING

Now here's something very important: although Taiji is not a dance in any sense, there is a kind of physical rhythm to the performance of the set. It involves *the constant change between left side/leg heavy vs. right side/leg heavy.* 'Heavy' here means supporting over 50% of the body weight. In the ZMQ37 form (and most other correctly put-together styles), the sides/legs alternate between right heavy and left heavy, changing with each succeeding full posture and transitional move. I've covered the *yin-yang* energetics of this fully in the previous section on the accelerants. But there's a more overt consideration here too. Prof. Zheng mentioned this alternation in motion as a certain kind of *momentum*, in which one side's weight provided an energetic impetus to the subsequent alternation over to the other side. This is not so easy to feel at first, but it is absolutely crucial to understand.

I call it 'sloshing'. It has a feel somewhat like water sloshing side-to-side in a large, heavy bucket that's half full of water. Imagine carrying such a bucket. Imagine how the weight of the water would feel as it shifted side-to-side with the rhythm of your steps. It never slows down to the point of stopping, and never speeds up to the point of splashing. As long as you keep walking, slow and steady, the water would never go still and never splash up out of the pail. It would just shift its bulk continuously and rhythmically side-to-side. That's the feeling.

You need to keep the shift point low, no higher than the *dantian*. The power sloshes from one leg, 'across' the lower dantian area and then straight down into the other leg, over and over. (As the rhythm shifts to the next leg, that leg becomes the support leg and is 'staked in' temporarily, as discussed in the previous section on the accelerants.) Let the power and rhythm of this process become the main engine of the physical aspect of your form practice.

At first this will seem like simply a somewhat challenging but not unpleasant physical aspect of your form work. Later you'll see that it's the basis for another ultimate mind-blowing energy cascade. Sloshing is the quasi-physical basis for controlled, rhythmic, rational movement in the form. The hands and upper body ride on this fundamental rhythm, assuming their proper respective shapes with no tension at all. You can see from the sloshing example that real Taiji doesn't completely eschew physical correlates altogether. But the genius of it is that leveraging of maximal internal energy from a minimal physical basis. What feels more relaxed is correct, what feels less relaxed is wrong. No style politics or economics or lineage pride needs to come into it at all.

CAT STEP

Now, there's an important physical element to the constant alternation between sides in the Taiji form, something you need to do in all transitions between postures. It's written in the Taiji classic writings: 邁步如貓行 (*maiburumaoxing*) which means 'step like a cat'. Here again we have an easy self-check, but now with movement instead of the posture self-checking introduced earlier. When you need to step your foot to transition from one posture to another, are you stepping like an elephant, with body weight added, or like a cat – lightly, softly, with no weight whatsoever?

You can test your cat step by attempting to raise your stepped foot immediately after you've touched it down. If you need to adjust your upper body for a balance reset as you raise your foot, then you've stepped like an elephant – with body weight. You should be able to easily and freely raise your foot off the ground after the step, but before committing your body weight to that foot. Your upper body and your overall balance shouldn't need to move at all to accommodate this little test. Basically, if the final stance looks long, most likely it wasn't a true cat step. This is the beauty of the objective standard in the Taiji classic writings.

TURN AND KICK

The 'suspended head' concept covered in the previous section is another theoretical point that can be verified in movement. In most forms descended from the Yang family Taiji, there's a movement where you first turn a half-circle on your heel and then kick straight out with the other leg. Usually it's called: 轉身蹬脚 *zhuanshendengjiao* or 'turn and kick', a heel thrust kick. For testing, the best version of this has your kicking leg bent 90 degrees at the knee at the start of the turn, with your thigh raised parallel to the floor, not sagging. That's how you should start and finish the spin portion. This movement is an ideal guinea pig for testing the suspended head. You must resolutely eliminate all physical tension and all BRUTE (random) *qi* power from your neck and head in order to perform this stably - without any wobble at the end. There should be no wobble, no undershoot, no overshoot, and no foot replacement (that little hop to regain balance is the result of excess tension). At the same time, you must keep all the rest of your body, below the neck, completely activated with the 'light and lively energy' mentioned in Yang Chengfu's original description of the suspended head concept. If you play with this move repeatedly, you'll start to catch what is meant by my re-formulation of 'suspended head' as 'detached head' in the previous section. It's as though this movement was designed specifically to teach and test that idea.

CRESCENT KICK

The crescent kick is another interesting targeted type of movement. It can be used to strengthen the *lingtai* energy assemblage. What I call the crescent kick is found in most Yang family derived systems, including ZMQ37, under the name: 轉身擺蓮 (*zhuanshenbailian*). It basically means: *Turning body lotus (kick)*. Although the physical dynamic of the kick is generated via the waist and hip (same as the physical aspect of all Taiji moves), the longest range of motion in a moving part is primarily the lower leg, from knee to foot. You need a teacher to learn the dynamics of this, so get on that. For now, since as you know I don't care much about the physics of it, I want to emphasize that this move is uniquely effective in working your *lingtai* energy hotspot.

Once you reach this posture in your form, you can stand in place and repeat it as many times as you like (but not to the point of physical fatigue). In the kick, you sweep your foot directly across your hands. (I'm assuming that your prior Taiji practice or yoga or something has made you at least limber enough to reach your toes with your hands. If not, ignore this section until you're able to do so). The requirement to reach your feet means that you naturally curve your mid-back very slightly. From this kick you'll get the feeling, maybe not visible outwardly, of a very slight convexity of the mid-back, centralized at the *lingtai* point. If you totally relax during the kick, make it light, crisp, and almost 'fast' (by Taiji standards) your *lingtai* point is forced to respond with amped up energetic output. Then – wow. It's great. Play with it. Be careful with this one though. One of the main signature principles of correct Taiji is: *keep your body upright*. You don't want to lean, strain, or reach for the feet excessively.

By the way, I'm not much into so-called 'applications' of the various Taiji moves. I hate it when Taiji books say stuff like: *If he does attack A, you respond with counter B*. That's boring and mostly useless (I know Professor Zheng's writings have a bit of that. He's an exception. When you become a one-in-a-billion Taiji master I'll make an exception for you too). But if you want a little toolkit of techniques, this dinky-looking kick is well worth considering for inclusion. It has some awesomely powerful functions in certain self-defense situations. Overall, it's a great move, one well worth calling out for special attention. Have fun with it.

THE FOUR FACETS OF ENERGY

Now that you know about the NEXUS Point, the ARC, the ARC accelerants, and so on, you're soon going to be feeling the Fully Activated Body, what I've tagged as FAB. It'll click in more and more, in your Taiji practice or when merely standing or sitting. You'll soon begin to sense the internal spirit power. I assume you have, or are acquiring, a decent grounding in a principled Taiji form under a qualified teacher. Therefore, this section covers more the *what* than the *how*. That's because the Four Facets phenomena emerge spontaneously when your Fully Activated Body (from the ARC process, described in the previous chapter) has kicked in.

These are what I've experienced. I've also found that they cohere with a close reading of the Taiji classic writings, and with other core materials. There's nothing new here. My value-added is that I'm writing directly about my personal experience, using accessible language. Of course, your own development won't overlap perfectly with my Facets as presented here, but you'd better be able to at least recognize everything I talk about or else you're barking up the wrong tree. Just remember though: if you don't *relax*, *none* of this is gonna happen.

The ARC activation is based on natural processes, but in practice it's something you train. You use the Taiji form, with the mild mental stimulants and images I've already covered, to try to promote a certain state (the FAB). Now I'm going to discuss things that initially emerge spontaneously from the Fully Activated Body. These are waves of energy that course through the body. There are two types of those. There's also a further advanced state of integrated energy, basically revisiting the FAB state in a more subtle form. These various facets of wave energy are spontaneous. They aren't

142

something *you do* (at least, not at first), rather they're something that *does you*. After you've had a full spontaneous taste of them, you slowly learn to collar them and harmonize them to your directive mind and will. The Four Facets of Energy are: STATE-1, SURGE-1, SURGE-2, and STATE-2.

STATE-1

The ARC process activates an integrated condition, in which the energy fills all channels from the feet through the fingers. When that is achieved, you're full of what I'll call *Static Tessellated Agglomerated Transparent Energy* (STATE). Because there is a later development to a more powerful and more subtle state, I'll designate this starter condition as STATE-1. I've discussed this condition, and the requirements for achieving it, extensively in the sections above on the ARC process and the Fully Activated Body (FAB).

It may seem from the earlier discussion on the ARC that I was talking about a *flow* – from feet to hands. This directed flow image seems to naturally fit the initial training experience. And most people need that idea of a directed vector to get started with the work – hence the rebound and catch teaching. But a better way to think of the result is as a *linkage* from feet to hands. At first it does feel like a directed current of electrical energy. But the end condition of Fully Activated Body is actually more a state of *integration*, described by Professor Zheng as 全身通 (*quanshentong*) or *whole body permeation*. It's only a beginner state/stage but already way beyond where most people ever get in physicalized or theatrical Taiji. This state is the basis for what's referred to in the Taiji classic writings as: 一身之勁練成一家 (*yishenzhijinglianchengyijia*) - *the internal power of the entire body is honed into a single functional unit*. That's the Fully Activated Body, or STATE-1 in my terms, which has been introduced already in prior sections.

In the more limited pre-stage of feeling the microcosmic orbit, the energy is restricted to a particular channel with a particular direction (up-back, down-front). But in the Fully Activated Body or STATE-1, you can make your energy go anywhere in any direction - it gets to be as though your whole body is a soaked sponge, no one part or channel any more important than another. There's also no inherent direction except what you may momentarily impose (just as a soaked sponge has no inherent flow direction, but if you squeeze it you can temporarily impose one).

SURGE-1

The next of these spontaneous energy facets was called out by the great internal boxing master Sun Lutang (1860 - 1933) when he wrote that, after long practice: 有真陽发动之语 'you *perceive the spontaneous movement of the real yang resonance'*. The "real *yang* resonance" refers to a fundamental concept of Taiji internal power development. The original Chinese word真陽 (*zhenyang*) in the above quote is from Master Sun's essay on his experience of cultivating his own superb internal energies. (see Appendix A: Are You Experienced? for my original translation). Note that *yang* here does not refer to the Yang family Taiji system, rather it is the *yang* of the concept I've already covered exhaustively, the ancient paired philosophical terms '*yin-yang*' (陰陽) meaning the counter-balanced dualities of sun/moon, male/female, day/night, etc.

The trick for Taiji is to learn to harness the spontaneous impetus of the 'real *yang* resonance'. The 'real yang resonance' is initially a subtle experience, yet at the same time very definite. You need to recognize its first subtle appearance, because it strengthens with conscious recognition. At first it isn't something you *do*, it's something that *happens*, just as master Sun has written. Remember this is not one of the normal, easy *qi* sensations that we all know and love (the BRUTE level of *qi* signs: warmth, tingling, buzzy feeling, soft doughy feeling, localized bubbling-well types of pulsations, etc.). This is a different, higher-order animal altogether.

The "real *yang* resonance" is experienced as a series of jolts, pulses or waves deep inside your body. If you've ever been through an earthquake, you'll be able to relate to the basic idea more quickly (I don't mean you'll feel the actual "real *yang* power" sooner than others, but you'll have some idea what I'm talking about here). It feels like something is 'discharging' as a jolt of motion streams through a joint, limb, or section of your body – or your entire body from foot to head. At one point in his essay, Sun uses precisely that term - 'discharge' - to describe it (see Appendix A). If you had any success with the Edwardian Fop power check drill presented in Chapter 2, I can now tell you that was a minor league look-ahead to this fuller energy dynamic. But the depth of pulsation from the Edwardian Fop drill is vastly inferior to the first spontaneous manifestation of the true *yang* resonance. In addition to the *yang* resonance, there are several other varieties of these pulsation effects. What Sun called the 'true *yang* resonance' is the first of these. I could also call this a kind of *yang* surge. I'll introduce a *yin* surge later (of course) so hereafter I'll designate the '*yang* surge' as the *Serial Undulating Resonant Groundswell Energy - Type 1*, or SURGE-1.

Whatever your core Taiji practice may be, you will probably first notice the SURGE-1 phenomenon when you aren't moving. For example, both Sun and I noticed it first during moments of quiet standing, in between active set practice (Taiji in my case, and *Xingyiquan,* another internal style also based on Daoist concepts, for Master Sun). You will most likely first experience the SURGE-1 in your joints or limbs, because you have a lot of conscious attention there. In addition, there are two autonomously moving systems inside the body – the diaphragm and the pulse. These also, if sufficiently relaxed and imbued with light mental awareness, will attract and host the SURGE-1. When both of these have begun to attract the SURGE-1, you're nearing the stage beyond FAB Fully Activated Body, which is full body *permeation* by mind, included in the higher Facets of energy.

Don't fool yourself though. No matter how many decades you may think you've put in, you probably, in my experience of those I've met and practiced with, haven't begun to shed even the most elementary layers of your surface tension (not to mention deep tension) and you're most likely still far from anything I'm talking about here. But I want to cover it, for completeness.

THE KEY RING JINGLE CHECK

Eventually the SURGE-1 will extend throughout your entire body. If you stand upright, very quiet, totally relaxed, and are able to initiate the ARC flow state of Fully Activated Body, then you should begin to spontaneously get the experience of the SURGE-1. Try standing upright and quiet, with your hands naturally dropped by your sides. Loop a ring of keys or a key chain over one finger, just loosely hooked over one bent finger of one hand. Without any *physical* initiation of motion whatsoever, just *change your mind* such that the SURGE-1 kicks in.

At that point, the keys should begin to jingle in your hand - *without you applying any physical energy, deliberate motion, or conscious intent* to your hand whatsoever. It's crucial that *your hand does not move independently* in this state. This isn't automatic writing! Nor is it a Kriya-style total physical freak-out (as covered in the section above on The Fallacies). The *entire body* is uniformly experiencing the same entrained SURGE-1 resonance. The SURGE-1 of your body as a whole creates a spontaneous light jingle in the keys you're holding. This is the beginner's first test of the basic form of the 'real *yang* power'.

Atomic physicists have written that the binding energy liberated from splitting a single atom is about enough to pop a Ping-Pong ball half an inch up from a tabletop. Point being, a single atom doesn't really have all that much energy. When you first begin to experience the SURGE-1 effect (the 'real *yang* resonance' in Sun's terms), coincidentally that's pretty much exactly the degree of kinetic energy you'll feel internally – about enough to physically move a Ping-Pong ball or jingle a key ring. Just the little bounce of a Ping-Pong ball... but now imagine that internal energy pulse layered, re-combined, fed-back, and re-amplified many thousands of times over. The result in the case of nukes is obvious (Fat Man and Little Boy bombs). In the case of internal training it's not so visually dramatic, but the same kind of combinatorics are at work. It may start soft and subtle, but you need to respect its amplification potential. Don't kid yourself that you already understand this if you haven't experienced it. It is totally different from any other kind of athletic and/or spiritual experience, yet at the same time not at all vague or speculative. It's absolutely concrete.

The SURGE-1 resonance will recur many times at ever greater strength in the course of your Taiji training. It recurs in cycles of an ongoing tempering process. It isn't a one-time *level* in a linear ordering. It's not something to be attained once and for all and then left in the rearview mirror. But even though the SURGE-1 phenomenon isn't a single straight progression, I think it's useful to cover what you may experience the first time through.

Stage 0: Fully Activated Body (FAB)
Stage 1: random jolts
Stage 2: *dantian* anchored - on inhalation
Stage 3: *dantian* anchored - on exhalation
Stage 4: *dantian* anchored - linkage across breath cycle
Stage 5: feet anchored - linkage across breath cycle
Stage 6: feet to head – the full SURGE-1

STAGE 0: FULLY ACTIVATED BODY (FAB)

You begin to become aware of the SURGE once you have the basic integration of energy linkage from feet to hands that I call Fully Activated Body or FAB. Even before that though, you will occasionally get some wave-like sensations, even when you are still in the BRUTE energy stage. An example is the localized forearm power wave that the Edwardian Fop drill introduced in Chapter 2 generates immediately. But those are all pre-SURGE effects.

STAGE 1: RANDOM JOLTS

After some time working with the ARC process , as the Fully Activated Body kicks in, you will notice occasional random jolts of internal energy discharge. They will feel like brief bursts or short periods of longitudinal vibration through a restricted body part. As previously mentioned, the most common sites for these are limbs and joints, but they could also be linked to the breath movement of the diaphragm or the pulse. They may happen in practice sessions and/or daily life activities. This is your first experience of the 'true *yang* resonance', the sharp power wave I call SURGE-1. You might feel slightly spastic at first, or think it's a case of bad nerves or even Restless Leg Syndrome (RLS). Your limbs may kind of jump a little from time to time. But don't worry, in the Taiji context this is just the real *yang* resonance wave warming up. It's not Parkinson's Disease, and be careful not to get carried away in this mild initial phase and veer off the road into the Kriya Fallacy either. It's just a bit of energetic discharge. But notice it for what it is, don't be oblivious. Again at this early point it isn't something you consciously *will* to happen, you merely notice when it does.

STAGE 2: DANTIAN ANCHORED - ON INHALATION

The key point in this next stage is that the SURGE-1 wave becomes correlated to a given body point for the first time. In Stage 1 you may feel random short internal jolts in any joint of the body - neck, wrist, shoulder, hip, spine, etc. Two things distinguish this next Stage 2.

First, now for the first time the energy vibrations become organized into continuous surge, an unbroken series of *waves* instead of one-off jolts or a short run of pulses. More significantly, the signature event of Stage 2 is that you feel the waves arising specifically from, or rooted in, the *dantian* (lower abdomen acupoint). Strictly speaking, this is the first stage where the term SURGE-1 really should be said to apply.

These waves of internal pulsing will be about 3 to 5 cycles per second (Hz) - very slow in electromagnetic terms (by the way, popular science to the contrary, *qi* is not truly an electromagnetic phenomenon. Scientists who conduct *qi* studies based on the EM assumption are like the drunk searching the nighttime sidewalk only under the lamppost for his lost car keys, because: *the light is better here*). In this stage, you'll feel continuous slow waves of vibration washing over your upper body, but originating from the *dantian*, rising up to the solar plexus at first and later all the way to the *baihui* at the crown of the head. Initially this effect will be strongest on the inhale.

The overall effect is so similar to being in a slow earthquake that you should check when you first feel something like this - are pictures falling from the walls, crockery off the shelf? If so: duck and cover! Otherwise: congrats, you're getting into stage 2 of the SURGE-1 effect. Reaching this point could take just a few months for a correctly-taught natural genius, but typically may require years or more because you've got to learn to truly relax for this and achieve the Fully Activated Body. Sadly most of us are far too tense to get to this as quickly as we might otherwise. The jolts at this point feel discrete, and though definitely originating from beneath the skin, they are somewhat shallow, more so than the SURGE-2 waves that come later.

STAGE 3: DANTIAN ANCHORED - ON EXHALATION

The next stage is the same as the prior stage in that the wave begins at the *dantian*, but now you have the SURGE-1 initiation on exhale as well as inhale (but they're still two separate SURGE-1 events). The exhale seems to be a bit harder to notice and then control than the inhale was. Normally you'll experience and understand the inhale-linked SURGE-1 first. Although the SURGE-1 will have begun for you automatically (the unconscious result of your prior ARC practice), at some point you'll feel a degree of control over it, or at least the possibility of facilitating the right conditions to prime the pump. From only catching the wave on the inhale, but having it die as the next exhale kicks in, you'll find it starting up again on its own with the following exhale. From then on, you'll be able to generate the waves from either stage of origin, inhale or exhale.

STAGE 4: DANTIAN ANCHORED - LINKAGE ACROSS BREATH CYCLE

Now it starts to get really interesting, because we're moving farther and farther away from direct physical correlation. In this stage, the vibration pattern becomes *continuous and undifferentiated* across the change-over in the breath cycle (inhale to exhale, exhale to inhale). This is a really crucial point of potential advancement but one where people sometimes get stopped. It seems to require a subtle shift in your mental focus. You need to center your breath at the *dantian* to initiate the wave cycle, but then as the SURGE-1 kicks in, you shift your mind to the wave pattern itself, forgetting about the breath altogether, in order to both strengthen the waves and also to link continuously across the breath phase boundaries (inhale to exhale to inhale, etc.)

Again, total relaxation of both mind and body are essential prerequisites. But it goes beyond relaxing. You'll also need to play with your mind to catch just the right feeling of *bridging over* the breath phase change with no effect on the wave pattern originating at the *dantian*. It may sound identical to the Stage 3 description above, just a combination of inhale-initiated and exhale-initiated wave cycles. But this stage is different because it has only a single one-time initiation. After that it carries on continuously, without a reset and restart at the breath cycle boundary.

STAGE 5: FEET ANCHORED - LINKAGE ACROSS BREATH CYCLE

Now it gets even more fun. At some point the origination focus of the wave pattern will drop from the *dantian* to the soles of your feet. The wave pattern will now run, independently of breath phase (see Stage 4 above) straight up from the soles of your feet to the *dantian*, which now becomes the terminus rather than the origin point. It thus begins to follow the true energy path of the Fully Activated Body (accomplished via the ARC linkage process described earlier). At this stage it's only going halfway up (to the *dantian*), but the more important difference is that the result of the original ARC process is a kind of integrated energetic connection or substance feeling (STATE-1), while the SURGE-1 you get now is a sequence of pulses of energy. This stage is kind of wild because when you really get the SURGE-1 going, and you stand in a simple easy stance like ZMQ37's Preparation Posture, you'll feel all and only the *muscles* of your legs, feet to groin, whomping in synch to the SURGE. Meanwhile the *bones* of your legs and all the *rest of your body* can be completely still. A truly bizarre but not unpleasant feeling. At this point you are nearing the ability to move the SURGE-1 anywhere in your body with your mind, to mentally control its intensity, to consciously include or exclude the bones themselves from the vibrations, and so on.

STAGE 6: FEET TO HEAD

At Stage 6, the wave pattern greatly intensifies. It also 'overflows' upward from the *dantian* (terminal point of previous stage) all the way to the crown of the head (*baihui* point). In this process, the key point is the true crown of the head. As in some of the earlier phases, this will initially be most apparent during the inhale, but you will quickly re-establish the right mindset to de-link away from the breath phase tie-up altogether, as you needed to do in Stage 4. At this point you may well be wondering: what is the subtle difference between the unconscious, uncontrolled phenomena that you merely 'notice' vs. the training process of learning to 'initiate' and 'control' the different energy states? It may seem I'm being a bit slippery in jumping back and forth on this point.

That's because it's really subtle. In the long run *everything can be fully controlled*. In the beginning, the important take-home is that the ARC process is a *conscious* training discipline, and its *result* is the natural 'involuntary' initiation of the SURGE-1. After that, every effect that begins by your merely noticing something can later become controlled with your mind. Everything in radical Taiji energetics is based on that paradigm: *Notice first, then control*. Once you have the ARC activation going, and you feel the SURGE-1 wave a few times, you are pretty much good to go. At that point, all the rest of this book becomes just icing on your cake. I said in Chapter 2: *if you can't feel it, you can't feed it*. The corollary now is: *when you can feel it, you can feed it*. Thereafter, the only limit is how hard you choose to vamp. Nothing can slow you but your own degree of commitment (or lack thereof).

May you take it way past me, way past everyone else, even past Yang Luchan's high water mark. That sounds competitive, very un-Taiji, doesn't it? But hey - *somebody's* gotta throw this art a ring, get it off life support, and restore the proud place it held in the Yang Luchan era when Taiji truly was: *The Supreme Ultimate Boxing*. It's up to you to teach the human race a lesson – that violence and raw physical power won't *always* carry the day. It's worth getting it just for that. And if not you, then who?

SURGE-2

At some point the experience of the wave or resonance undergoes a qualitative shift. It becomes noticeably softer, slower, deeper and warmer. I'm sure surfers have terms for radically distinct wave types in the ocean, but I'll simply call this SURGE-2. Where the SURGE-1 wave is maybe 3 to 5 pulses per second, the SURGE-2 wave is about half that or less. The SURGE-2 wave is a very advanced effect. Once you've made it this far, you truly don't need this book any more. Not only does the SURGE-2 wave feel softer than the SURGE-1 wave, it's also more generalized. The SURGE-1 seems to run along a local channel within the body. The SURGE-2 wave, in contrast, seems to spread out through much broader body sections. For example, where the SURGE-1 wave is often felt running narrowly up along the spinal column, the SURGE-2 wave will typically spread itself across the entire trunk or torso of the body. Rather than running through the inside of the bones of an arm or leg, as the SURGE-1 wave seems to, the SURGE-2 wave will cause all the tissues of the entire limb, including the bones, to feel as though they're made of the softest cotton or finest goose down.

If you've been through lots of earthquakes, you may relate to a comparison with seismic wave types. The Sharp Wave is like an internal version of the seismic Primary (or P) wave – fast and sharp like a sonic boom that bumps and rattles windows. Then in most earthquakes, some seconds later, the secondary (or S) waves arrive, which are much slower and deeper, with their up-and-down and side-to-side motion, shaking the ground surface vertically and horizontally. The broader point is that the SURGE-1 and SURGE-2 waves, just like the Primary and Secondary seismic waves, are two distinct experiences.

STATE-2

Finally, we get to the really primo stuff - the SURGE-2 wave eventually becomes so intense and also speeds up (paradoxically, since the SURGE-2 is experienced initially as *slower* than the more forceful SURGE-1) to the point that the perception of the effect as pulses, as a wave, completely disappears. Just as when an airplane propeller speeds to the point of continuous sound and uniform appearance rather than cycles, the SURGE-2 energy waves fuse into a single undifferentiated continuous pure state or field effect, from feet to crown, your entire body.

The transition from the previous wave thing to this near-final state/field condition will be your most intense experience of the classic Chinese adage: 物極必反 (*wujibifan*) – *every extreme leads directly to its own opposite*. I will call this very refined unified condition *Static Tessellated Agglomerated Transparent Energy* 2 or STATE-2. It's the culmination of all the previous work, though paradoxically, once you begin to get it, you'll see how simple it really could be to achieve. The entire process of getting here, all the prior verbiage of this book, all the stages and states and energy experiences, all of it boils down to merely this:

- *Withdraw all tension from the body*
- *Fill the emptiness with mind*

As the summary above implies, I still faintly believe it may be theoretically possible to channel the universal energy directly from the NEXUS Point intake to and through your relaxed body, thus achieving STATE-2 on your yoga mat, meditation cushion, or Barca lounger. But many, many fakers claim to be able to do that. Almost none of them can. Reason is, *they aren't actually relaxed*. To bypass the ARC work and jump directly to STATE-2, you need to achieve absolute relaxation. Sure, some people *feel* all enlightened and everything, and maybe they are, but it has no relation to

STATE-2 as defined in this book because STATE-2 is an energy condition. I know they aren't there yet, because I've pushed with hundreds of them. The problem is that when you're lying down in *shavasana* (corpse pose) on your mat, you can relax to some degree, and concentrate on intaking and infusing the energy through your body, even without Taiji's ARC process.

That's ok for cultivation. But Taiji is more, it includes persistent states and deployment as well. As soon as you stand up, bang! Your tension all floods right back in, ruining any chance for effective deployment. But more than the deployment problem, the fact that so much latent tension remains means that you never really absorbed the energy very thoroughly to begin with. Even the cultivation step was sub-optimal. So for now, until somebody makes a pill for it, if you wanna play you have to go through all the ARC and accelerant training already described.

And be careful here, accept no substitutes. It's very easy to fool yourself if you haven't actually and fully experienced all the prior stages. It's easy to kind of feel good, just doing ordinary Qigong, or standing on a pretty mountain looking at the distant scenery, you're on top of the world, it's a mystical moment... NO. That ain't it. This is a very different, very specific, unbelievably powerful energetic experience. It's not mystical. You won't be talking to a burning bush or anything. But every cell in your body will be puffed out with pure cosmic energy. It seems strange, doesn't it, to be explaining something as puffed out or filled up with energy, and yet... empty? That's the paradoxical mystery of it.

Guo Yunshen (Xingyiquan master who was cited in Theory section of Chapter 2 and teacher of Sun Lutang) has stated (using different vocabulary) that in the STATE-2: "无声无臭···呼吸似有似无···虚空灵通之全体": "*there is no sound, no smell, you do not feel you are breathing, and your whole body is imbued with lively emptiness*". This is actually the borderline to *huajing*, the mysterious energy. But I classify it as correlated with *shen* or spirit level energy, because there's just a touch of that paradox again – we talk about total *emptiness*, yet also a feeling the whole body alive with something. It empties, yes, but then immediately refills with something. There's still something there. Just as the *mingjing* energy ranged across a spectrum from the BRUTE superficial sensation to the sharp waves of SURGE-1, so the *anjing* ranges from the soft wave of SURGE-2 to this incredible experience of STATE-2.

But try not to get confused – STATE-2 is not the absolute nothingness linked to *huajing*. STATE-2 feels as though your body substance has been completely replaced with something else, something a lot better than the original construction. It's as though the outline of your body, once emptied out, is repacked with a warm, soft, silky, yet firm fine substance. STATE-2, once achieved, doesn't ever weaken or fade out even when you are doing other things (not specifically engaged in your cultivation practice) it just kinds of puts itself on the back burner, from whence it can be called up instantaneously any time. This is not an exercise. You're not imagining it, you're just experiencing it. Less work!

And there are two major versions of STATE-2. One is a full field effect, where you feel an infinite sheet or plane of undifferentiated energy. You can also use your mind to in effect "roll up" that sheet or plane into a tight cylinder of pure STATE-2 soft power. You can then do things internally with this cylinder. For example, you can run it between the NEXUS Point in your head (see Chapter 1) and the *huiyin* point in the lower groin, or between the NEXUS Point and the *weilu* point in the coccyx. It feels like a column of neon velvet straight through your core.

Or you can run such STATE-2 energy cylinders through your arms. The great Meiji-era spiritual swordsman Yamaoka Tesshu wrote in a training poem that: *If your mind is not projected into your hands even 10,000 techniques will be useless.* Well this is where that happens, your mind projects itself through your arms in the form of an amazing energy injection cascading down your arms, totally unlike all the other little flows and buzzes you've been getting all along from any Qigong you might have picked up. It's really different. You'll know it when you feel it. You first experience it as a cascade, but then it quickly settles down to become more like a true STATE effect. It's as though the whole-body soft STATE-2 has been localized into your arms. At that point, you can mentally switch at any time between the wave or pulsation condition (SURGE-1 or SURGE-2) and an arm-specific STATE-2 effect. This is the most fun work of all and it can have application to real-world work and games such as Taiji push-hands or *kuzushi* practice (unbalancing, see next chapter, Push).

Beyond that you can now apply your refined arm energy to pretty much anything. For example, if you know Xingyiquan you'll quickly find that the practice of Xingyi at this level is totally out of this world, a revelation utterly unlike the physical arm-flailing or calisthenic performance of Xingyiquan you may have experienced in the past. (Hint: try out *hengquan* 'crossing fist' in this mode, and you'll find you can 'spiral' the arm's STATE-2 condition with a most intriguing effect. You might also try Chinese calligraphy with the writing arm charged with the STATE-2 energy).

The Taiji energy work is really profound. It's up to you alone how deep the rabbit hole can go. But most people, even Taiji players, haven't yet realized it. For example, when your game is running at a certain level, you'll experience your energy body not only tactilely but visually. It will come to the point that a wireframe laser-outline colored light image of your energy body will manifest itself moment to moment like a graphic FX in your third eye, tracking your real-time movements in the Taiji form as you do it. This can't happen if you take a 'drive to the finish' approach to the form sequence. You can't be thinking of the next move and the one after that, feeling *I gotta get through to the end of the sequence.* You must feel that this

157

move, the one you're on right now, is the only move. There is no next move to do, at any given point. There is no next place to go, and nothing else to do or be (*I-am-the-Universe* type of mentality).

Then the laser-bright graphic energy lines will suddenly flash up onto your visual screen and shock the heck out of you. But it's fun. You'll realize that there really is a 'luminous egg' through and around humans, just what that poetic hoaxer Carlos Castaneda wrote about. You'll have direct visual confirmation and self-perception of that. I'm not talking about seeing your aura here. The aura is a subtle but *external* radiance. With advanced Taiji form work you're getting the *inner energy lines* flashed up in Vegas style neon. It's like the movie *X The Man with the X-ray Eyes*, where the guy sees through to the girder substructure of a skyscraper, rather than the surface. Or hang on, I'm dating myself there – it's like the green dripping substrate of reality in *The Matrix*. Except in this case, it'll be your own body represented to yourself.

Now let's revisit the table of energy types and levels presented earlier, but now adding in a column for the Four Facets. You'll notice I still haven't said much about the final level of *huajing*. That's because it's total absolute emptiness, *without* the refill that you had in STATE-2. Anything I say would be gilding that invisible inaudible untasteable impalpable lily. I include it just because it's a part of Guo Yunshen's original framework, but let's work on the feast we have set in front of us now before we worry about dessert.

Summary Table of Traditional Terms

Level	Functional Category	Energetic Experience	Facet
精 jing	muscular	physical athletics	N/A
气 qi	*mingjing* obvious	sparky, spiky, electric, hydraulic, edgy, firm, sharp	STATE-1 (FAB full energetic linkage) SURGE-1 (faster, sharper waves)
神 *shen*	*anjing* secret	pneumatic, seismic, subtle, silky, soft	SURGE-2 (slower, softer waves) STATE-2 (substance change)
虚*xu*	*huajing* mysterious	undifferentiated Total nothingness	Universal merge Nothing at all

BREATHING

The whole breathing thing really courts misunderstanding. I could dismiss this area altogether and leave you none the worse by saying: *Just breathe naturally; let your breath take care of itself.* That's the wisest way forward. But I'll offer a few specifics beyond that.

BASIC PRACTICE

For purposes of daily Taiji form practice, you can forget about all the fancy stuff like reverse abdominal breathing and yoga's Ujayii breath or the breath of fire, and all the other mystical breath practices. Just as you can't make a plant grow faster or better by yanking up on the leaves, forcing the breath in any way at the beginning is not going to do you any good in Taiji development. (Other arts, of course, may require various different practices, which are entirely valid in their separate spheres and traditions. In this section, I am discussing Taiji alone).

Beyond that, once you've achieved the Fully Activated Body described in the previous chapter (via the ARC mental training), a bit of attention to breath will re-enter the picture. You will at some point experience the breath-linked initiation of the wave energies described in the previous section (The Four Facets of Energy). As mentioned earlier, you will *find* (not *force*) that some of the wave resonance phenomena are initially linked to the start of an inhale or exhale breath action (as covered in the previous section). At first, this is just *noticing*, not *controlling*. Later, you will once again transcend the breath linkage as you find that the wave cycles extend beyond the breath cycles, bridging them and finally obscuring them altogether. When you reach STATE-2 you won't feel you're breathing at all.

Even though Taiji is in no sense a mechanical system, the energy does necessarily manifest somewhere (or eventually, everywhere) in the physical body. The first stirrings of the 'real *yang* power' or SURGE-1 resonance are usually experienced in the joints and limbs. But the spontaneous movement of it can and eventually (with correct relaxed practice) will manifest anywhere in the body. For now just keep a relaxed, soft, aware and observant practice going. Breath will take care of itself in this very interesting way - if you just leave it alone. Natural breathing along with consistent Taiji practice naturally kick-starts the process described in Sun's writings (Appendix A). The breath operates with its own natural intelligence to smooth, temper, and forge the wave energies to the point that they fully permeate the body under the instantaneous control of your mind. That culminates in the STATE-2, transcendence of breath altogether.

CHAPTER 4:
PUSH

MINDSET

UNBALANCING

He's a magic man...
He got magic hands.

- Heart

I despise violence. That's why I got into martial arts in the first place, to try to figure a way out of it. Not just for myself but for all humankind. Unfortunately I later found humankind is not in the least interested in a serious answer to this question. Humankind is only interested in the Three F's: Feeding, Fighting, and er ... Finding a mate. Anyway, I despise it. So don't think that Taiji's push hands exercise is necessarily leading you in the direction of combatives. It's deeper than that, as we'll see.

When you start to feel the internal powers, you'll want take them out for a road test. Taiji's push hands (推手 *tuishou*) practice can be seen as a type of testing. It's a well-known basic training exercise in which partners stand facing one another and each attempts to unbalance the other. I stated earlier that internal energy work has two aspects: *cultivation* and *deployment*. We've talked a lot about cultivation via the Taiji form, now deployment comes up via the push hands or unbalancing exercise. It's important to do push hands practice as a reality check. Otherwise it's too easy for us to fool ourselves about how relaxed we've become through our form work, or, at the more advanced levels, how much energy we've cultivated.

But you have to be careful, because while high skill with relaxation and energy will result in greater push hands ability, the inverse conclusion isn't necessarily valid. There are many ways to be great at push hands without dabbling in the internal energies at all. Large people sometimes have a natural advantage in pushing smaller people. People with a naturally aggressive psychology can have an advantage over even a fairly experienced Taiji player, depending on his/her level. People with a deep background in contact games and martial sports like wrestling or rugby can sometimes use their skills to good effect. People with naturally strong bodies and fast reactions usually do better. The list goes on and on. So I have to emphasize: *Skill with push hands is a necessary but not sufficient condition for assessing internal development.*

So, partners stand facing each other and each attempts to unbalance the other – but without stepping the feet at all, either to push or evade. To do this, you need to keep yourself relaxed, and also stay sensitive to any excess tension in your partner's body or arms. But beyond just *checking* your energy level, push hands is also a drill for *developing* the attributes of relaxation and sensitivity. I want to emphasize the word *attributes* as opposed to *techniques* or specific fighting *skills*. I know that many Taiji programs like to emphasize their techniques and the (supposed) applications of those to fighting and self-defense. To me this is another example of Taiji people being coy without really stepping into the ring. I don't think there's any special value to a random collection of arbitrary fight-like moves hanging in a vacuum.

As physical combatives, none of the Taiji techniques is anything special. If divorced from the internal content that is the focus of this book, are they somehow more effective than Muay Thai, Western boxing, Judo, Sambo, or Brazilian Jiu-jitsu? Not really. And if you do have the energy running, then any touch can be your technique. Taiji techniques are probably worse than the martial sports, because they depend on a fairly civilized application setup, two people evenly facing off on a clean flat surface, no groundwork, no buddies coming up behind with a crowbar, all kinds of assumptions.

The combative sports also make some assumptions, but within their restrictions they're more realistic as fight scenarios. I've written one or two positive comments about a few of the Taiji form's outward moves, but overall I think any special attention to them as fight moves is a waste of time. Both the form and the push hands exercise have the deeper purpose of developing greater attributes. To consider Taiji as mainly an inventory of techniques is like buying a Rolls Royce for the hood ornament. Or worse – it's like driving a Volkswagen bug with one of those joke Rolls Royce hood ornaments mounted on front.

Push hands isn't fighting or combat in any form. It isn't even like boxing which is also a highly restricted, artificial format (like push-hands), but where you have the potential to really get hurt. In boxing you must protect yourself at all times. In push hands however, if you feel you have to protect yourself at all times – for example, protect your feet from a sneak stomp, or your head from a sudden butt – then you're working with the wrong partners. There's definitely a place in martial arts training for reality-oriented combative work. You can begin by sparring at your local boxing club. But don't bring that mindset into your push hands practice or you'll never get anywhere with real Taiji.

All kinds of people, not just Taiji-ster's, can play push hands. In any given year, I practice the Taiji unbalancing work with students and teachers of a large variety of martial arts including Aikido, Jiu-Jitsu, Judo, Wing Chun, wrestling, etc. Though push hands seems to be a very narrow drill, it's actually about the broadest and most fundamental skill of all, applicable to any martial art or sport – keeping your balance under pressure. In fact sometimes, in order to remove the suspicion that these partners are merely 'playing my game', I use the Japanese word *kuzushi* (崩) to refer to what's called push hands or *tuishou* in the strict Taiji context.

Kuzushi is a generic term meaning 'unbalancing work'. In Japan there are so many traditional and new flavors of Jiu-Jitsu, Judo, Aikido, etc. that when people get together they often use this term to describe the general process of playing with each other's balance, yielding, rooting, energy, etc. It's like the first stage of a Judo throw – the setup action of controlling or taking your partner's balance, but without the need to follow through with the actual slamdown (Judo throw or sweep) to the ground. What I'm calling *kuzushi* has the same goal as traditional Taiji push hands: make the partner lose his/her balance (so that s/he has to take at least one involuntary step to maintain him/herself). In general, push hands or *kuzushi* provides a simple, safe, straightforward, no-sweat method of minimal Taiji testing that obviates the need for mats, headgear, mouth guards, gloves, suitable ground surface or any other special setup.

The use of the word *kuzushi* rather than *tuishou* may seem like mere semantic quibbling, but it's important because of what it excludes. It excludes post-facto controversies based on claims such as the following:

- *I could've punched you in the nose!*
- *I could've touched your throat!*
- *I could've stomped your instep!*
- *I could've kicked you in the groin!*
- *I could've spit in your mouth (I'm HIV positive)!*
- *I could've been holding a knife!*

When you enter into a traditional push hands configuration with anybody, the above actions are all theoretically possible. They are not really useful as a check of combative ability though because basically they say: *anything goes now* and that's a very different situation, because if anything goes for *you*, then anything will go for *me* too, and instantly we're in a different space altogether. For example, if you attempt to 'touch my throat' I might snap your elbow joint as you do so, etc. So to introduce the above types of considerations is inappropriately mixing apples and oranges.

My version of ZMQ37 push hands (a good basis for real Taiji work), has absolutely nothing to do with any of the following:

- *two-person formal pre-patterned* **choreographies,**
- *specific quasi-grappling or striking types of* **techniques**
- *physically* **powering** *your partner out*

Those don't have to completely constrain my partner (though we should be working roughly with the same assumptions). But for me, on my side, the emphasis is entirely on relaxation. There is no inventory of techniques. Technique merely arises spontaneously to achieve the unbalancing goal, as circumstances call it up, like a whitecap on the ocean. It recedes without trace or memory when that goal is accomplished. We gradually learn to control both our own and our partner's tension, ego, and fear. The emphasis on relaxation naturally yields all the attributes required for push hands and which can contribute to self-defense: sensitivity, neutralization, and instant elastic power that emerges naturally as required by a situation.

Now, even though push hands isn't combative, it isn't cooperative either. It's a highly restricted game, but it still adversarial within a very limited, specifically agreed framework. It's a work of genius, designed to blast our energy and sensitivity spaceward if we can get past our hang-ups. Hang-ups tend to be of two types:

i.   Taking push hands practice as some kind of ersatz combat simulation (see above discussion)
ii. Taking push hands practice as a fully cooperative, or even choreographed, gentle dance game.

Both are wrong. It's true that push hands is merely a drill - but it's a special one. Let it do its work for you. Let me re-emphasize that although push hands superficially *resembles* some kind of ritualized 'combative' setup, it has no direct connection to a combative type of interaction or setting. In particular, it doesn't much matter where you put your hands, as long as you keep contact with your partner. Conventionally I like to say that your hands can be placed:

- anywhere on your partner's *hands or arms*
- anywhere on their body *between the collarbone and the hip bone* (with obvious restrictions based on partner's injuries or any special sensitivities)

As for 'defense', you may choose to mimic 'protecting your head' (as in boxing) or not. But remember that this is a *pushing* drill. Pushing *a person's head* is only meaningful within the drill if:

- touching the head can be done without injury to the partner
- by touching the head, you can move the partner's entire body (exact same goal as in pushing or touching any other point).

Unbalancing the partner, thus forcing him/her to take a step (move his/her foot), is the immediate point of the game. The longer term point is to develop your ability to sense and issue internal energy. Because push hands, in my framework, is not a combative skill game (it is attribute development work), there's little point in crowing that you have the ability to touch your partner's head, or throat, or other anatomically vulnerable areas as you push. If we're going to play hypothetical imaginary real combat (if that makes sense at all) then we might as well go further, for example, fantasize that we're each holding a knife. If I had a knife, *any* area of contact on your body would be vulnerable to lethal attack. There'd be no special reason for pride in my being able to touch your head. But in any case, that kind of thing isn't the point. The point is to trigger loss of balance, *with the lightest possible physical touch.*

If somebody thinks s/he can move me by pushing my head, or other vulnerable areas that aren't normally the focus of push hands practice, s/he can certainly try that. It can become a small part of the drill. But I don't think that adds much to push hands practice. The key point remains: if your *touch* or *your push* is good enough to move me, then you can easily touch my torso and pop me, no need to touch the head. Nor in that case will you care where I place my hands on your body (within common sense parameters), or what part of my body I'm guarding or not guarding, or how high or low I hold my hands. *If you're more relaxed than me, you touch me anywhere and I'm gone.* Conversely, if you cannot move my body with a simple touch or push on a reasonable target zone, trying to emphasize my vulnerability to 'real' attack by reaching for the throat or head (or groin, knees, feet, etc.) won't prove anything meaningful, nor will it help develop your own sensitivity and relaxation in the least.

Let's think dentistry for a moment: 'protecting your head' has little relevance when you are having dental work done, and it's the same in push hands. Of course this assumes your dentist isn't some kind of maniac who'll slap you upside the head once he's got you in the chair and in a compliant frame of mind. In martial arts *attribute* training, you need training partners you can minimally trust - just as, in getting a root canal, you need a dentist who isn't a pathological scumbag.

We can see how absurd the logic would get if we took push hands as a serious combative drill. Then we'd also wish to protect our *feet*. You never know, somebody could do a hard *flash stomp* on the instep – and that really hurts. In the standard push hands configuration, you're leaving yourself wide open for that. And then, we'd also have to watch out for *head butts*. Because even if we take push hands combatively, and thus try to protect our head with our hands up, still, standing as close as we do for push hands it's very easy for the guy to sneak in a head butt – which is quite a nasty move. While I was in Beijing training other Chinese martial arts that have a more combative emphasis, I saw many bloody and broken noses from head-butts. So to me, combatively oriented push hands is neither fish nor fowl. Even with its supposedly hardcore combative focus, it's still too limited to mimic a real street encounter, or to prepare you for real bar brawls or cage fighting, while conversely the paranoia and stress of it tend to choke off your relaxation and sensitivity.

So the point stands: push hands is an *attribute* drill. It serves to develop sensitivity to tension in yourself and another. It's true that Taiji *as a whole* can possibly become, or may contribute to, combative training, but push hands, at least in my *kuzushi* interpretation, is not combative per se. The Marines Corps is a fighting force, but Marines do a lot of pushups in training - and pushups are not a direct combat configuration (because your head isn't protected…) Just because two people seem to kind of 'square off' in setting up for push hands, don't jump to an adolescent combat fantasy based on appearances alone, or again you'll be like a primitive tribesman who thinks the tiger or shark teeth painted on the front of a fighter jet represent a real live animal. The real power and point of the work is not on the surface.

If you *do* crave more combatively realistic training, for quick results I suggest Western boxing, Sambo, or Muay Thai - get down, go real, have fun (of course we all know these have rules too, but they *feel* a bit more real at least). These can all be practiced concurrently with your Taiji. There is no inherent conflict, they're apples and oranges. In fact I'd strongly recommend that you get involved with one of these combat sports, so that you never end up fooling yourself about your fighting power.

In Chapter One, I questioned the common motivations for practicing Taiji, including the drive for 'power' i.e. fighting and self-defense. Personally, I view Taiji as a vehicle that trains you to embody the ecstatic energy of the universe. If you choose to view it as a martial art that's fine - but in that case it's *essential* that you have an entirely distinct, more reality-oriented training framework as a check so you don't end up fooling yourself. You may become skilled at Taiji push hands, and you may be feeling a lot of internal power. At that point you may well conclude that you've attained some kind of supreme martial arts ability. That's when you really need some rough and skilled guys playing under totally different rule sets to keep you grounded. Good candidate arts for playing this reality anchor role include: Judo, Western boxing, Muay Thai, Russian Sambo, or Brazilian Jiu-Jitsu. Of course these aren't *real* as in *street survival*. But, if not exactly *real*, they are certainly *rough* enough to keep you from getting a swelled head.

And by the way, when I advise that you do something more 'real' such as boxing (for example), I am *not* talking about having the whole Taiji class suddenly tie on boxing gloves like a bunch of dorks. That's a joke. You need to get to a genuine boxing club (and not a boxercise weight-loss class either), say nothing about Taiji, and get in the ring with real fighters of all types at all levels, anybody who's willing to play.

Push hands, just like the Taiji form practice, ultimately is not physical, nor structural, and not mechanical. It's an energetic interaction. Push hands, in addition to being a progress check on your internal development, is also plain fun. It may seem that I'm arbitrarily defining my own special idiosyncratic version of push hands, an eccentric emphasis which nobody else would ever go along with. That's possible. But I couldn't care less about such judgments. I'll continue to treat push hands as simple unbalancing – a drill for developing the attributes of relaxation and sensitivity – rather than either some kind of combat simulation exercise or an oddball Chinese ballroom dance step. If nobody else has their head in that game, that's fine. The great Japanese swordsman Tesshu Yamaoka once said he would hold to his own interpretation of Zen even if nobody else in the entire world did, and that may well be what it comes to.

THE LOSS INVESTMENT PRIZE GAME

Push hands: *A Taiji-based cooperative but non-compliant drill for developing attributes of balance, sensitivity, energy issuance, and for plain fun.*

Professor Zheng often admonished his push hands students with the famous Taiji adage: *Invest in loss*. D. H. Lawrence asked the question: *Are you not willing to be sponged out, erased, canceled, nothing?* Great philosophy. And I've often wondered whether there's a royal road to push hands. Is there a way of developing it further? Is there some elaboration which could constrain our naturally violent and completive/combative instincts even further, yet retain a bit of non-compliant realism? Towards that goal, I've created a game framework for push hands. I call it the *Loss Investment Prize (LIP) Game*. The prize in the LIP Game is *money*. (But only on a small, playful scale.) I try to keep it fun, nothing too serious. It's a non-symmetrical game, with a designated Defender and Challenger. Basically it involves keeping track of foot movements (which represent unbalancing) and paying out accordingly. But there are some important details:

The LIP Game Rules (for two players, a pre-designated Challenger and Defender)

1. Start position is facing one another, in standard push hands stance. Challenger can move feet freely - but for setup and offense only (not to save his/her balance in defense).

2. Defender may not move feet at all, beyond minor comfort adjustment. Defender may unbalance Challenger at will, but must not move feet to do so, and accrues no points for doing so.

3. Every time Challenger is able, via push, or via movement generated from a lock or hold, to force Defender to move one or both foot involuntarily, unbalancing him/her, that's PLUS ONE point for Challenger.

4. Every time Challenger is forced to move feet, involuntarily, in a defensive move triggered by unbalancing actions of Defender, that's MINUS ONE point for Challenger. But Defender accrues no points.

5. Players reset to Start position after every Exchange (one or two attempted moves) whether a point is scored or not. If a point was scored or decremented on that Exchange, it is recorded on paper and next Exchange begins from Start position.

6. After 10 minutes or total 30 Challenger points (whichever first) Defender will pay out sum of (mutually agreed amount) for every Challenger point.

7. If Challenger points total less than or equal to zero after 10 minutes, Defender makes no payment.

8. Points will be written on a sideline paper after every PLUS or MINUS point event, but a Point is only recorded PLUS or MINUS if *both* Challenger and Defender agree that it was a true and clean point.

9. To avoid strength jams and muscle tussles, either Defender or Challenger can at any time during an exchange, before a point-scoring foot movement is made, call 'JAM' and then the players reset to Start position with no points added or debited for that exchange. However, neither player may abuse JAM call to save him/herself.

10. In this first pure version of the game, no throws, sweeps, tackles or shoots are allowed, but maybe in later versions these could be added in. Arm locks and arm/upper-body oriented submission types of holds are allowed but not scored, thus they can only be useful as a *setup* maneuver for achieving an unbalancing, not for forcing a tap-out directly.

At first glance, this may look like merely a weirded-up version of a fixed-step push hands tournament rule set, so ...why bother? But you may be failing to appreciate some innovative nuances here that you'll never see in a competitive tournament format. These are features that emphasize the attribute development aspects of the practice, while stripping out some of the irrelevant ego and muscle. This rule set embodies the true spirit of Taiji more explicitly than most push hands practice or competition frameworks.

First, this game is *asymmetric*. The Defender has to pay out for his losses, and s/he cannot "win" anything. *Invest in loss.* Second, the direct use of money helps to keep it psychologically real enough, without requiring or encouraging injury or damaging submissions as in other martial sports. Third, notice that unlike a tournament format, no referee is required. Two people alone can play this game, and the *point agreement* rule helps to keep it friendly and peaceful, unlike the adversarial atmosphere of a tournament. Of course this game won't work if either player is acting in bad faith. I take as a given, that you are starting with quality people (of whatever Taiji skill level).

FIXED FOOTWORK

The reasons for having this first version focused on fixed step are that:

a. foot movement gives a pretty clear scoring criterion - avoiding the need for a referee, and eliminating arguments about who did what, which need to be supported by instant replay. Moving step can have clear scoring if you allow throws and sweeps, but moving step play can also be more ambiguous in scoring, more complex, more dangerous, and require more space, as well as possibly mats, etc. All that doesn't fit the light-hearted spirit of the LIP Game. Further, and more importantly:

b. believe it or not (most people don't), fixed step push hands allows for the development of energetic skills that simply can't be developed any other way.

Most people don't understand the true purpose of the fixed step restriction. That's understandable if you are looking at push hands as some kind of combative training framework, because mobility is the first and most important principle taught in any kind of fighting system. From that point of view, it may seem strange to have movement removed by stipulation. But remember that push hands, in my conception, is an *attribute drill*. In attribute drills, even military trainers sometimes adopt artificial restrictions.

Of course if somebody punches at you, the best thing is to *move* (perhaps with a simultaneous counter), which generally implies *foot* movement. That's basic boxing practice. But in the deeper work of Taiji push hands, we observe that if you deal with incoming force by foot movement, your body never seems to develop the extreme sensitivity and power that are the distinguishing hallmark of Taiji. I am not disparaging the art of fighting footwork. It can be deep. Really brilliant Pacquiao-style fighting footwork requires years of ring experience or radical natural talent. Nevertheless, for most average people it's still much easier to learn to simply move your feet as opposed to Taiji's deep relaxation and yielding response.

A boxer with whom I used to spar regularly, one of the best I've ever been in the ring with, had a fantastic ability to instinctively roll off any incoming punch (and counterpunch) instantaneously. I asked him about the origin of his freakish level of skill with that. He told me that often, throughout his childhood, his dad would stand him against a wall or in a corner, forbid him to move away, and proceed to punch him hard and fast from all angles. His dad said this would toughen him up. He learned from that early age to slough aside impact by turning with the punch, since he couldn't move away. That skill has stayed with him even though footwork of course became a major part of his later boxing toolbox. I don't condone child abuse, so I offer Taiji push hands as a kinder, gentler avenue to a similar result.

PUSH HANDS IMPROV

Within the strict limitations (fixed foot position, limited target area, and minimal 'attack' move inventory - basically just push and pull), there's still a great deal of depth to explore. Despite all the restrictions, the work has its own kind of freedom. In various Taiji styles there are types of push hands that involve choreographed initiatives and responses, but I don't hold with that. By contrast, the real ZMQ37 style push hands is totally free within the general terms of this section's description.

Guitar great Jimi Hendrix once stated the following about musical improvisation:

> *My stuff exists outside the lines. I'm free. As long as the bass player stays in the root, I can do whatever I want. If it starts feeding back, then fine. The strings and notes and tones are fighting against each other, but the guitar is still tuned to E, so it's going to be at least in that area. I could be playing a lead way up high, but that low E string could still be feeding back. So there are two tones going on. It's like you're playing two guitars at the same time. You have to let it go, but still control it. The guitar is pretty open. You can't really hit a bad note unless you don't know how to bend it and shape it into all the other melodies and tones going on. It's all about recovery. That's the most important part of soloing and improvising.*

- (from *Jimi Hendrix: A Brother's Story* by Leon Hendrix)

That's kind of how it is with ZMQ37 push hands. As long as you can stay relaxed, there's really no such thing as a bad position. Roll out, catch his tension, and you're good. That's why my approach differs from other Taiji styles in that I have no interest in push hands techniques.

So the approach in summary is:

1. **Total relaxation** (as opposed to any kind of structural mechanics)
2. **Internal energy** as the triggering power source (as opposed to clever application of physical, muscular, or tendon force)

Keep a silent, soft, detached mind. The goal in serious push hands work is not to win but just to watch calmly and see what happens. It's something like this kind of attitude:

> *When the grey heron is pursued by its enemy, the eagle, it does not run to escape; it remains calm, takes a dignified stand, and waits quietly, facing the enemy unmoved. With the terrific force with which the eagle makes its attack, the boasted king of birds is often impaled and run through on the quiet, lance-like bill of the heron.*

> - William Jordan

As for the *results* of this wise and serene mindset, why don't we let genius boxer/rapper Roy Jones Jr. help us out with a freshly updated 21st century version of Taiji's classic *Song of Push Hands*:

> *Can't be touched,*
> *Can't be stopped,*
> *Can't be moved,*
> *Can't be rocked,*
> *Can't be shook -*
> *We hot.*

> - Roy Jones Jr.

That describes push hands skill in a nutshell.

TENSION

Can you play their games?
Without losing track,
and coming down
a bit too hard?

- The Guess Who (*Share the Land*)

TENSION TYPOLOGY

Some Taiji teachers, those of a therapeutic bent who look to sidestep Taiji's martial arts legacy, like to use the kinder gentler term *search center* rather than *push hands* to describe the exercise. That does sound less combative. But *search center* doesn't get us descriptively any closer than push hands. So if we really need another name I go with *kuzushi* (unbalancing) as described in the previous section. But actually, I think the most descriptive name of all would be something like: *search tension*. Or, as we'll see later, sometimes it's even: *trigger tension*. Those two things are what we're really doing.

Once you identify your partner's tension, regardless of whether it's on his/her center line or not, and regardless of your respective body positions, you've got 'em. That brings us to the main topic – tension and relaxation. Tension is a central concern of push hands practice. In my world, and to my hands, there are two kinds of tension in a partner. The push hands adept will immediately sense both kinds of tension in most people's bodies, and both can be exploited.

The tension that appears and disappears quickly is *superficial tension, either conscious or unconscious*. It's very easy to work with. You can manipulate that kind of tension with about the same ease as lifting a teapot by its rigid handle. An example of *conscious* superficial tension would be a partner's deliberate attempt to muscle you out. The other sub-species, *unconscious* superficial tension, usually arises from carelessness, laziness, or habit – a hunched shoulder or tight wrist, that kind of thing. The diagnostic feature for superficial tension is that your partner is able to drop it quickly, whenever you point it out (assuming s/he wants to). Superficial tension lends itself to on-the-spot teaching and correction, just by drawing attention to bad habits. And just as it can easily be fixed, even by a relatively unskilled person, it can equally easily be exploited by a relatively unskilled person. Even somebody who has little knowledge of, or interest in, the deeper energy game of Taiji can take advantage of it in a partner. If you've got a bit of brains, you can become fairly good at push hands just by learning to detect and exploit superficial tension.

Deep tension is different. I'm not a psychoanalyst, so I can't say whether it has more profound emotional or psychological roots than superficial tension. Like superficial tension, it's also available for an experienced Taiji player to use in unbalancing. But unlike superficial tension, deep tension normally isn't anchored to a particular strong muscle or habitually concentrated in a single body area. Deep tension is a holistic, almost inherent property of a partner's body (or mind?) overall. So to whatever degree a partner's body harbors it, it will be available to the experienced Taiji adept's touch anywhere on his/her body. (That's why you might as well push in the safe, legal zones as opposed to the unconventional danger zones such as head, neck, groin, etc. Since the deep tension is everywhere, why not just use the nearest and most convenient spot?)

Deep tension tends to be entirely unconscious and cannot be dropped on instruction. Becoming aware of it and shedding it is a long-term process. Unlike superficial tension, it can't be significantly reduced in a single training session, or with a teacher's one-time verbal correction or posture fix. Deep tension is like a dye which pervades or permeates the entire cloth, while surface tension is like a sudden coffee spill on your pants or shirt – it comes and goes. It's interesting that people can seem superficially relaxed, not at all obviously uptight or muscle-bound, and yet they'll have this deep, unconscious tension. Deep tension can only be fixed by training the Taiji ARC process through a good Taiji form over a long period. Deep tension is not only hard to get rid of, it's also harder to detect. You need to have a much greater level of Taiji development to detect and exploit deep tension than was required in the case of superficial tension. I've done this unbalancing work with hundreds of partners across Japan, China, and North America, in addition to my work with my own students who are typically experienced martial artists from a wide range of styles and backgrounds. In all of these many people that deep, unconscious tension has been *always* present and apparent.

THE TRIGGER EFFECT

From this section onward, unless specified otherwise, whenever I write about issuing energy in general, I'm using that as shorthand for either the FLASHOUT of STEEL energy from the NEXUS Point, or the shortcut issuance of energy from the *lingtai*, which are all covered in Chapter 2. The energy may be tuned to more of a *yin* quality or to more of a *yang* quality, as we'll see, but for brevity I'll often just refer to issuing energy. Please review Chapter 2 if you're unclear on the details.

Now we get to a really deep subject. *What exactly is happening in (what I'm calling) real push hands?* If there really is no essential physical power in the movement, what exactly is causing your partner to stumble or hurtle back? Those who aren't as committed to the internal paradigm as I am, but who are mindful of the general Taiji zeitgeist, would say that you *sensitively exploit your partner's bad moments*. A bit of over-extension, too much of a turn, inability to sit back far enough – faults in physical kinetics and configuration can be exploited to affect a partner's balance with minimal physical effort on the pusher's part. That's the prosaic explanation, and it works well as far as it goes. Then push hands becomes a game of learning over many years to be sensitive to bad body angles and other subtle positional criteria. As I say, that's a fine approach and many a talented push hands player has been produced by sticking to that program.

However, this book isn't going to talk about that kind of thing. That's not what I'm about. In keeping with the overall theme of this book, my interest lies strictly in *applying the internal energy to the basic problem of unbalancing a partner*. My fundamental principle however may seem a bit surprising, in that unlike some committed internal stylists, *I do not assert that the internal energy per se is doing the work of blasting 'em back*. It's a bit more nuanced than that. The key principle of internally-oriented push hands is the following:

> *The applied internal power does not act directly to move your partner's body, rather it acts as a trigger applied to his/her tension, like a spark on gunpowder, which causes your partner to unbalance (or throw, or knock down) him/herself.*

The force that propels people back when popped is not 'my' internal energy, *it's simply their own deep internal tension.* Weird as it sounds, that's all it is - their own activated tension is jumping them back. Their body is jumping back without being entirely under their conscious control.

The tension to which your internal effects are applied can be of either type above: superficial or deep. But essentially, your partner is always moving him/herself. Or to be most accurate, your partner's tension is doing the real work, the 'heavy lifting' so to speak - triggered by your application of energy. The results of touching a partner's tension can be compared to the interaction between a really hot oiled saucepan and a raw popcorn kernel. The kernel's going to pop regardless of which part of the kernel first contacts the oil physically, or at what angle or trajectory it lands, etc. It's the heat that does it, not the positional interaction. All that matters is the simple fact of contact - which allows for the transfer of the triggering property. In this example, the triggering agent is the heat, but the heat is not the direct and proximate agent of the kernel's explosively kinetic reaction as it pops and slams the side of the pan. The true agent of motion is the kernel's own stored chemical energy.

The deep unconscious tension (which everyone seems to have, apart from great Taiji masters) is not permanently localized to a particular area of the partner's body. It's everywhere and never leaves them altogether. So you might as well work simply with his/her arms and upper torso, there's no need to touch the head or other sensitive places (unless, acting from extreme anxiety and tension, s/he wildly whips your relaxed arms or hands to those areas of his/her own accord). It also doesn't matter what kind of patterned circling *choreography* s/he tries to use, nor does it matter if s/he attempts any kind of *technique* such as a lock or sophisticated Chinese *qinna* police holds, or how high or low s/he holds his/her hands, or whatever s/he does. Since the deep tension isn't localized or transient, as long as you're in contact, you're good.

Since the deep, unconscious tension is always present everywhere in my partner's body, it may occur to you to wonder: *Why don't I pop him/her out every single time?* If you watch me push, for example, I only pop my partner now and then in a given session. For one thing, doing that is very monotonous for both parties. It's true that every time they step up and we touch I could just - *blammo* - rock them back a few feet or as long a distance as I want (though really all you need to do is have them move their foot, no need for pyrotechnics). But that gets to be incredibly monotonous for both of us. I want to chat while pushing, to put myself in awkward little imbalances as a puzzle for them to figure out (poking gentle non-verbal fun at the fact that most of them are mentally bound to the idea of physical configuration as determinative in push hands) and just enjoy a little interactive game to pass the day.

For another thing, people react emotionally to having their deep tension touched. It's primal. When somebody is moved via *transient surface tension*, their reaction is either to shrug it off and get on with the next interaction, or maybe even gratitude at the little mini-lesson. It's within their current purview of understanding and all is well. But in the case of being popped by somebody touching their *deep tension*, emotional reactions range all over the spectrum.

Sometimes, it could be joy and gratitude. But often enough it's a kind of primal anger, fear, resentment, a desire to punish, etc. I have seen it all. When people experience being moved by their own tension, without understanding it, that's when they get scared and seek to convert the drill of push hands into some kind of mutant 'martial arts' thing, or combative type of exercise - which of course it was not meant to be. It's only a drill (the point I've beaten to death throughout this chapter). But the emotional body will attempt to do that when 'threatened' in this way (of course there's no actual physical threat or pain at all, we are talking about a deep-seated emotional effect). And that's when minor accidents can occur (but fortunately nothing too serious most of the time).

To take just one of hundreds of experiences I could cite, once as a class visitor I was invited to do push hands with a famous martial arts sensei in Japan, a master who teaches a blend of Chinese and Japanese martial arts. I knew in an instant that he had the same deep unconscious tension as almost everybody else, and I was easily able to move him around. After just a minute of that, it seems his ego was threatened at a deep level - so he lashed out with a sudden kick targeted at my groin. Normally, everyone understands that in push hands or *kuzushi*, kicks are a foul. So this was a typical 'conversion' reaction, meaning the attempt to re-interpret push hands as a (pseudo) combative practice rather than a mere drill. Because I've been brutally schooled over decades of other combative practices, I easily evaded the kick, then bowed, thanked him, and politely terminated the interaction. But I understood his reaction and I don't fault this master for it. That's a primal body thing, coming from a very deep place (sorry to get all psychoanalytical on you.)

So then - what exactly *is* the role of the internal energy? I've been discussing internal power through the whole book - yet I may seem to be almost denying it now (by claiming that people in effect move themselves). I'll get deeply into details in the following sections. For now I'll say you use your energy as only the *primer* not the *powder*. Just like a bullet fired from a gun, the cartridge's *primer* has only a small physical triggering force. But the primer ignites the much greater physical power of the *powder* charge, which is what actually propels the bullet out the barrel. The 'powder' in this image is your partner's internal tension, and the 'bullet' (the thing that's ultimately moved) is his/her physical body.

You will sometimes read great masters writing about blasting opponents with their internal force. I will maintain however that in all cases, what these masters or anybody else is really doing is all that can be done with '*your*' internal energy: to trigger or ignite '*his or her*' tension. It is quite possible that what I'm calling deep tension here is actually some tangled hairball of physical tension plus the emotional or energetic substrate. I call it their (deep) tension for convenience, but I don't actually know exactly what it consists of. So you may be actually triggering not only a partner's physical tension to do the work, but further, his or her entire *being* may be hijacked for just a moment. I'm calling it deep tension, but maybe a better term for what a skilled adept triggers might be the *inherent energy mass*.

186

No matter what, though, it's simply not the case that your internal energy per se is directly picking up and moving your partner's physical body. It doesn't work that way. Your partner is being involuntarily moved by some element of his/her own being, which you've caused to react internally. The conclusion is that you never need to issue any kind of direct kinetic power – neither external physical power nor any sort of bazooka barrage of your own overwhelming internal energy supposedly sufficient to blast them off their feet. Conclusion: stay soft at all times. Mentally and physically.

In this section I've introduced the idea of chronic deep pervasive tension, and also used a couple of crude metaphors to illustrate the basic trigger effect: bullet cartridges and popcorn. But the best metaphor for all this, strangely perhaps, is *nuclear*. That's the most profound and evocative metaphor for the deepest processes of push hands and I will develop it more fully in the next section – SHELL Interactions. But there are a few more basic considerations of push hands interaction to get out of the way first.

PARTNER WORK

Rubbin' is racin'

    - NASCAR speedway traditional wisdom

As your skill deepens, you may begin to feel a lack of skilled practice partners for your continued *kuzushi* improvement. Never fear. You can easily and instantly upskill any partner to almost any level desired to make things spicier for yourself. Here are just a few of the ways that I often use to apply extra hot sauce when the partner is too far below my level. It's basically just applying an objective constraint that dials down your own relative ability.

How to Instantly Upskill Your Push Hands Partner

1. Use *one hand* while s/he uses *both*. Hook either your lead or offside hand behind your back into your belt and unbalance with just your one hand against two.

2. Use *no hands* while s/he uses *both*. Hook both hands in your back belt and yet remain immovable.

3. Let him/her stand in fully braced "bow" type of elongated strong stance while you *just stand upright*, feet shoulder width, like waiting-for-a-bus mode.

4. Let him/her stand in normal push hands "bow" stance, braced mode as in Point 3 above, while you stand in bow stance - but on your *heels* only. You remain immovable.

5. Let him/her stand in normal push hands "bow" stance, braced mode as in Point 3 above, while you stand in bow stance - but on your *balls of feet* only. You remain immovable.

6. *Tie your upper arms* flush against your body with a karate *obi*, secured just above your elbows so that only your forearms can move freely. S/he works with full freedom (within the framework) as ever.

7. Let *him/her move freely* around your front and sides, or even step in back of you if you're that confident, like moving step push hands, while *you* don't take a single step – neither in defense nor offense.

8. *Combine* any two or more of the above restrictions.

Those are a very small sample of what can be done within the basic *kuzushi* framework without additional risk of injury, and without any need for any change or upgrade whatsoever in terms of facilities, available space, surfaces, safety equipment/accessories, special clothing, etc.

SAFETY FIRST AND LAST

As your *kuzushi* skills improve, you must always remember: Safety First. Sometimes, because I only bump people a little in push-hands practice, or I merely jolt their balance gently so they have to take a small step, they assume that's the limit of the real Taiji power. But nothing could be further from the truth. The reason I just bump people a little, make them take a step here and there, is because people can get hurt. If you've never seriously injured somebody in sparring or some martial arts context, you don't know the feeling. It's absolutely horrible. Especially when there's blood all over the floor, a body is down and out, EMT's have been called in - it's just horrible. You may think that would apply only to MMA or boxing. You'd think Taiji would allow one to really rip loose without fear of the consequences. But it isn't so. The real Taiji power is potentially destructive. I'm not saying the real Taiji power will *explode an attacker's internal organs* or any of that Ninja nonsense. Remember the Taiji power is only a trigger. I'm talking about something a lot more prosaic.

Ever since the time, years back, when I, without even realizing what I was doing, blasted a large aggressive guy pin wheeling backwards over twenty feet - into and through sealed fire doors, out onto his butt in the parking lot, resulting in setting off the building alarm and the mandatory facility evacuation by firefighters - I've learned to err on the side of absolute gentility. The topic has been well summarized by an anonymous writer on an internet martial arts forum:

> *From my experience as a lawyer, the most permanently damaging or fatal situation in real life comes not as a result of any pressure point or exotic maneuver. The worst nightmare is simply a bouncer/drunk/nitwit punching someone who is rendered unconscious and then falls, striking his head on the pavement. I have had 3 clients victimized in that fashion with catastrophic results. And another 2 beaten by police with*

flashlights and then falling unconscious and striking the back of their head on the ground. When the victim does not die outright, they lead the rest of their life as a shell of their former selves.

Of course, he's talking raw street stuff. Nevertheless, random falling can be horrifically dangerous in any context. *Falling in an uncontrolled way can be incredibly dangerous regardless of what person or technique triggered that fall.* In Aikido, where there are mats and students are trained to fall (basically launching themselves into choreographed, controlled rolls), it's safe enough. And in ordinary Taiji push hands it would be safe enough. But when you learn to really trigger a partner's tension, I can't stress it strongly enough – you've got to back off. Just play with little nudges, here and there, so they can feel their own tension.

SHELL INTERACTIONS

Generally you will want to affect your partner's energy using your own energy. The well-known Taiji term for this is發勁 *fajing*, literally "issuing energy". It's a briar patch of a term, lending itself to all kinds of interpretations all over the map. In keeping with the physical/mechanical revisionism of current Taiji teaching, you often see explanations of *fajing* in terms of 'proper posture' and 'body mechanics'. For a soft version of physicalized *fajing*, we can consider something called ballistic striking. One net commentator (posting only as DdIR) has summarized this style of issuing power very well:

Ballistic strikes operate by allowing both flexors and extensors to remain relaxed, the arm (assuming we're talking about punching) is effectively a dead weight, unsupported by the muscular tension required to maintain linear skeletal alignment. It's like a medieval ball-and-chain, as opposed to a battering ram. ... the ballistic [punch] is thrown with very little tension, the power being generated by a weight shift from foot to foot and delivered by a "dead arm" swing.

That's a good summary of a certain view of *fajing* (which isn't directly mentioned in the quote, this is me talking now). And this physicalized approach scales all the way up from the loose style outlined above to more serious combative work, such as the optimal balance between muscular tension and relaxed power propagation of a pro boxer's punch. It all works as a kind of *fajing*. After all, physical or kinetic energy is a kind of energy too. To see the application of 'proper posture', 'body mechanics', and 'kinetic force propagation' as the foundation for practical striking, just Google practically any photo of boxer Rocky Marciano KO'ing an opponent. That shows all you need to know about relaxed and yet fully coordinated propagation of whole body power for concentration on a given target. That's how you get those *manos de piedra* (yes, I know that was Duran's tag, but Marciano had that quality too).

That fast-and-loose-yet-unstoppable power comes from a whole-body physical coordination, a beautiful thing to see in (or better, from outside of) the ring. Most of the true Greatest-Of-All-Time candidate boxers consciously or unconsciously mastered that kind of work. Other good examples were Roberto Duran, Roy Jones Jr., Mike Tyson, and Ali. Outside of boxing, in other martial sports and arts, people have tried to replicate those abilities, with varying degrees of success. For example, methods for vibrating the tip of a long white pine staff (pole-shaking) are based on similar ideas. Sometimes these principles are even applied to push hands, with a result that sometimes resembles Taiji. It's all very well as far as it goes. That's all a kind of *fajing*. I'm a recreational boxer myself, so I have not the slightest quarrel with it. But this is a book about Taiji, so I won't be covering that kind of training here.

You also may sometimes see another type of work labeled with this pathetically overloaded term *fajing*. There are methods that require you to build up a big storm head of physical pressure in your abdomen which you then release all at once with a shudder through your arms and maybe a big HUH kiai sound or other such Dolby effects. That's great stuff too. If you want to work that way, be my guest, enjoy. But that kind of hard *qi* work has absolutely no relation to anything I'm discussing in this book. Please don't confuse the two.

As I've been at pains to emphasize, this book is about real Taiji. It isn't about boxing, or Judo, or any other art where normal body mechanics apply. Nor is it about conditioning your abdomen to steam boiler toughness for explosive strength emission. Rather than copy-and-paste physical principles from other arts and sports, I'm going to write here about the meaning of *fajing* within real Taiji, the mental and energetic art. But before we reach the juicy stuff, I need to cover some preliminaries.

From the crudely physical point of view, there are three initial stages of development in evolving toward the ability to deploy the Taiji internal energy in push hands. They are the Three P's:

PUSH hands
PROBE hands
PLACE hands

In PUSH stage, your hands are actively trying to push the partner off balance. You may attempt that by means of some technique, or possibly by just raw bulling the guy over. Either way, this is pretty much all physical, the lowest level. It implies a near total lack of sensitivity to the actual internal state of the partner, just an attempt to force your will over them. It often works well, especially if you know some standup wrestling basics, and it works even better if you outweigh your partner by 50+ lbs.

In the PROBE stage, you've learned to use a physical push as a diagnostic tool rather than always as an offensive assault. You've become able to send out gentle probes of light physical force. Like a bat's sonar these probes rebound back to your fingers with information about the partner's state and locations of tension. You then launch a physical push action based on the tension information returned from such a probe. This is the level of what I called above: *exploiting a partner's bad moments*. This phase, while more sensitive than the prior Push phase, is still physically based and therefore a low-level skill.

In PLACE stage, you merely place your hands passively anywhere on the partner, doesn't matter where. You don't use any physical strength, not even 4 ounces is required, and you don't initiate any physical technique, nor do you send out any physical probe. Merely by placing your hands on him, he will seem to throw himself off balance, often with surprising violence. This is where real push hands begins. It's a complex space with many interesting ramifications, which will reward a closer inspection under the hood, in the next section. All the remainder of this chapter assumes that your basic mode of initial physical engagement in push hands is at the 'place' level, not 'pushing' or 'probing' as defined above.

THE TAILOR'S TOUCH

They acknowledge and perceive that even while they lived in the body, it was the spirit that sensated, and that although the faculty of sensation manifested in the body, still it was not of the body, and therefore that when the body is cast aside, the sensations are far more exquisite and perfect. Life consists in the exercise of sensation, for without it there is no life, and such as is the faculty of sensation, such is the life.

- Emmanuel Swedenborg

What are the considerations of high quality 'place' mode work? Professor Zheng sometimes told students that they should touch, and even push, as though their partner were made of tissue paper, which the slightest over-exertion will tear. It's an evocative image. Now I'll go a step further in that general direction.

I've heard that there are blind tailors in Istanbul and throughout the Middle East who can tell everything about a piece of fabric by simply touching it. With a single feel they know the quality, the origin, the type of yarn, the texture of the weave, possibly even the color. They know what kind and quality and value of garment or rug can be made from this bolt of cloth. That's all due to their sensitive skilled touch. You want to approach push hands with that kind of attitude – literally. Usually when you're doing push hands, unless you are out on Venice Beach or in a nudist colony, your partner will be wearing some kind of upper body garment. You should approach push hands as though you are going to push with an empty shirt or sweater or jacket or whatever they are wearing. That makes your fingers more sensitive and your pushes less forceful. How much force does it take to push an empty suit of clothes?

In other words, while strictly maintaining physical contact with your partner you *push the clothes not the body*. Yet you retain the same ultimate goal as ever – to unbalance your partner, forcing him/her to take at least one step or fall over. Don't open an actual gap (that will transform your push into a strike, which is a foul), but learn to appreciate this image, which forces you to be gentle and to use essentially no physical force whatsoever. This type of pushing is difficult. You may complain that since it's physically impossible to move someone by pushing their clothes alone, this is an unrealistic and counter-productive visualization. True, but despite that, the effort is great mental training. Be aware of your partner's clothes, more so than his or her body. Don't worry whether s/he's physically strong or not – muscles don't matter when you're focusing on clothes.

Imagine you're a master tailor who's been hired to appraise and put a figure on this fabric for a potential buyer who wants to make a good bargain. What's the quality of this cloth? What's it good for making? How does it really feel to you? What would you pay for a bolt of it? Asking these questions (to yourself please!) is, strangely, much more important for really deep push hands skill development than worrying about their body posture or tactical intentions. So in addition to the other candidate re-wordings for 'push hands' that I've cited in the previous section, such as 'search center', here's another one: instead of 'push hands' we could say: *'push clothes'*. But of course we aren't really talking about clothes at all. I've promised this book won't overload you with any more theory than strictly necessary, and that when theory *is* introduced, it will be in the most functional possible context. Now comes a moment when I think it's helpful to go a step further into the human energetic architecture, because it bears on our understanding of push hands practice.

The human body is encased in a close fitting *Superficial Hi-frequency Energy Laminal Layer* (SHELL). It fits around you with about the same closeness and thickness as a sweater or a loose shirt. Here's the point: you want always to be working with your partner's SHELL, not his/her body. This is how you train for smart hands. Admittedly by working this way you're going to get bounced out a lot at first, but stick to your principles. Your hands are quietly educating themselves about the energy SHELL that surrounds every person just like a suit of clothes, but which we normally shove right through, as we blunder blindly forward seeking the body.

In the previous section on Tension, I defined the operative effect of internal energy in push hands as *triggering* – just igniting your partner's inherent tension (or tension/energy bundle). In the upcoming section on the various SHELL interactions, it gets tedious to continually refer to the trigger effect explicitly, even though that's what it always is. So in this next section when I talk applying energy to unbalance your partner, please understand it as that same kind of trigger effect.

THE SPIKE

There are three related yet distinct experiences in applying internal energy for push-hands. We'll look at each in turn, moving from a lesser scope to the most total engagement.

In the simplest case, you merely follow your partner's moves passively, then occasionally (or continually, depending on the partner's level) you will feel something almost like a little spark or twinge in your fingers and hands. If at that moment you simply push very gently, quickly or slowly, you will find you've caught his/her tension at a maximal point, and it takes almost no physical effort to knock him/her back. Of course, as I've explained, it's only a trigger effect. Your partner is actually moving him/herself with his/her own tension. You'll feel as though s/he is (unconsciously) actually *trying* to maneuver his/her area of greatest tension directly to your hand. In this case, a simple, not overly forceful, physical push is all you need to unbalance your partner. The internal aspect of this was merely deciding a convenient timing for your gesture. No technique or physical strength should be applied at all.

In one of the most ancient and venerated classic books of the traditional Chinese medical canon, the *Huangdi Bashiyi Nanjing* (黄帝八十一難經 *The Huang Emperor's Canon of Eighty-One Difficult Issues*), often called simply the *Nanjing*, we find the concept of *deqi* (得气). It means something like *acquisition of the crucial energy point*, or essentially *nailing it*. This is usually mentioned in connection with acupuncture, referring to the distinct sensation that an acupuncture healer, or more commonly the patient, feels when the needle has just entered the perfect spot to address a given complaint. I'd like to hijack this term to describe this mode of push hands. So some new vocabulary for you: *deqi* – which means: *nailing it*. But because the Chinese word *deqi* is a little hard for English speakers to say, from now on I'll refer to this relatively straightforward style as the *Sudden Percussive Instantaneous Knockback Energy* (SPIKE) touch. Li Yaxuan has written about the SPIKE (using other vocabulary) as follows:

> *Whenever the right opportunity comes to your hands, your internal energy's automatic reaction instantly sends him sprawling out. Therefore, in pushing hands you need not seek out a particular time or chance to push him, no need to force anything. When the chance has perfectly developed on its own, you'll feel it jump straight to your hands.*

MICRO-FAJING: YINJECTION

There's also a more pro-active way to work. Instead of mindlessly waiting for your partner to blindly impale him/herself on your hands as in SPIKE mode, you can precisely craft and control everything about the interaction, including the timing, intensity, form, and direction of the resulting jolt back. This is very sophisticated work and gets to the living heart of the Taiji mystery. When you begin to understand this process, you'll be amazed and amused that some Taiji people continue to think of push hands in terms of either athletic attributes or physical techniques - no matter how sophisticated.

To get into this topic, I'll elaborate the nuclear metaphor touched on in the previous section, where I also introduced the idea of pervasive, chronic deep tension. Think of your partner's chronic deep tension as a chunk of fissionable material, like uranium 235 – something that can sustain a fission (atom splitting) chain reaction. Most people are carrying this chunk of fissile material around within themselves all the time. It's very powerful but they aren't much aware of it because it doesn't 'go critical' under normal circumstances. Your application of energy is like the neutron bombardment that triggers a chain reaction within the unstable mass of their own fissile tension clump. From this, you can easily grasp the key fact that obviously *the neutron bombardment itself has no physical energy comparable to the fission reaction it triggers.* The neutron bombardment that kicks off the show is only an initiating agent – a trigger effect. The neutron beam is narrow, physically weak, and invisible – everything we want our Taiji touch to be. This is the true meaning of the trigger effect. (And before you ask, the answer is: NO - of course I'm not saying that either you or your partner are ever *actually* radioactive in Taiji practice! I know people are very literal these days, but gimme a break, this is a *metaphor*, ok? But it's an illuminating one.)

Continuing the metaphor, you can not only trigger their energetic reaction, but you can *shape the charge*, controlling direction and magnitude of the final physical effect, in the same way that blast shapers are incorporated into nuclear weapons. Now, again let me stress that *there is nothing actually destructive* about this process. Although Taiji is said to be a martial art, push hands is merely a pleasant attribute drill, and nothing more. But this metaphor is designed to be so unconventional and shocking that you *never regard push hands as a straight physical interaction ever again.* In actual effect, push hands is totally harmless, and a *jing*-trigger touch can actually be therapeutic to your partner, even as s/he's hurtling backward. The danger, if any, in push hands is not atomic blast but only unintentional falls, which I've already covered in the previous section, 'Safety First and Last'.

So, you can trigger tension where and when you wish, and control your partner's resulting energy release. Let's get into how this is done. The *Nanjing* (see above) offers a key idea, which is normally thought of in a medical context, but which I will co-opt for describing this kind of Taiji push-hands work:

陽隨陰入 (*yangsuiyinru*)

Literally this means *the yang enters following the yin.* It is also sometimes translated as *yin leads, yang follows.* I'm not going to get into the medical interpretation of this line, which is very abstruse. You can get any number of Chinese medical textbooks to explain that. I'm adapting this interesting observation and terminology to the energy dynamics of Taiji push hands.

It works as a two-stage process. In the practice of push hands, your proper relaxed following of your partner will occasionally result in a good placement of your hands on his/her body, a position from which it's reasonable to believe a good push (to unbalance only, not to otherwise harm) could be launched. At that moment, the average push-hands practitioner will just physically go for it. If they've heard that Taiji is all about soft strength and relaxing, they may try to somewhat moderate their physical force - a bit. But most likely they'll just go for it and enjoy the guilty pleasure if it happens to work, knocking the partner back. But regardless of the result, whether "successful" or not, that approach isn't Taiji. It has nothing to do with Taiji.

To see what real Taiji would look like, we need to rewind the tape a bit, back to: *a position from which a good push could be launched*. That's the key moment (for a higher adept, *all* moments are that). At that moment, when the untutored would just go for it, the Taiji adept initiates two closely linked, but absolutely distinct, stages.

> *Stage 1: Issue triggering yin energy into the partner's body with a touch.*
>
> *Stage 2: Guide the reaction toward the desired directional focus with a light physical nudge.*

In terms of our nuclear fission metaphor, Stage 1 is like the neutron bombardment into your partner's clump of fissile deep tension. Their inherent energetic tension is like a big unstable hunk of U-235, as already discussed. This is the trigger that sets off the reaction in their deep tension. Obviously your *yin* energy per se has no power whatsoever to move the lumbering meat mountain that is your partner, right? Just as a thin stream of invisible neutrons has no inherent power to blow away a city. Stage 2 is your control over the magnitude, direction, and shape of the physical results – like the charge-shaping mechanisms (reflectors and so on) in a nuclear device that control, constrain, or direct the blast effects. Stage 2 functions to achieve what Wang Zongyue (Taiji classic writings) termed: 專注一方 *aim in one direction*.

It's really crucial that you understand and deploy these two actions as distinct phases. When you're just learning the process, you can separate the stages by what feels like a musical half-beat. Over time as you gain proficiency, the little gap between the two phases will lessen to the point of disappearance. Then they will *appear* to be simultaneous and instantaneous (see 'Fire' mode, described below). Nevertheless, apart from the SPIKE mode (above), it's always two stages operating – otherwise it isn't Taiji. The Tailor's Touch introduced earlier is crucial. You want to 'break' into your partner's SHELL, but only with your *yin* energy (the imaginary neutron stream issued in Stage 1 application) at first. If you thrust your *yang* (crude physical) energy directly into and through the partner's SHELL, then you may move him/her but it won't be Taiji. You will have learned and gained nothing.

I call the Stage 1 application of your *yin* triggering energy "*yin* injection" or *yinjection* for short. As your hand touches any accessible portion of your partner's body (in practice it's usually clothing), you just imagine that the neutron beam (or a healing beam of soothing light - beautifully pastel colored, if you wish), is issuing from your fingertips and/or palms, and that these beams are streaming invisibly into your partner. Some people are so sensitive that they'll spontaneously pop themselves, merely from their body's percept of the *yin* energy trigger, *before you even apply anything in Stage 2*. That tends to happen more often with a female partner because women are more sensitive to the triggering energy than men. It results from an interesting combination some people have, particularly women, of extreme sensitivity accompanied, paradoxically, by plenty of deep inherent tension. In general, micro-*fajing* is like sawing down a tree – sometimes it's a two-stage process of sawing through the trunk, then pushing or pulling the trunk to the ground. Other times, it's a one-stage process of merely sawing through the trunk. Even a thin cut that goes all the way through will sometimes bring the whole tree down spontaneously without the need for any further tipping action at all.

The Stage 1 issuance of "lightly disruptive *yin* energy into the partner's body" may sound esoteric or even scary (especially with my nutso nuclear metaphor). But it's nothing of the kind. We are all constantly interacting with one another at the energetic (sometimes called the 'etheric') level, throughout the day. That's all happening randomly and unconsciously. In push hands practice, we have the opportunity and permission to play with these elements in a controlled and purposive setting. Nothing scary about it. This action is only an innocent feather touch, far less aggressive than the gross physical straining, shoving, wrenching and near bludgeoning that goes on in your typical push hands match between two strong men.

So, no matter what metaphor I may throw at you, don't think of your energy trigger as some kind of Dragon Ball Z organ-exploding *ki* ball. It's not that at all. It's much more like the paralyzing bite or sting of a venomous insect which savagely disables its prey before gorging itself on .... Just kidding! Yinjection is totally harmless. It's merely a feather touch of directed *yin* energy, of lesser intensity and milder intent than 99% of the random dirty energies that the average person receives and issues all day long without batting an eye. In fact, a close cousin of this simple yinjection thing is often taught as an energy healing technique. In this case, we are adapting it to the Taiji push-hands attribute training. That was the genius of the founders of this great art – they saw that an essentially medical concept could be adapted to martial arts, and be practiced pleasantly with no ill effects. In fact the chance of any kind of injury, internal or external, under the Taiji practice modality described here is far less than that of your average Brazilian Jiu-Jitsu or Muay Thai sparring session.

It may seem that yinjection boils down to little more than a feint. But that interpretation is wrong. A feint, whether in boxing or in ordinary push hands, is a physical gesture. It may be minimal but it must be physical because you need to "sell" the move, as they say in boxing. In boxing, the feint depends on visual interpretation by the opponent. In pushing, a feint would correspond to the 'probe hands' level of work, which has been discussed earlier in this chapter. But yinjection is operating at the 'place hands' level and has no physical component to it at all. It does not depend for effect on any kind of visual or tactile interpretation by the partner. Rather than depending, as a feint does, on positive identification and interpretation by a partner of your intention, it depends on the opposite - innocence and inability to be interpreted. Crucially, your partner should not notice that you have issued your *yin* energy. At Stage 1 there is no accompanying physical gesture. Just your hand placed on his/her body surface. You don't make Bruce Lee grimaces, whines, or snarls. At this stage in fact, your partner should feel nothing consciously and may even feel extra confident for just a half-beat, before his/her tension 'goes critical' as the chain reaction is triggered, priming the pump for Stage 2.

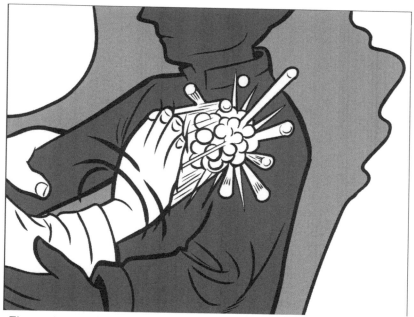

Figure 11 YINJECTION: Your *yin* power leads off, in order to trigger the latent energy of your partner's inherent tension. The illustration depicts the yinjection trigger effect, symbolically and metaphorically, as a neutron-beam bombardment of a fissionable mass which, in the illustration, represents your partner's deep tension, located for this example in the shoulder area. It is only your partner's own inner tension which reacts to provide the energy that physically moves his or her own body.

So in Stage 1, you pierce your partner's SHELL to trigger his/her tension, and in Stage 2, you control or at least influence the nature of your partner's physical reaction. There are three main Stage 2 modalities. You choose one of the following as your follow-on action after yinjection:

a) Application of follow-on physical energy
b) Application of follow-on *yang* (internal) energy
c) Linking via continued transmission of *yin* (internal) energy

Let's consider these in turn. First, the Stage 2 modality (a), a very light guiding physical gesture. Use your Tailor's Touch to be sure you don't overdo things. The physical push gesture is only needed to give your partner's reaction a focus direction. It 'tells' his/her body which way you want it to go out. So it has a purely directive function. As we know by now, that light Stage 2 physical push is not the actual motive energy that moves your partner's body. In Stage 2, modality (a), you finally *could* get just a little physical, with your follow-on push gesture – but crucially you need to *keep it light*. Just a feather touch - but this time a feather touch of very light *physical* energy, rather than purely etheric or internal energy.

Here's the guideline: with modality (a) you should know that your push was nowhere close to moving him/her on a purely physical basis. If you suspect, even slightly, that your push would have moved him/her physically, without the Stage 1 yinjection trigger, then it was too strong. The Stage 2 physical move should be light contact – not a whole lot more than the Tailor's Touch itself. This is a form of physically gentle *yang* power that I call the *Nonthreatening Unconcealed Directive Guidance Energy* (NUDGE). It merely shows his/her body where to throw itself. This very light physical energy can also be considered a very low-level form of *yang* power application, so it fits our general guidance for this type of pushing: *yin* leads, *yang* follows. In most cases, the NUDGE is all you need to know or do. The other two Stage 2 modalities (b) and (c), are purely for reference and research purposes.

With modality (b) as your Stage 2 follow-on, you intensify the energetic 'chain reaction' that you already triggered in your partner with the Stage 1 yinjection (the 'neutron bombardment' of our nuke metaphor). This can be analogized to the use of 'boosting' elements in nuclear weapons, where additional nuclear energy components or special feedback mechanisms are used to intensify a chain reaction that's already underway. In most cases, just as with a nuclear device, the energy liberated by the straightforward application of the triggering energy is more than sufficient. Believe me that most people already have plenty of compressed tensile energy inside them, such that when it's triggered no further amplification is needed to jolt them back very strongly.

But still. Taiji was once considered a martial art, so I do need to cover this intensification angle, for completeness. The boosting energy is your own *yang* internal power stream. It takes the form of a wave transfer from you to your partner. The energy wave could be of type SURGE-1 or SURGE-2. In the heat of the moment it's not easy to control or even notice the difference. It's just an augmentative pulse.

The type of result to expect from the boost is controlled by the basing location. If you issue the boosting *yang* SURGE from a shorter, closer point (such as your arms or mid-back) your partner feels a sharp, short jolting effect that the old masters called *leng jing*, literally cold power. This results in a very abrupt but relatively short jolt back of your partner's body. If you issue it from a deeper location in your body, from your lower back, *dantian*, legs, or feet, the effect on your partner won't be instantaneous but will be a kind of slow motion, long distance tumble-back effect. This kind of SURGE application is sometimes called *chang jing*, long power. This is neither a physical/kinetic nor an imaginary (visualized) power wave.

It's crucial to remember that even with your *yang* boosting, the primary energy for the final physical outcome is still your partner's concentrated chronic tension. Lacking that you can stream *yang* energy into him/her all day til the cows come home and it won't have the slightest effect. Even in nuclear weapons, the boosting components require an initial energy release from the chain reaction triggered within the fissionable material. But introduction of additional *yang* energy boosting takes over control of the chain reaction triggered by your initial yinjection. This can allow you to modulate the final effect as follows:

If you apply 5% of your power, s/he'll experience (his/her own tension as) a nudge.

If you apply 20% of your power, s/he'll experience (his/her own tension as) a jolt.

If you apply 30% of your power, s/he'll experience (his/her own tension as) a blast.

And so on...

We could say it's like those Orca trainers, the young women at the water shows. The girl raises her arm to waist height, and the Orca jumps to a certain height; for a chest high hand signal, the jump is a higher; and an overhead hand signal results in an even higher jump. The girl is not throwing the Orca up into the air with her own power. The Orca is flinging himself around. She's just indicating to it how high it is to propel itself. That's what this is. Of course, by comparing this reaction to an Orca performance I don't mean to suggest that the jolting effect in push hands is voluntary or cooperative. It's involuntary, and often surprising (and even irritating) to those who experience it, though some people find it amusing as well. Generally it comes as a revelation, something they hadn't understood about themselves.

This modality (b) of *yang* boosting-energy is what Li Yaxuan was talking about in passages such as this:

> When you spontaneously issue relaxed instantaneous energy
> from the dantian, it can cause your partner or opponent to jump
> out, or collapse when it penetrates deeply into him. You may

push him far away, or you may hurt or even kill him. This is not
ordinary physical energy. It is deeply sunk, completely relaxed,
and issues instantaneously without any chance of detection or
interception.

But even in this passage, you should understand the 'hurt' and
'kill' stuff as references to the *yang* energy *boosting* effect only. The
outcome is always powered by your partner's own deep tension
reacting with itself. If a partner has achieved deep relaxation (i.e.
is a Taiji master) none of your energy issuance will have any effect,
because in that case s/he's relaxed and there's nothing to trigger.
By the way, we can see from this whole discussion that there's a
systematic ambiguity in the use of the term *yang* energy, not only in
my presentation but overall in the Taiji world. The term '*yang* energy'
is sometimes used to refer to plain old overt physical strength, and
at other times it refers to the active aspect (as opposed to the yin
aspect) of internal, non-physical power. Hopefully in this book the
context has made the intended usage clear.

With modality (c) as your Stage 2 follow-on, you merely continue
the application of the *yin* energy beam or stream that initiated
the trigger effect in Stage 1. This achieves a kind of union of
your partner's SHELL and your own. I will cover this effect more
thoroughly in the next section.

If you apply only the Stage 2 physical NUDGE, without having
set the stage properly with the initial yinjection, then you aren't
doing Taiji unbalancing. That can be considered a good sporting
practice, maybe some kind of sumo hybrid thing. But it isn't Taiji,
so let's not have confusion of names. That ordinary physical push
may work sometimes, may fail other times, depending on you and
your partner's relative size and weight, experience at the game,
knowledge of techniques, sneakiness and speed, determination
and ruthlessness, etc. No matter. Succeed or fail, I don't care to
hear the result, because it has absolutely nothing to do with Taiji.

Keep in mind, all these teaching directives are targeted to *'you'*. Don't use this idea to bash your partner - scolding that what they're doing isn't real Taiji because you don't think they're following this process in their pushes. Nobody likes a nag (ha! This whole book is one big nag. But you know what I mean.) Beyond suggesting they buy this book, keep these ideas to yourself as you practice. This teaching is for 'you' not 'him' or 'her'.

Cherish your partner's natural creative push style. Let your partner do whatever s/he wishes – as long as nobody pulls a gun you're good. S/he may use strength, may be physical, may push you hard, or resist your pushes with tricks, force, and speed. No matter - no lecturing on the spot. That will mess up your energy. Keep quiet about that kind of stuff while you're in the game, unless s/he asks outright for instruction. (There's always the internet for griping after the fact.) This is something you work on privately and quietly in the session. It's your secret practice in plain sight. If somebody else is using ordinary physical force - perhaps even with great skill - that's fine. That's just another opportunity to try to stick to the real art under challenging conditions.

Let's summarize Micro *fajing* again, in a nutshell:

Stage 1: YINJECTION

Stage 2: NUDGE, or *yang* boost, or *yin* continuation

This idea *'yin* leads' idea shouldn't freak you out as something exotic, wild, dangerous or radical. If you're practicing push-hands at all, you're doing this anyway. You are always issuing *yin* internal energy (that everyone has in them) along with your physical push. It's just not yet real Taiji, because with the huge amount of physical tension and roughness most people employ, the *yin* energy is swamped, ruined, and contaminated beyond repair every time. The push itself may succeed or not, but it isn't Taiji. Actually, even in daily life, whenever we shake hands or hug or clap one another on the back in congratulations, we have a similar experience of issuing and receiving energy. It's merely three things that differ: the accompanying physical gesture; the explicitly controlled separation (or integration) of stages; and the quality and quantity of the resulting energy. So this *yin-leads-yang-follows* thing is pretty natural. It's basically just an energy application of the old idea of a pointed drill bit. Be a wedge, not a wall. And always remember:

> If the camel first gets his nose in the tent, his body will soon follow.

MACRO-FAJING: YINFUSION

Let's begin with some definitions so you can see where this term *yinfusion* came from:

infuse: v. to introduce, as if by pouring; cause to penetrate;
perfuse: v. to suffuse or permeate (a liquid, color, etc.) through or over (something);

Got the idea? This mode is the ultimate deployment of Taiji skill. In the Micro *fajing* of yinjection, your *yin* energy trigger and the subsequent unbalancing action (NUDGE or *yang* SURGE) are both directed along a particular vector. They are local actions. With yinfusion, you take over the steering wheel completely, by 'thickening' your SHELL to the point that it includes your partner. With that, s/he is within your SHELL entirely and is effectively energy-neutralized. This is when your partner will feel as though s/he has no strength to resist or escape. At that point, your partner's body is merely an unpowered rag doll, and you can do whatever you want with it – for the moment or so that the effect lasts.

It's done by your mind, as ever. It's an action of your *yin* power, with no physical accompaniment at all. And just as with yinjection, there's no royal road to this one either. You have to keep working on it til you get it. And even after you get it, it may not work with full effectiveness every time on every partner – same as a physical technique in that respect. But this is Taiji. This is the kind of thing we work on if we consider ourselves serious Taiji players.

The yinfusion effect is just a continuation of the application of *yin* energy in the trigger Stage 1 as described above. You use your mind to continue to pour in the *yin* and thicken it around your partner until your SHELL's are temporarily fused. Actually for a brief moment there's only one SHELL – your own – within which you can lightly and easily control your partner. A single yinfusion impulse yields a few seconds of SHELL inclusion, permeation, and consequent physical neutralization of your partner. Within this brief time window, any technique or gesture you may care to try will work. You don't need to add much hot sauce at that point.

The NUDGE concept already introduced for yinjection is fine, or you can use a locking and immobilizing technique, as in jiu-jitsu. In the case of yinfusion, once you've learned how the process works and how it feels, the *yin* energy can even come directly from the intake NEXUS Point into your partner's SHELL via any area or degree of physical contact, no matter how light or incidental.

Figure 12 Yinfusion is the complete subsumption of your partner within your SHELL, done by expanding your SHELL circumference. Eventually this can be accomplished with **yin** energy channeled from the NEXUS Point as shown in the illustration.

You can get a little feel for how this effect feels from the dojo visit report of Kiyokazu Maebayashi, a professional martial arts instructor who visited the Daitou-Ryuu style class of internal martial arts grandmaster Sagawa Yukiyoshi in Tokyo (also see Appendix C).

> *When I am on the receiving end of one of Sagawa Sensei's techniques, I don't feel any power from the point at which we are connected, but I feel an energy which penetrates my whole body to affect my center and break my balance. ... This is how I lose my power and am thrown easily by Sensei.*

- Aikido Journal, September 10, 2011

That's the absolute peak of yinfusion skill. This mode of work is called application of the 'aiki' power (合気力 *aikiryoku*) in their style. For our purposes, the term yinfusion is the best "translation" of *aiki*. Just as in Taiji, Sagawa sensei absolutely ruled out the use of any physical force whatsoever in the practice of his art. A similar experience of yinfusion or aiki is reported by Li Yaxuan, describing the push hands experience with his teacher Yang Chengfu:

> *Whenever I practiced push hands with grandmaster Yang Chengfu, I had a most peculiar feeling, which I've always remembered. Every time when I began by merely touching his hand, I felt drained of all resistance, every part of my body became utterly weak. When grandmaster Yang simply touched my arm, I can't explain it but I felt that every part got absorbed into him somehow. It was as though somebody had thrown a giant net over me. No matter how I moved I couldn't get away and my every movement just put me at a further disadvantage. Even though I knew grandmaster Yang's hand was just placed on me lightly, still it felt incredibly heavy. I couldn't really move, but I couldn't not move either. Trying to power my way*

out of it was hopeless, but trying to get out gently didn't work either. Whether I tried to move quickly or slowly it was all equally useless.

Remember, your SHELL in yinfusion is like a bell-jar (SHELL-jar?), except it is *full* all the way through. Your partner is trapped in your thickened shell like a prehistoric bug in amber. It's an expansion of the thickness of the SHELL, and not merely throwing it over to cover like a net or bag. It's this thickening or inclusion effect that creates the momentary total helplessness by permeating and suppressing your partner's SHELL absolutely.

Always remember that the yinjection or yinfusion actions have no visible or physically perceptible effect on your partner whatsoever. To put it most strongly: if an action has a visible or perceptible effect, it wasn't yinjection or yinfusion. The visible result is always the effect of the follow-up energy, whether used for control or boosting. You can now understand that these basic SHELL interactions are not exactly discrete internal 'techniques' in and of themselves. They're building blocks that can be combined in many ways, sometimes resulting in dramatically divergent final physical results. In the next section, I'll list a few of the most basic and typical usage effects of combined SHELL interaction application. Listing out the full internal 'recipe' for every type of effect is beyond the scope of this book, but in this next section I'll indicate what kind of NUDGE underlies the characteristic final effect.

ELEMENTAL MODES OF ENERGY APPLICATION

How shall I elude on foot one who chases me on wings?

- Archias

You need to have mastered all the Taiji energy elements discussed earlier in this chapter and this book before you can hope to get anywhere with the distinct modes of push hands energy application. To get anything beyond a bit of physical experience that allows you to fake out beginners with mechanics, technique, and clever use of ordinary strength you must have thoroughly understood all the points on energy training discussed previously.

Once you have that going, you'll begin to discover the basic energies or modes of push hands energy application. Traditionally, there is a large inventory of interactive energy types in Taiji. And there are much higher energies of interaction than those discussed in this chapter. Those are beyond the scope of this book. Though the basic modes presented below can be tagged with fancy ancient Chinese words, I'm not going to do that. I'm not here to play word games. When it comes to Taiji, words just aren't the thing. So I will simply identify them by the classical elements whose deepest quality they seem to embody – *fire*, *water*, *earth*, *air*, and *metal*.

Although this association with the classical elements overlaps a bit with the Five Elements (五行 *wuxing*) of traditional Chinese philosophy, it isn't a perfect matchup, because it was never meant to be. I don't use these elemental terms to force-fit any given abstract system. And I admit that cataloging them this way is kind of Ninja-cheesy. What can I say? I have a streak of inner cheese a mile wide. Ever since Musashi picked up this Elements riff for his

214

classic Five Rings book, it seems everybody has dog-piled on, and I'm no exception. I find that the element names express my gut feeling as I deploy the various modes. But I could as easily have tagged them A, B, C, D, and E. Words are just fingers at the moon, look for the *feeling*. In the documentary film *This Is It,* at one point the stage director challenges Michael Jackson:

> Director: *"Michael, if you insist on having the cue come from the rear-side stage where you can't see it, how are you going to know when to move?"*
> Jackson: *"I'll feel it."*

That's the attitude you want. The most important thing is to understand that these are emphatically not five techniques or five families of movement, or anything like that. Seen from the outside, any of them could resemble any other. In fact, all five can be deployed through *any* physical motion, or through practically *no* physical motion at all - just a single simple touch of the hand. *They are not techniques or patterns of movement or styles of physical motion.* That would be meaningless to me, as I'm all and only about energy. These are just different expressions of energy. They are recipes of multiple compounded SHELL interactions.

I realize that the relation of these pushing Element 'modes' to the fundamentals of SHELL interaction presented earlier may be unclear. I agree it's confusing and hard to explain. For now, think of the SHELL dynamics presented above as a discussion of automobile fuel injection, internal combustion, transmission, drive train, and so on. Real bare metal fundamentals. These five Element modes, on the other hand, are more analogous to styles of driving: highway; residential neighborhood; professional closed course and racing; city rush hour; executive protection and motorcade; and so on. But the SHELL dynamics are always operating, under the hood.

Or for a less macho example, it's like the difference between a presentation of how to operate basic cooking equipment (oven, stovetop, pots, pans, knives, etc.) vs. actual recipes that produce a final customer-facing result, a dish somebody eats. Another comparison would be to that beast of a software app, Photoshop. Taiji's SHELL interactions are like the essential components of Photoshop operation, what you must know to accomplish anything, like 'layers, 'alpha channels', 'blending modes' and the 'clone stamp tool', etc. You'd need to know what these are and some of their basic functioning to do anything. The Element modes of pushing, on the other hand, are more like the final graphics you create. You use all that operational stuff in sometimes complex and subtle combinations to produce highly articulated graphic results. These analogies are inexact but I hope they convey the basic idea. Keep in mind that there's not always a one-to-one mapping between a single type of SHELL dynamic and one of the final push results (the Five Elements). Some of these Five Elements are produced with combined and multi-layered use of SHELL dynamics.

To map out the exact multi-step SHELL interaction recipe for each one of these Element push types is beyond the scope of this book. (Watch for 'JUICE 2: THE SEQUEL', due in 2013). You need to find your own personal style of using these energies anyway. What I can do is provide an overview of the 'look and feel' of each push Element. With that in hand, and a good understanding of the basic SHELL interactions, you can probably work out these recipes or something else even better, on your own. That said, below I mention rudimentary considerations for creating some of these Element effects from the basic SHELL work.

FIRE - REBOUNDING

The Fire mode is instantaneous rebound at the very first micro-second of contact. You SPIKE the partner's energy/tension and ricochet it instantaneously right back at him/her. This has the effect that his/her entire body will be jolted back - but crucially you are only blasting him/her with his/her own energy. S/he's blasting him/herself. That's really important. The Fire effect can be dramatic, but if you try this as a strength move, or as some kind of macho combat thing, it won't work. You may move him/her - more or less - but it won't be the real thing, it feels totally different. The Fire mode is also the basis of *tifang* - complete physical uprooting of your partner's body. Generally, Fire mode works best if your partner's incoming touch force is more than four ounces, because you can throw that back too.

Almost every single person you ever practice with, no matter what their training background, will always be touching you with more than four ounces. That's one expression of their deep unconscious tension mentioned earlier. On your side though, the Taiji classic writings teach us that *not even a fly can alight (without setting it into motion)*. The Fire mode is where that lofty idea hits the pavement. All you need to feel is a fly's weight impacting you, anything weighing more than 4 ounces and - *blammo* - you sling it right back. Just a touch on your part is all it takes, but the effect is dramatic. However, you must be careful not to overdo this.

When I practice with pretty much anybody, I only sling 5% of his/her own power back at him/him (or I could also say, I apply only a very small fraction of my triggering energy to his/her tension). Any more than that could be dangerous. Not because of some death touch *dim-mak* organ explosion thing, but because as his/her body hurtles back, up, or down, s/he might slip or fall, and hit the wall, floor, or a glass door too hard and cut or split his/her head open. That's when blood goes everywhere, 911 must be called … it's all bad. I've done this kind of thing to aggressive push partners in the past, but now I never sling more than 5% of their own power back at them in Fire mode and I mean *never*.

But even if you keep it this way, using under 5% power for blowback, don't do Fire mode very often. Or frankly don't really do it at all -

unless you're an 80-year Chinese man with a long white beard and big sleeves and stuff, or you're built like a sumo wrestler. Those surface attributes help people accept the Fire mode experience better. Otherwise, people don't really like to feel this mode from somebody who pretty much, on the surface, seems just like them. It jars their pre-conceptions. I do however sometimes demonstrate a mild form of this privately for my students.

In terms of SHELL interactions, the Fire mode is accomplished in any of several ways. One is the simple SPIKE described in the previous section. Fire mode is essentially the visible outcome of a SPIKE. Fire mode can also be more deliberately applied, as Micro *fajing*. In that case, the NUDGE of the micro *fajing* action can be either a plain mild physical shove, in which case your partner's own degree of tension will solely determine how far s/he's thrown. Or, if the NUDGE is applied as a *yang* energy impulse, the power of his/her tension will be modulated by you (so you need to very careful doing that. Basically, don't do that.) Doing the NUDGE with *yang* energy impulse (the SURGE-1 under conscious control, see Chapter 3) is usually what accomplishes *tifang* (total body uprooting). In any case, the quintessential quality of Fire mode is instantaneous reaction. So when the micro *fajing* approach is used, you need to have refined it to the point that the two separate components of micro *fajing* (yinjection and NUDGE) are practically simultaneous. Finally, the *yin* energy version of the NUDGE has no real application to Fire mode work.

Fire mode can also serve as a diagnostic tool for level in an initial push hands session with a new person. If when you first touch any part of his/her body you can instantly rebound him/her back a step with a single Fire mode touch, your level is superior to his/hers. If s/he either yields or roots you, or if s/he bounces you back from your light Fire mode touch, his/her level is superior to yours. If you have any doubts about the outcome of the Fire mode test, then your level is equal or inferior to his/hers. If you feel you need to repeat the test to be really sure what happened, again your level is equal or inferior to his/hers.

WATER - YIELDING

Water mode is just the classic Taiji yielding, which can be perfected in absolute fun and safety in ordinary fixed step push hands work. But here's where it's most important that you understand the crucial fixed-step restriction. Because if you get out of incoming pressure by moving your feet, your body will never develop the Water mode yield reaction. But if you can keep the stationary foot discipline your Water mode skill will emerge naturally. This is the safest mode for both you and your partner, and in a way the most fun. It feels the most Taiji-ish of the basic modes discussed here. Once you've yielded him/her, you can do whatever you want with his/her body, just don't *over* do it. Unlike the Fire mode with its instantaneous, invisible speed, water mode can be slow and soft. It strictly tracks to the exact speed of his/her motion.

The are two sub-types of yielding in Water mode, macro and micro. In macro yielding, your partner's entire body is affected. S/he will go sailing past you as s/he grasps at shadows and struggles with smoke. The macro yield response directly achieves the stated objective of (this type of) fixed step push hands – his/her entire body is moved off balance, obviously requiring major foot movement to recover – if s/he's able to recover at all.

Micro yielding is different in that you do not substantially affect his/her balance, nor do you force him/her to move his/her foot. In micro yielding, you merely give way at the small local area s/he's pressuring, for example, your hand or arm (though it could be any legal target area). This is a very educational way to work in that you can get your partner to feel the effect of his/her own strength without the shocking full body dynamic that sometime overwhelms the teaching. The micro yield is almost invisible to onlookers and may be a bit perplexing to your partner at first also, as s/he can't quite figure out why s/he isn't able to get a purchase on you. With this mode you can work toward the famous objective of preventing a bird from flying off your palm as the elder Yang family masters were able to do.

In terms of the SHELL interactions, Water mode is basically *fajing* without the *fa* (issuing). That is, you link energy via yinjection or yinfusion, but then you follow up with merely a gentle physical pull rather than any form of the NUDGE.

EARTH - IMMOVABILITY

This is the famous Taiji "rooting" thing. Rooting means simply letting his power pass directly through your body and through your feet, right into the ground. It's the most basic and least fun of the four modes, but of course a must-have checklist item. You might think this Earth Mode rooting is the entire point of fixed-step push hands, but that's not true at all. Read above on Water mode again - *yielding* is really the entire point of fixed step push hands.

Many people mistakenly believe that working in fixed step mode directly entails rooting as the primary response. That's mistaken. The ideas of 'fixed step push hands' and 'rooting' should be separated in your mind. You can practice a lifetime of fixed step push hands without ever rooting. In fact, rooting is the closest response to plain old physicality – like an NFL linebacker. Rooting is a quasi-physical skill, almost mechanical. So, although you must understand it and be able to perform it, don't take any special pride in it. Rooting is just a skill you need as part of your foundation package, not that big a deal. It is however probably the first of the four modes discussed here that will begin to naturally emerge for you with correct and diligent practice of the ZMQ 37 method.

In terms of SHELL interactions, you don't need to do anything for this one. As long as your overall energy level is stronger than your partner's, his/her energy will always be magnetized to the floor through you, and any power he may have will be lost like a candle in the sun. And of course there is no NUDGE action required, as you just stand there.

AIR - IMPALPABILITY

Air mode is in some ways the strangest of all five basic modes. This is an 'offensive' move, meaning you are initiating the action. It's essentially a very slow-motion version of the Fire mode. But it feels so different in practice that it deserves its own category. It can only be performed once you reach a fairly high plateau of Taiji skill. In this mode, your physical pushing action, the NUDGE, is extremely slow, giving him/her all the time in the world to neutralize your push. Unlike Water mode, where you match your partner's speed of action, in Air mode you always move slowly regardless of how slow or quickly s/he responds.

Tell him/her to take his/her time, encourage him/her to do anything (within the push hands context, no switchblades please) to free him/herself from your pressure. Just tell him/her: "Don't move your feet." On your side, simply place your hands anywhere on his/her legal target zone and move into him/her slowly - very slowly. Give him/her all the time in the world or it isn't real Air mode. Even offer him/her five dollars if s/he can keep his/her feet in place if that's what it takes to motivate.

But you go slowly – without changing the placement of your hands, you track his/her internal tension. You follow whatever s/he does, however s/he wriggles or struggles, until his/her own tension takes him/her off balance. This may be compared to the boa constrictor - which are said never to struggle nor hurry to choke out the missionary in their coils. Instead they relax into him/her just a notch tighter every time s/he exhales, until it's all over (Air mode does not explicitly follow the partner's actual breath, it merely has a boa kind of *feel* to it). Though s/he feels no more explicit pressure than just the air around, s/he can't stay on his/her feet.

As far as the SHELL interaction aspect of this, it requires a high level of yinfusion skill. Normally in macro fajing, you'd thicken your SHELL to include your partner, as a kind of setup, then move on from the yinfusion action to the NUDGE (various ways to follow up with an unbalancing, locking, or even striking action). But in the case of Air mode, you have to consciously maintain the yinfusion condition for the duration of the final unbalancing stage, no matter how long that may take. Air mode is an advanced skill.

METAL - MELDING

In this mode, you meld together your energy and your partner's so there's no distinction between the two energies at all, they are seamlessly welded. This differs from Fire mode because you don't bounce him/her away; it differs from Water mode because you don't yield to him/her; it differs from Earth mode because you don't root against his/her energy, in fact there is no distinction between your energy and his/hers. Finally, it differs from Air mode because instead of feeling nothingness, emptiness, s/he feels s/he's been incorporated into a larger feeling of substance that includes both you and him/her.

You and s/he are like two figures joined only at the point of touch, but cast as a single piece of bronze. This is the mode in which you can "walk" your partner around the room with your hands continuously on him/her, against which s/he's powerless – even though you are merely touching, not gripping. S/he must stumble around with you as though you two are one slab of metal.

The SHELL interactions involved in Metal mode are beyond the scope of this book. If you can do everything else I've talked about, you can work that out for yourself. If not, get cracking.

Those are the five basic modes of push hands energy work. There are many other kinds of interactive energy you can learn, but they're beyond the scope of this book. Anyway, if you haven't mastered these modes you aren't ready for the others. And these are all you need to have a lot of fun with Taiji partner play.

The five Element modes are all initiated by 'you'. That is, you can decide what you want to achieve, how you want to react, which of the five Element modes you want your partner to experience. I sometimes rotate through all these in (semi-private) demonstrations. But I should say a word about a different kind of configuration: what your partner will experience when you are completely passive and haven't mentally chosen to do anything. This could be a surprise 'attack' (not really, remember it's just push hands, but you know what I mean: a very sudden unexpected aggressive action by your partner), or just a moment of daydreaming or inattention on your part.

One possible result is – s/he may get you out! Yes, even after you've achieved a high energy level, if your attention wanders and your inherent energy level isn't quite *there* that day, and you have a bit of internal tension for whatever reason, than a very strong, very sudden, fiercely committed attack may cause you to step out. That's fine it's all part of the game. But more likely, if you have a high level and are reasonably attentive, another metaphor will apply, just plain *water*. Water has three phases – ice, liquid, and vapor. If your level is high enough, what your partner will experience when you're passive will depend entirely on his/her actions. A very strong attack will be rebound as though hitting a solid wall of ice – or like the hard impact on water when hit from a height or with great force. A softer smoother attack will be accepted and redirected as though by a mass or current of water. A tricky attack like an attempted lock or grab should seem, to your attacker, to land on nothing – vapor.

THE SHELL REVISITED

As with everything in this book, the SHELL discussion is nothing original. The idea of a close energy double of the physical body has been common in esoteric circles and mystery schools for thousands of years, and of course is now a New Age staple. It's also well-known to some martial artists. For example, in his book *Discovering Aiki: My 20 Years with Yukiyoshi Sagawa* (*Aiki Shutoku-e no Michi*), Professor Tatsuo Kimura talks about grueling, repetitive Aiki Jiu-Jitsu exercises he learned from his famous teacher, grandmaster Yukiyoshi Sagawa:

> *I wondered what it was I was training. Then, suddenly, I realized that I wasn't training my muscles, but rather something inside my body. I gradually understood that **something very near the core of the physical body that is not the body was strengthened***

(my emphasis; for more on affinities between Taiji and Aiki Jiu-Jitsu , see Appendix C) So there's nothing surprising in the concept. We just need to keep finding better and better ways of training and talking about it in a martial arts context. In view of all the above discussion, we can finally understand why the founder of modern Taiji, grandmaster Yang Luchan, was reported to say:

太极拳惟有铁石人不击，凡是血肉之躯，无不可当

> *The only man that Taiji cannot defeat is one made of iron or stone. Against any creature of flesh and blood, Taiji will always prevail.*

Most people take his meaning superficially – just another way of boasting that he could beat anybody on earth in a fight. But in fact it's a much deeper and more trenchant comment. When seen in the light of *yin-leads-yang-follows*, grandmaster Yang's statement is illuminated as his coded way of saying that due to the purely energetic (non-physical) nature of true Taiji, *it only works against living things*. That's because only living things have the refined energy structure (the right kind of SHELL), which produces the desired energetic chain reaction. Taiji gives primacy to mind. But it isn't exactly mind over matter. Taiji is mind over meat. This is the crucial difference between a truly internal art, such as Taiji, compared to an external art like Karate, where the punches work with equal destructive effect on both living opponents as well as on bricks, ice blocks, and boards. Yang Luchan's art, by his own admission, worked only against living things. But it's worth noting that he was also famous for never injuring or killing anybody he faced.

TROUBLESHOOTING

勝可知而不可為 *(One may know how to conquer yet be unable to do it)*

- Sunzi, *The Art of War*

After all this, I can hear you still wondering: *But… how do I actually do this stuff?* I don't know how better to say it than to simply repeat: *visualize and imagine*. It all starts in the mind. The most important thing is simply to know what can be done. Then with some personal experimentation you'll find your own way to it. Did you learn to ride a bike from verbal instruction? Certainly not, but you needed to know that such a thing was possible. These Taiji special effects are the same – *the what is the how*. You have to trust just a little, believe in the possibility enough to get started with it. Then tune your mind according to the results: Hotter results? Do more of that. Colder results? Do less. It's not really much different than Olympic high-jumpers and pole-vaulters clearing the bar in their mind's eye. You just use your mind to channel and manipulate the energy in the ways described. The only real impediment to at least getting started is your own doubt. Maybe you tried some of this stuff a few times and it went nowhere, convincing you this is BS and can't possibly work.

Time out for a sports quiz. Floyd Mayweather is, by the stats alone, possibly the greatest boxer of all time. In his 2009 win over lightweight world champion Juan Manuel Márquez, he landed a career high of 59% of his punches thrown (more than double or triple the average of many successful professional fighters), while 41% of his punches in that fight missed. Some of the missed punches were left hooks.

Pop Quiz:

If we see a video clip of Floyd Mayweather missing an attempted left hook at some point in the 2009 Márquez fight, we can logically conclude that:

  a. *The left hook is not an effective boxing technique*
  b. *Mayweather is not a competent boxer*
  c. *Márquez in that fight was awesomely far beyond Mayweather's league*
  d. *Mayweather should have pulled a .45 and shot Márquez instead*
  e. *None of the above makes any sense*

The correct answer is *e*. And so it is with yinjection and yinfusion and all the other methods described here. Sometimes they aren't going to work for you. It was said in ancient times: *the fortunes of war are various.* All kinds of factors affect any attempt to do anything. If it doesn't work *this* time, you should just keep trying to improve it for *next* time.

But for some reason, when it comes to this Taiji internal stuff, when somebody hears it, tries it, and fails at it – once – their immediate reaction tends to be: *Oh that stuff's totally fake.* But in fact it's no more fake than a missed left hook. This kind of energy dynamics, not physical pushing, *is* the method of real Taiji, just as the left hook *is* one of the true fighting methods of boxing. You don't give up and walk away because it doesn't work the first time, or every time, or on every opponent.

226

In fact, the micro and macro *fajing* the others probably won't work for you on the first try, and probably not on the hundredth either. And maybe not the thousandth. Nonetheless, *this is Taiji*. This is what it is. Even when you think you've really got it under your belt, a surprise new partner who can deal with you handily could pop up at any time. No matter. This is Taiji, and these things are what we have to work on, no matter how difficult. Professor Zheng famously said: *Invest in loss*. Don't blame the method. Keep working on it and you'll improve.

Of course, if it seems *never* to work for you, you're going to get suspicious. So let's look into possible impediments more closely. When your partner is able to either yield or turn out of your attempted push, or else able to simply root it into the ground, the trouble is likely one of the following:

- *Running on Empty*

  If you haven't developed your internal energy via the basic standing and moving practices described in Chapter 2 on cultivation of power, you won't have enough gas in the tank to use for push hands.

- *Unnecessary Roughness*

  Even if you have a good internal energy level, if you apply too much physical force in your NUDGE, or if you forgo the yinjection (or yinfusion) step and just go for a direct physical push, you'll jam yourself and fail against a stronger or more experienced partner.

- *Bad Tactics: Position*

  Especially when beginning to work with this two-stage method, you still need to calmly wait for the right time, when your partner's motion brings him/her into an optimal position. Your hands will know if you don't over-rule them.

- *Bad Tactics: Timing*

  Again, as with Position above, in the beginning don't force the push, let your hands feel the moment when it comes around.

DEFENSIVE SHELL - THE SLIDE

The SHELL interactions and the five elements presented so far probably all strike you as oriented more to offense than defense. Even the Water mode, which emphasizes yielding, ends up with you throwing the guy around, in one direction or another. The other modes all seem to emphasize unbalancing your partner, rather than preventing your own unbalancing. It's often said that a strong offense is the best defense. And we could just leave it at that.

All the interactions and modes presented so far don't really allow for a defensive need to develop. You've either SPIKE'd your partner, or yinjected or yinfused him/her, in various ways and combinations and the result has ended up looking like one of the five Element outcomes. Once you have successfully yinjected or yinfused your partner, s/he is temporarily drained of power. His/her 'attack' potential has been totally jammed, and you can do whatever you want to him/her at that point. So there's not much need to train for anything that really looks and feels defensive. However, in the spirit of dialing down the practice to meet on a level playing field when working with any partner at any level (such as the games in the list of ways to upskill your partner) I will mention a few defensive ideas. Working these has more to do with learning about your SHELL's inherent properties than it does any functional need for these kinds of defensive tools.

The main property or technique you want to pick up is the *SHELL Lubricated Internal Defensive Energy* (SLIDE) technique. To get this going, you need to begin thinking of your SHELL as a membrane, more than as a force field. It's a slightly different mindset than what's called for in using the SHELL for yinjection and yinfusion. In the SLIDE mindset, we conceive of the SHELL as a thin membrane around our skin. We imagine this membrane as coated with ice, oil, or water – anything extremely slippery.

This works particularly well when you are in a 'hands-on-hands' situation. That means a partner who mostly focuses on controlling your hands alone by placing his hands over yours at all times, as taught in other Chinese martial arts. Normally, that kind of push situation turns into a simple twitch-fest. Both sides keep tension in their hands, and each tries to use superior reflexes to lull or fake the other for just the fraction of a second it takes to whip their own hands out from under the partner's control and whack him or her. Kind of a video-game mode. It's fine if your partner does that. But you as a student of Taiji, are committed never to wallow in that kind of physicalized mud. Right?

So you don't get into the twitch-game at all. Let your partner cover or 'control' (from his or her point of view) your hands. You don't need to think about techniques or counters at all. But, no matter what your partner does, you have the idea of maintaining the membrane, a thin but absolute barrier of extreme slipperiness between your skin and your partner's. It's like a sheen of wet ice between you guys, at the contact point(s).

With that in mind, your partner will be absolutely unable to get enough purchase or friction on you to launch anything substantial. Everything will seem to slide right off you, even when you make essentially no anticipatory or countering response at all. This is similar to the 'micro yielding' mentioned in the Water section of the five Elements. It only differs in that 'micro yielding' still requires a bit of (local) physical movement to achieve the unbalancing goal. Whereas in SLIDE work on the SHELL, you just let him slide off your SHELL membrane. When the climber slips and tumbles down the alpine slope or glacier, the mountain has done nothing. Another way to think of the SLIDE is as a FLASHOUT or STREAMOUT of the STEEL energy from the NEXUS Point to your entire SHELL, as an undifferentiated whole.

DEFENSIVE SHELL – THE SLURP

The SLIDE works best as a kind of preventive defense. When it's done right your partner will never get any purchase on you to launch a push. At times however, you'll find yourself stuck in an Earth mode type of standoff. Let's say you have a strong root, and s/he's pushing right into it and you aren't moving. But s/he isn't giving up. How to resolve this? Best way is just to push him/her off you. But to set up for that, you need what is essentially a defensive maneuver that I call the *SHELL Leaching Uptake from Retractive Pull* or SLURP for short. This move is absorptive. Instead of yinjecting your partner, or SLIDE'ing him or her off you, you SLURP up the outer edge of his shell, which disrupts his or her energy framework enough to give you an opening to work in.

In practice it really feels as though you are just using your hands to take a lick, slurp, or taste of the outer edge of his/her SHELL energy. You don't need any accompanying physical gesture, or at most you'd use the very slightest back-away of your hands but without losing contact. Keep your Tailor's Touch. Just create a mental feeling of swiping your hands very light and briefly over the surface of his SHELL, right in place as your hands are situated, without actually moving them. This will momentarily clear the 'hard' outer edge of his or her SHELL, and you can then counter-push with a NUDGE as already discussed. Again I can't give you a rigorous formula or exact recipe for this, but you don't need that. You just need to know that this is a possibility, and then you can easily work it out in practice for yourself. Try it a few times with a few different people and you'll start to get the hang of it.

Imagine that somebody overfilled your drink cup at lunch. As the root beer runs down the side, you give it a quick lick to clear it off the edge of the cup. That lick is both a *yang* action in the sense of your tongue going forward into the dribble of liquid. Yet it's also *yin* in that it's retracting, taking something away rather than adding anything. Anyway that action clears the edge of the cup. That's the feeling of the SLURP. Only difference is that in push hands, you're doing it with your hands *in situ* coupled with your energy, not with your tongue. Although… now you mention it … you *could* do it with your tongue I guess (I'd better not restrict the body part or I'll get pinned with my own *Structural Fallacy*).

CHAPTER 5:
SWORD

BASIC PROJECTION

Taiji has inherited a bunch of weapons stuff from its ancestor arts. You'll see Taiji versions of at least the following: straight sword, saber, short staff, long staff, halberd, and others. That's all well and good for show, but I've emphasized throughout this book that theatrical focus is a lethal, show-stopping error. And although these weapons forms are for the most part physically very vigorous, I've also cast doubt on the idea of Taiji as an optimal route to ordinary physical fitness. So why bother mentioning weapons at all?

Before I answer that, let's stand down the armory a little – we need a reduction in force. That list of traditional weapons above is both too *short* and too *long*. It's too short in that once you know what you're doing, anything can serve as a weapon. One of the oldest martial arts clichés out there is: *any weapon is just an extension of the hand and body.* Medieval samurai Miyamoto Musashi (宮本武蔵1584 – 1645) famously used a handy boat oar to bash down a skilled opponent (Musashi wasn't packing that day). So there's not much percentage in obsessing over the particular set of traditional hardware listed above. A Russian folding infantry shovel could do all the same practical work in the right hands. The list is also too long in that it really only takes working with one weapon to get the point (so to speak) of the work. And that one weapon is the Chinese traditional straight sword. Of course, it isn't strictly necessary to do any weapons training at all, sword or anything else, to reach your full energetic potential in Taiji. But it makes such a huge difference in practice that it may as well be called mandatory.

We could get into all kinds of Chinese sword arcana: different styles of blade and hardware, all kinds of cutting techniques and angles, offense and defense, and all that. But as you should know by now, I don't care about such things in the least. All that matters to me is the energy, the power. That's the focus of this book and this

235

chapter is no exception. So forget all that medieval minutiae for now. Professor Zheng practiced with the straight sword incessantly, for one reason as far as I can tell: *sword practice, if done right, can hyper-accelerate your realization of one true purpose of Taiji training - mind/body unification through energy*. For that, once again just as with your primary Taiji training, any basic Taiji sword form that adheres to the overall guidelines of Taiji will suffice.

Hold your palms facing each other, but about one inch gap apart, not touching. That's the typical relationship of *mind* to *body* of an average person. Now touch your palms flatly together. That's that result of intensive Taiji training over a fairly long period. Most people think that's all there is. But now, now press your palms together and completely *interlace* your fingers. Now you're getting closer to symbolizing the ultimate Taiji integrated state. You may think your mind is already permeating your body, just because you can wiggle your fingers on command and you can feel a breeze (or a brick) contacting your toes. But not so, there's a whole different level of integration out there, which brings its own special power and pleasure. I've covered a lot of that already. The sword work isn't introducing any new form of energy or state, it turbo-charging what's already been introduced.

Achieving that unified state is the purpose of sword work, not looking slick or mastering esoteric gymnastics or arbitrary movement patterns or trying to role-play ancient Chinese soldiers. For energy integration, straight sword practice is *almost* a required course of study. It's like travel - theoretically you *can* take a boat from New York to Auckland, but in practice for most people an airplane is the only reasonable way to get there. The Taiji sword is your jetliner.

But still - what is the real point of it? Having read this book to here, you *know* it's worthless to mindlessly learn sword as a mere physical movement drill, right? But there's a very important Taiji technical point that sword helps you 'get'. In Taiji, all physical movement is powered by the waist. That's what allows you to keep your arms relaxed, because the waist power does the main physical work. But you need to keep your *mind* extended and projected through your *hands* while you refrain from applying any physical power through them. That's the hard part, and the basis of the ARC training process.

I quoted a core teaching from the Taiji classic writings earlier: the waist leads. Something about sword practice helps you understand that much faster and more fully than the empty hand form, though it applies equally to both. If you've ever chopped wood logs or cut down trees with an ax, you probably remember the first time you tried it, somebody must have come up to you and said something like: No, you're doing it all wrong. Don't use your arms and shoulders, use your hips (or waist or trunk, etc.) They showed you and you tried it and found the real difference it makes. But if you hadn't been working with that tool, the ax, to try it out with, do you think you really could have understood the point?

Taiji is non-physical but in the very beginning we do need to get the right feeling from the physical as a foundation for relaxation and energy projection. Working with the sword is the super-highway to getting the point that the waist leads. In the beginning, when you're still working with the physical aspect of the form, try to really feel that your waist is powering the cuts. Remember that feeling clearly, and next time you do your empty-hand form, re-create exactly that feeling without the sword. This greatly accelerates your grasping the principle of the waist leading.

Most students fail to one side or the other. They either put too much physical power into their hands and arms, thus not allowing the waist to do the power generation, or else they totally give up their hands and arms, not only eliminating all physical tension (which is necessary) but going too far and shutting down *mentally* as well (which nullifies the entire point of Taiji practice). In the latter condition, when the mind is not engaged and projected, the hands get floppy and you think you're doing Taiji but you aren't. You've mentally collapsed, and you aren't projecting anything. Being mentally weak or unengaged is as unproductive a path as being physically tense. I don't mean to sneer - it can be tough to get that perfect 'zone' - removal of all physical power while retaining mental extension and activation. It's a really tough state to achieve but that's the job of Taiji practice. Richie Havens had a good lyric: *I'm up on a tight wire, one side's ice and the other's fire.* That about says it, the razor's edge between tensed and collapsed.

So how does all this relate to sword? Sword work helps you understand and develop this delicately balanced state. You need to power the sword through your waist - just as in the empty hand form - but in sword form, you are less likely to commit the error of *floppification* - letting your mind go out of your hands/arms because you imagine you're super cosmically relaxed. Practicing the sword, you must at least keep the sword from falling out of your hand. So to that extent at least, you must retain some degree of *mind* in your sword hand (and likewise, that one touch of mind is essential for maintaining the constant peculiar 'pointing' shape of the fingers in the off-hand). This is the first essential feature and benefit of the sword training. Far from theatrical art or for impressing your buddies, sword work develops and reinforces the key technical premise of Taiji. Once you really understand the Taiji sword, even just *thinking* of a few sword moves will instantly trigger the *'yang resonance'* aspect of your *qi* power (the SURGE-1 wave described in Chapter 3, Form) to flash through your bones and tissues like a mega-volt electric surge.

But be careful with sword work. There's something about the sword, the implement itself, that seems to bring out everybody's inner Zorro. Some people who have good, relaxed Taiji basics lose it all once they pick up the sword. Their limbs go rigid and straight, they seem to lunge agressively forward, and so on. It's some kind of tension blowback thing. I don't know what's up with that, but watch out for it. The sword form is physically every bit as relaxed, soft, and gently upright as the empty hand form.

In Chapter 2, I talked about the ARC training process for extending your energy from feet to hands. Now I'll discuss that in a little more detail, in a sword context, and focusing first on legs. Most teachers and commentators try to describe the legs' role in structural, mechanical, or physical support terminology. But in the pure Taiji context, those physical things aren't the key point about the legs at all.

For Taiji the legs are part of an energy connection, and also perform a storage function.

The legs are like a huge hyper-charged battery system for energy. That's part of the meaning of the injunction in the Taiji classic writings that 'power comes from the legs and manifests through the hands'. As I've said throughout the book, they aren't talking about 'ground path' or any physical/structural stuff like that. They're talking literally about internal energy storage and flow. You'll be totally amazed the first time you experience the legs' function as described here. It's an especially mind-shredding hallucinogenic experience when you get that going from your feet *up through the sword*. That'll really rock your world.

You may think any kind of martial arts weapons work would achieve the same thing. After all, don't they all go on about weapons being an extension of the hand and so on? But again, in practice things are different. I trained traditional Iaido (the Japanese art of seated sword drawing, cutting, re-sheathing) for many years. The Iaido masters also emphasize that the sword is an extension of your body and mind, and talk about powering cuts with the core and back, not the arms and shoulders, etc. That sounds like Taiji, and certainly it's a great art in its own right. But in fact it's very far from the profundity of Taiji. If you train that way you'll probably never understand the points I'm making here, because you need to begin the work in an even more delicate state of mind and body that possibly neither Iaido nor any other traditional weapons art can instill.

The correct starting point of Taiji feels kind of weak, it's not a real he-man type of vibe. You must feel physically weak but with your mind strongly extended. When you can achieve that feeling as your starting point, you're ready to take your first step on the long road to serious Taiji power. Unfortunately, in our current global culture of winner takes all, 'roiding ourselves to the gills, and stomping the losers, who wants to *invest* in that kind of *loser* type of feeling or mindset, no matter what we're told may come from it later? It's really hard for us to overcome our cultural conditioning in these areas.

Anyway, for Taiji you don't need to own a full arsenal of weapons like some kind of Mexican drug cartel - just work on straight sword, as Professor Zheng did. And, by the way, try to avoid any kind of hardware fixation on the sword or fetishization of the implement per se. That's totally irrelevant – remember Musashi and the boat oar. It can be a serious distraction for students, most especially for men (we love implements). Any lightweight reasonably balanced practice weapon will be fine, even a wooden sword is fine for Taiji. Just don't use anything too heavy or too long for your size (don't be macho) and don't use a sparkly but wobbly Wushu tinfoil sword (Theatrical Fallacy).

HAND & MIND

For the next sword teaching, I need to digress for a moment into the empty-hand form. In ZMQ37 style Taiji we have a basic principle for correct practice of the empty-hand form called 'Beautiful Lady's Hand' (美人手 *meirenshou*) or BLH. It is a simple flat extension of the hand and fingers from the wrist, straight but not stiff. Fingers including thumb are lightly aligned together, all pointing in same direction. The ZMQ37 style insists on this position for both hands at almost all times. The question everybody asks, or should ask is: *why?*

The usual answer is that this facilitates flow of *qi* energy to the hand and fingers. True as far as it goes, but is there anything more to be said? And if that's the only answer, then why in ZMQ37 Taiji do we *bend* our knees and try to sit low? And if we believe in physical determination of *qi* channeling, how would the *qi* ever reach the feet and toes, given that the feet themselves are naturally angled at 90 degrees to the ankle, in almost every posture, and in daily life?

The real reason for the BLH, like many things in Taiji, can best be understood from looking at the sword form. In sword form, the right hand lightly holds the sword, and the left hand is in a peculiar formation, index and middle fingers aligned together and pointing straight forward, other fingers curled and lightly gripped together behind. Let's tag that left hand shape as SPH (sword pointing hand). If more people knew sword form, then even more people would be asking about this than about BLH. Again the usual explanation for SPH is a vague statement about *qi* projection. Again it's true as far as it goes. But if we look a little deeper into the actual experience of sword practice, the reason becomes clear in greater detail. Let's digress for a moment and return to sword *per se* down below.

241

In all types of Taiji practice you need to catch energy through the entire body from feet to fingers. That is the entire game. To do this you need your body and arms to be totally relaxed, yet at the same time, your *mind* alone needs to hang out at the fingertips in order to serve as a kind of goalpost or greyhound mechanical rabbit for the *qi* to target. Without that little bit of minimal mind-dust at the hands, the *qi* (or *mingjing* energy which is *qi* in functional form) won't make it all the way, it will stop in the *dantian*. You want to drop it to the feet and then rebound it all the way up through the body, NEXUS Point, and the FLASHOUT to the fingers.

So, how do we get some mind in our hands? Actually it's easy, any kind of martial arts practice promotes that. Any kind of striking fist as in Yiquan, or Aikido's *tegatana* (karate chop shape), or the 'tiger mouth' hand variations in Xingyi and Bagua forms - all these help to lead the mind to the hands. You have to pay some attention to shaping your hands in these exotic ways. So that's half the game. But typically in the kinds of practices listed above the mind goes hand-in-hand (so to speak) with physical tension. Sometimes the required shaping itself inherently calls for physical tension, in other cases the tension is just a natural stowaway that the performer isn't really even conscious of. Either way, it's a death sentence for the energy function of real Taiji.

What to do? Some genius, either Yang Chengfu or possibly Prof. Zheng on his own, depending whose account you go with, sat down and asked a great question: what shape of hand most optimally *maximizes* presence of *mind* while jointly *minimizing* required or accompanying *physical* tension? In the sword form, the answer is very clear. The right hand holds the sword as loosely as possible without dropping it. Bingo that's an easy and perfect standard. The SPH in the left hand is then adopted to simulate that perfect natural right hand condition - the SPH forces just that little bit of mind presence needed to maintain the weird shape (Just Enough Mind, or JEM), but does not require or encourage any further tension.

If you practice the sword form with the above idea in mind, keeping your focus on totally relaxing the body (legs and torso) while leaving the hands and arms completely loose and totally relaxed - except for the absolutely minimal hand/mind presence requirement described above, it's a completely different experience. Try never to let the weight of the sword impinge on your hands or body at all – it feels very much like the membrane greasing or icing concept of the SHELL SLIDE defense of the previous chapter. In Taiji, we often talk about four ounces as the limit of physical pressure or weight you should be willing to bear. Any sword worthy of the name weighs more than four ounces, so as you go through the form, *don't ever bear its weight.* As you move in the sword form, you should feel that you're always just barely getting out from under the weight of the sword, by the skin of your teeth, so that your body never actually supports it – just as, in push hands you would never accept more than four ounces of pressure from your partner on your body. This kind of sword practice will bring home to you the feeling mentioned in the famous line from the Taiji classic writings: 一羽不能加，蠅蟲不能落. That is: *a feather cannot be added* (without you feeling it), *a fly cannot alight* (without weighing you down).

The BLH is the brilliant importation of the sword hands insight (the idea behind the SPH) to the empty hand practice. The BLH again gives us a single unvarying hand shape across all postures that again requires Just Enough Mind (JEM) for its maintenance, but without encouraging even the slightest hint of physical tension. Some Taiji practitioners in other styles are either *over-tensing* their hands (to get the more articulated, theatrics-oriented configurations required by their traditions), or else *under-minding* their hands, letting them flop around any old way, in the mistaken belief that flaccid collapse is synonymous with the true Taiji relaxation. The BLH concept, designed as it is to skirt both Scylla and Charybdis, is a gigantic breakthrough in the history of Taiji empty-hand training methods.

THE LINGTAI AMPLIFY

I introduced the *lingtai* (midback) energy hot spot in Chapter 2. This is one of the main areas of concentration of functional energy transmitted from the feet in the ARC rebound phase. In Chapter 2 I introduced the full ARC and also the shortcut wherein the power is concentrated at the *lingtai* point and projected outward to the hands directly from there, without completing the full ARC back through the NEXUS Point in the head. This discussion of the *lingtai* in sword practice is centered around that shortcut deployment - raising the energy to the *lingtai* and then out. When that shortcut component is really juiced and humming, it's a pure ecstatic feeling of absolute pleasure. And that's just from rocking your ARC in the empty hand Taiji form (ideally also incorporating the three main accelerants covered in Chapter 3, Form).

But if you want to super-charge that shortcut stage of integration, you need your sword – at least at first. Something about the traditional Taiji sword moves and hand positions, and something in the nature of the weapon itself, act radically to set that path on fire. Of course, as I said on the empty hand training, you will need a correctly structured basic Taiji sword form. Any one will do (you *know* I'm going to say it: *as long as it conforms to the Taiji classic writings.*) Taiji sword is typically done at a bit higher speed than the empty hand form. For example, the optimal time for the ZMQ37 empty hand form is anywhere from 7 to 12 minutes. The best timing for Yang/ZMQ sword form is 3 minutes. So it isn't quite as suitable a platform for going deeply into the most basic ARC development work. However, the sword program has a hidden jewel – that final projection torrent from the *lingtai* is goosed by 300%. It's your ARC finishing school.

Again, as ever, you ask: *How to do it?* Again, as always, I answer, *There's no royal road, just mentally open the door for it.* You only need to know that it's possible, be told once what to look for. The *lingtai* was made for sword, and vice-versa. You'll feel it. Once you know the kinetics of any Taiji sword form and can execute them correctly, you then keep your mind anchored on the *lingtai* throughout the form. Simple as that really. It will amplify your overall energy hugely. As you step through your sword set, keep your mind mildly on the partial path from the *lingtai* anchor out to your hands, one holding the sword, the other in the distinctive configuration 'sword pointing fingers' (index and middle fingers straight, thumb, ring and pinky fingers folded together). Then, because you've steadily worked through the ARC process in your empty hand form, your energy is primed – suddenly, BLAMMO the stuff will surge out from your *lingtai* into your hands and beyond, even into the sword itself.

Unlike the full RC process in the empty-hand form, with the sword you may not be quite as aware of the rebound phase of drop and re-ascent from the feet to the *lingtai*. The transmission is happening, make no mistake. All the basic stuff I've already discussed for empty hand form, such as the sloshing, etc. is working strong. But the sword is a light, quick, and lively beast, so you'll find yourself mentally working more directly on the short path from the *lingtai* out to the sword and hands for maximum responsiveness (as if, for example, you were really facing another swordsperson in a duel). That light and lively quality that only sword brings out is reflected in the *lingtai* energy concentration directly, with a huge *maxout* of throughput. (The *ling* of *lingtai* can actually mean 'light and lively' in Chinese anyway). Learn it, feel it, love it.

Figure 13 When practicing Taiji sword, concentrate on the energy connection from the *lingtai* (mid-back) energy point through the hands and beyond. The arrows indicate feeling of energy flow direction within the body – regardless of orientation of the cut, the major flow of energy will fill from the *lingtai* outward (there is a minor channel of return energy that's beyond the scope of this book. It operates naturally so don't worry about it.) Pose is Yang/ZMQ37 'Minor Literary Star'.

Do your sword form a few times in the *lingtai*-centric mode I've suggested, then do your regular empty hand Taiji form. You'll be shocked at the amplification.

THE HEART RADIANCE

I'm now going to reveal another deep potential of Taiji. It may be difficult to profit from it in your own practice right away, because you may not yet have the foundational precondition for everything I discuss in this book - *maybe you aren't yet relaxed*. But that's ok, file this away for later reference.

Among all the hot spots and channels where the energy can concentrate especially strongly, the one that feels the best, the one center that gives literally ecstatic/orgasmic type of pleasure is the heart/solar-plexus (膻中 *shanzhong*). I use that traditional point term, though in practice it feels as if the heart and the solar plexus almost merge into one big ball of heat and light. But this is one of the hardest to open. You'll have buzzing arms and legs and throbbing *dantian*, and electrified spine and powered-up arms and so on long before you'll understand what I'm saying here about the heart center. But when the heart center opens and admits the force, it's like no other sensation on earth - way beyond any illegal or legal meds you could snort. You'll know then why they call it the *solar* plexus, not to sound cheesy but it's exactly as if the 'radiance of a thousand suns' were to burst through there all at once.

Of course there are infinite ways to work on it, but one of the best - perhaps surprisingly because it isn't one of those mind-shreddingly complex Daoist *neigong* meditations – is Taiji straight sword play. Again it's a mental process, but the main clue is this:

the lingtai is opposite the heart. They can resonate together. Most of the energy projects out through the arms and sword, but enough of it sympathetically harmonizes with the heart frequency to achieve a huge amplification effect. If you know anything about sound structure, you'll feel the heart center is vibrating sympathetically at some high-multiple harmonic of the fundamental frequency generated up from the feet, which concentrates in the *lingtai*.

As with the empty hand Taiji form, it doesn't matter too much which particular style or form you play, all of them have the requisite basics. But it may be hard to detect the initial benefit because at first you may not yet be relaxed in your work. Don't rush to the closet, whip out your Chinese straight sword, swing through a few moves, feel nothing and toss it aside with a sneer. Recognize that you may not yet be sufficiently relaxed to feel it fully, and keep on trucking.

Though I've been to Tiruvannamalai in Tamil Nadu State and visited the Ramanashram, I was a few decades late to take direct audience the Maharishi. But another guy who did it for real has left us this account of the experience:

> *As I sat before Bhagavan, I became aware of an all- penetrating, all-conquering love that nothing in me was able to resist. But when I use the word 'love', I don't think I quite encapsulate the driving, unstoppable energy with which Bhagavan effortlessly radiated this dissolving force. If I say that I was repeatedly struck by jolting, shuddering, mind-dissolving bolts of lightning, you will get a better idea of just how powerful his presence was. Or perhaps you won't, because I have discovered that no one who has not experienced this kind of energy for himself can really understand what I am hinting at. You will get the idea of some magnificent being radiating light, but you will not have that experience for yourself.*

- Wolter Keers, as recounted in *The Power of the Presence*, by David Godman

Persistent sword work under the guidelines given here, followed by a few minutes of quiet standing will open the heart center. Then you'll come as close as any of us still can to: *having that experience for yourself.*

CHAPTER 6:
COMBATIVE TAIJI?

I loved something that I made up.

– Scarlett O'Hara

OK, I admit it. I've been waffling, haven't I? Despite every intention to be totally clear, despite my honest insistence that push hands is only an *attribute* thing, I've still somehow managed to dodge giving a totally unambiguous straight answer to *the most basic question* I know you have: *Is Taiji, taken as a whole, a serious combat training system or not? Just answer the question!*

I admit I'm a little schizoid on this question of the combative aspect of Taiji. But you've pushed me to the wall. Much as I'd love to keep hope alive, and go on dropping hints here and there that while push hands per se *isn't* a combat art, somehow Taiji overall *might* be, I have to level with you now: in its current form, with the kinds of training and training time that are available in the real world of today to most normal people, Taiji can no longer be considered a fighting art. Nor does it directly develop skills or techniques that can be readily applied to ring, cage, street, or jailyard (shank defense) without some additional … accessorization.

I hope you're satisfied, now that you've nailed my tail to the floor and got your straight answer. And yet… that said… like most Taiji teachers, I still want to have it both ways. We all love to hint coyly that we *could* kick your ass, we simply *choose* not to at this time. That's because the founder of modern Taiji, grandmaster Yang Luchan (楊露禪), was such a total badass. They called him Yang Wudi (楊無敵), Invincible Yang, because he was said to prevail in every one of the hundreds of challenge matches he fought, without ever killing his opponent. We all idolize him, and view our art's sad fall from that height with dismay.

Naturally there are those in the Taiji world who are still true believers that *their* brand of Taiji *is* a full fighting art. This fantasy is usually just another variant of the common physicalist fallacies I've been calling out all along. Essentially, some believe that Taiji basically boils down to some kind of efficient or sophisticated version of applying physical power. So they think that if they can seem relaxed as they hit, or if they violently rotate their bodies and limbs as they attempt a takedown, or if they strike at an unconventional angle, or in some unusual way - maybe with a slap or a crane beak or shoulder, something that seems derived from a Taiji form - that they're thus proving the ultimate combat utility of the art.

But to me, only the full-on unrestricted use of pure Taiji energy to *completely disable* any kind of unarmed opponent under any conditions *with one single touch* would qualify Taiji as a truly *unique and distinctive* combative art for street or cage. And at this time, sadly, the art just can't meet that condition. There are many great and powerful teachers out there who can do all sorts of amazing and scary things. But you'll never see any of them in the cage doing it for real, and for money, against the best UFC fighters or world title boxers. It's very possible that Li Yaxuan, who I've quoted elsewhere in this book, was the last of the true full-spectrum Taiji combat greats who would have met my condition. And even *that* standard doesn't begin to consider the final sorry truth that from knife to nuke, from Coke bottle to Claymore, from Taser to Tomahawk, reality is ruled by *weapons*. Maybe even Yang Luchan could have been machine-gunned into Swiss cheese just as easily as anybody else. You know, like they did to Sonny at the toll booth.

A real master player at a bare minimum would need to be able to survive *that*, without a vest, to justify our Taiji title: *The Supreme Ultimate Fist*. If that's really what we are going to call our art, we have a long way to go from where we are today. Boxing promoter Don King once replied to another manager reluctant to have his title-holding fighter go up against a tough challenger managed by King:

Hell, when you say the words 'world champion' that means you fight everybody.

In that light… *Supreme Ultimate Fist*? Questionable. I hope now I've finally been clear enough about my view. Despite that, I too, just like any other Taiji person, simply can't resist the temptation to opine about fighting and self-defense. It seems so tantalizingly near our art (yet in reality, so far from us …). I can only ask your kind indulgence. When you think about self-defense, you need to back away from Taiji or any other canned paint-by-number solution and survey the entire problem space, as it exists in the real world. So the first thing is knowledge.

1. KNOWLEDGE (for self-defense)

You need to understand all the legal and psychological ramifications of any kind of fight. For the psychology of real-world conflict, I always recommend Geoff Thompson's great memoir of "working the door" (night club bouncer gigs) *Watch My Back.* In his highly entertaining style he makes any number of essential points about the emotional, psychological, and physiological (e.g. adrenaline dump) aspects of inter-personal conflict. I have my own personal rules on this, to wit:

- COURTEOUS: Be courteous to everybody.
- QUIET: Keep your mouth shut around strangers.
- SOBER: Don't drink alcohol or hang around those who do.

Easy enough, don't you think? If you can hold to my simple three rules above, you'll have side-stepped over 95% of the typical triggers for any kind of inter-personal spat. I have no scientific citation for that figure but it seems right to me.

2. FEELING (for self-defense)

Then you need to understand how sensitive your body/mind already is to threats around you. Your body has a built-in Early Warning System. Please read the classic book *The Gift of Fear* by Gavin

Becker. This book has numerous case histories of people saving themselves by taking their body's instinctive reactions seriously – when a person or situation "feels like trouble" it is trouble, plain and simple. Get out. With that understood you may want to begin to build a bridge between the serious threats described in that book and the proximity sensitivity training described in Chapter 1 of this book. The proximity sensitivity discussed there is a more articulated, more sensitive, but less generalized version of that same Gift of Fear.

3. ACTION (for self-defense)

Understand that every environment is your Personal Armory. Please view Vladimir Vasiliev's (pioneer of Russian Systema martial art) great DVD on *Improvised Weapons,* covering the use of belts, credit cards, baseball caps, books, pens, jackets and other common objects in self-defense. If you absolutely cannot run or evade, realize you are already armed to the teeth. Throw and slash, poke and smash - using anything that's at hand – and then run.

The great classical philosopher Seneca noted that:

> *Men of the meanest lot in life have by a mighty impulse snatched up whatever was lying ready to hand, and by sheer strength have turned objects which were by nature harmless into weapons of their own.*

4. TRANSCENDENCE (for self-defense)

With the above background, you are ready to incorporate the benefits of a confident, relaxed body and mind fully imbued with internal energy as developed over time by dedicated practice of Taiji. I want to re-emphasize that push hands per se is not functional combative training. It is neither combative technique, nor method, nor skill training, nor in any sense a realistic configuration for unarmed conflict. Some Taiji teachers try to fool their students and themselves otherwise, but it won't fly. Push hands is strictly an attribute development method, one of the best for working on deep relaxation which in turn enables the free flow of internal power. If you're smart and you care, then later on, once you've got that power to some degree, you can spend a few decades figuring out how to work it into your "real world" martial arts or combat sport, be that Brazilian Jiu-Jitsu, Western boxing, Muay Thai or whatever you do for reality work.

But all that said, though push hands per se is definitely not a combat development system, it does border very closely on an incredibly effective and awesomely destructive mode of combative work. In fact, some people can slip seamlessly and instantaneously from push hands to this particular 'real world' mode, achieving a 99% overlap from the Taiji push hands attributes onto the nasty real world fighting skills of Russian Systema's *dynamic joint breaking* (refer to eponymous DVD available from Vladimir Vasiliev). Strange though it may seem, the dynamic joint break work, as masterfully exemplified by Vladimir Vasiliev, is pretty much true combat push hands by any other name. In this work, you control the opponent's joints and instantly destroy them (as opposed to slow submission). So despite my academic disclaimer above about the in-applicability of push hands to self-defense, for some people push hands-fostered attributes actually could translate into this kind of real world combat skill. It's not an easy thing to practice normally. Taiji push hands offers a safe and gentle, somewhat indirect, approach to this fearsome skill. But so few people have heard of Systema-style dynamic joint breaks that I normally state my disclaimer starkly, as below:

> *Taiji push hands does not directly foster real world fighting skills... but let those who have ears, hear.*

Even in more directly Taiji-specific terms, push hands skill has a limited but definite application to 'real fighting' (whatever that is). Here's how it works. In my style of very restricted movement, fixed-foot push hands, you learn a kind of instantaneous sensitivity and energy issuance that I called Fire mode in the Push chapter above. In a clinching type of struggle, you can use that to blast your opponent away, and if there's a wall or a sharp drop nearby, a Fire mode response of that type could be lethal. Alternatively, you could simply take his balance for just a moment. That momentary loss of balance would normally, during friendly practice mode, result in your partner/opponent simple taking a single step back or to the side, to recover his momentary loss of stability.

Triggering that small step is our only goal in the practice mode. But in the more combative mode, you would use that instant, the moment when they begin to take that step, to take them down, or to definitively break their structure and finish the fight with a more direct hit (not part of Taiji per se as I've said). I do not emphasize this mode in own teaching, but believe me – the potential is in there. However, even those who are able to take aboard my little hint above about dynamic joint breaks will do best to practice *as if* there truly is *no functional application of push hands* work. Because if you have even a slightly functional mindset, you will unconsciously but inevitably fall into the instrumental trap of trying for a lock, arm bar, joint break, neck twist, or choke. You'll begin to apply physical strength in your effort to reach that goal. And from then onward, your prospects for getting the real Taiji powers are totally nil. So this point about the morphing of attributive push hands into applicative dynamic joint breaks is a description (of something that naturally emerges) *not a prescription* (of something to try for).

Anyway, the most important practical thing for staying alive in one piece, as one poster to my old net discussion group AlasBabylon trenchantly observed, isn't ruling the ring at your local Fight Club, it's careful driving:

> *In your car, driving, anywhere, anytime, is where you are most likely to get hurt or killed. Terrorist crap is irrelevant compared*

to driving. The idiot on your tailgate is much more dangerous to you than [Jihadi extremists] will ever be. Death is at your fender, countless times every day. Pay attention when you are driving and drive like a person of sense.

CHAPTER 7:
THE BIG PICTURE

Consider this
the slip
that brought me to my knees

- R.E.M.

You can skip this chapter. There are no Taiji drills here. I'm going to go all existential on you. Most people don't like thinking about the big picture. And I don't blame them the least bit. But somebody has to do it, so here goes.

We've circled back to the first question: *why?* From a Buddhist point of view, everything in this book is trivial. It's all merely the pursuit of *siddhi*, any kind of magic power that helps you get a leg up in this vale of tears (for example, making yourself 'infinitely heavy', or 'almost weightless'). An Enlightened One scorns such child's play. Meanwhile, from a scientific point of view, this book's message is pure fantasy. If you can't measure or weigh it, consign it to the flames. Finally, pretty much *nobody* disputes James G. Frazer's long term forecast:

> *In the ages to come, man may be able to predict, perhaps even to control, the wayward courses of the winds and clouds, but hardly will his puny hands have strength to speed afresh our slackening planet in its orbit or rekindle the dying fire of the sun.*

- The Golden Bough

Even on a less cosmic scale, the human body is obviously obsolete. Within a few years, there may be total systemic collapse (due to food or fuel depletion, sun storm EMP hit, nuclear pyrotechnics, financial seize-up, etc.) leading to Mad Max zombie wars. Barring that however, people in the richer countries will start to be *mentally* augmented and neurologically optimized (say goodbye to: guilt, fear, madness, and remorse), with implant chips for panoptic military/government surveillance, enhanced memory, total-sensory-immersion virtual game worlds, and so on. Meanwhile on the *physical* side, there'll be exoskeletal devices such as robotoid pogo-stick limbs and suits for super strength, speed, and agility. Those and other after-market parts will click right into the new mental stuff, *et voila* – homo sapiens *per se* will be squeezed out from the middle altogether - done and dusted.

Author Vernor Vinge has summarized well:

> *It seems plausible that with technology we can, in the fairly near future create (or become) creatures who surpass humans in every intellectual and creative dimension. Events beyond such an event -- such a singularity -- are as unimaginable to us as opera is to a flatworm.*

The typical rhetoric of Transhumanism goes even further. Nick Bostrom has summed it up:

> *Substrate is morally irrelevant. Whether somebody is implemented on silicon or biological tissue, if it does not affect functionality or consciousness, is of no moral significance. Carbon-chauvinism, in the form of anthropomorphism, speciesism, bioism or even fundamentalist humanism, is objectionable on the same grounds as racism. Biology mandates not only very limited durability, death and poor memory retention, but also limited speed of communication, transportation, learning, interaction and evolution. Embodied (human) intelligence is imprisoned by biology and its inevitable scarcity. Intelligence ought to be free — to move, to interact and to evolve, unhindered by the limits of biology and scarcity.*

But it's interesting that even as we become increasingly mechanized, dehumanized, roboticized by all the high tech, the more things go that way in covert reality, the more, on the surface, we seem to crave news about, and immersion, in *body* stuff. The old fashioned, totally obsolete, over-the-hill human body. The more physical autonomy we surrender in terms of increasing lockdown via domestic aerial drones, synthetic telepathy (look it up), active-denial pain machines and virtual everything, the more we obsess over celebrity sex and baby bumps, steroid use by athletes, etc. And the more we obsess over our body's health and work out at 24-hour gyms and so on. Anything that recalls the body to mind is attractive to us.

There's obviously some kind of latent mechanical intelligence in the universe that sees us humans as now cooked sufficiently crispy to serve it as a bootstrapping platform into material manifestation. Though *why* it would want to materially manifest is something else altogether. You'll have to ask *it*, because I've not the slightest idea. Anyway, while that immaterial mecha-mind is working its way *in* to manifest as us, we material chimps are highly motivated to work our way *out* and meet it halfway. That's because from our human point of view the physical body is weak. Therefore humans are DNA-engineered to seek power. Technology seems to offer the greatest power trip of all. Freeman Dyson has explained it best:

> *I have felt it myself. The glitter of nuclear weapons. It is irresistible if you come to them as a scientist. To feel it's there in your hands, to release this energy that fuels the stars, to let it do your bidding. To perform these miracles, to lift a million tons of rock into the sky. It is something that gives people an illusion of illimitable power, and it is, in some ways, responsible for all our troubles - this, what you might call technical arrogance, that overcomes people when they see what they can do with their minds.*

How can the puny little physical semi-chimp individual body put on *that* kind of a smoke-and-light show? No matter how much *qi* you amass, you're always going to fall short. Within twenty-five years, we'll know the outcome: either the mecha's will have completely colonized us from inside-out, or everything will have broken back down to the Stone Age.

Which is all fine.

But it does raise a question: given the above sci-fi sitcom already in-progress, *why* do I continue to insist on the value of training up the Taiji internal energies? Before I answer that let's take in some historical perspective. This obsolescence-of-the-body thing probably started way back with the capture of Stone Age fire, but if we need to pin a historical tail on the donkey I'd go with the introduction of the *gun*, which took off seriously about year 1500 CE or so. Fast forward 500 years and now look at how martial arts movies all labor under *the shadow of the gun* - meaning, they all need to contrive somehow to make their essential defining action (fistfights) somehow meaningful, despite the fact that even if the legendary creator of martial arts, Zhang Sanfeng, were levitating up above he could be Uzi-ed out of the sky with the merest trigger pull.

So every martial arts movie is required, as the first condition of its plausibility, to finesse the *gun* thing either by pushing the story back in history (as in Mifune type samurai drama), or by taking a heroic approach (making the central action into in effect a sport match, with rules barring guns), or by bald fiat (as in *Enter the Dragon*, where guns were not allowed on the tournament island, or *Billy Jack,* where people just never were quite able to get their gun sites onto Billy most of the time).

So then, given that martial arts are totally obsolete, and considering that these internal energies weren't ever much use for anything *but* that (*if* that) then - what's the point? Three reasons:

1. The quick answer is what I stated in Chapter 1: it feels better than heroin. As you scale up the energy ladder from the *mingjing* through the *anjing* to the *huajing*, it'll totally blow your mind. It's truly available out there, or I should

say *in here*, it's real, it's not physical or structural in the least, and it'll totally blow you away. When you finally *really* get it on (if you do) you won't believe you were ever so foolish as to assert otherwise (if you ever have). Alexei Melnick, the author of *Tweakerville* has described the first experience of crystal meth as follows:

I remember thinking, all this time I was lied to. I get it now. Here's what they don't want you to know and I don't want to tell you. If God made one more pure thing than that first peak of clear he kept it for him self. Forget your first time. Forget what's her name, she made the sun shine. Forget that guy was supposed to be for ever, who? Forget when your kid said dad for the first time. That was the old world, your old life, the old you. You just cracked out your shell. Taste air for the first time. You just got born again. You just put on your cape. You can hear every thing. Every thing zoomed in, tweaker vision. This is the real world, that other world was the lie. This is the more real world. No fear. No pain. Just clear. Until each breath is clear, clear. And each heart pump is clear, clear.

I realize that kind of comparison is deeply offensive to many readers. So here's another one, take a toke of Bill Clegg from his book *Portrait of an Addict as a Young Man*:

The smoke billows out into the living room like a great unfurling dragon. As he watches the cloud spread and curl, he feels the high at first as a flutter, then a roar. A surge of new energy pounds through every inch of him, and there is a moment of perfect oblivion where he is aware of nothing and everything. A kind of peace breaks out behind his eyes. It spreads down from his temples into his chest, to his hands and everywhere. It storms through him - kinetic, sexual, euphoric - like a magnificent hurricane raging at the speed of light. It is the warmest, most tender caress he has ever felt.

Seriously, I don't know how to make the point any more forcefully that the natural internal energy can give you just that same kind of experience without the horrific social, legal, medical, and financial hassles that dog Melnick's and Clegg's drug-addled worlds.

2. But so what? Just a better legal high? Is that *all*? Not quite. I also practice because Taiji holds out, in this violent world, under the bristle of the guns, in the glare of the shells, beneath the shadow of the *strange fruit*, the promise: *there's something beyond the physical*. There's another power that's 'real'. Real in the sense that it can under limited demonstration conditions overcome the physical without stooping to it. But notice that I've still got 'real' in quotes. That because *actually* only guns, flame throwers, Tasers, Daisy Cutters, Fat Man, Little Boy - only those are *really* real. Without quotes. But. I cling to the sophomoric idea that Taiji has, if nothing else, *demonstration value* down here below.

3. I further assert that there *is* a deeper meaning to it all, which is that maybe - just maybe - the whole point of having a physical body in the first place is precisely that it does allow the possibility (rarely effectuated) of cultivating this stuff. And even though the energy per se isn't exactly physical, you *do* need a body as a supporting platform for the work. The Darwinian dog pile has coughed out this interesting toy – the human body. It'd be a shame to toss that on the evolutionary landfill without even opening the carton. It's even possible that, per Buddhism, getting a chance at human physical opportunity is rare in the overall energy-based scheme of things (spirit dimensions and astral planes). If that's true, the physical body may offer some things that no amount of chipped-up simulacra

can provide. So quite apart from the *ecstatic* motivation for pursuing energy work and studies, which I've discussed at length throughout the book, I have a more *instrumental* motive. I have this totally weird idea: even though these non-physical or quasi-physical internal energies are pretty much useless down here below, still it's possible that buffing up these internal energies while entombed down here (in a physical body) might have some kind of payoff for your re-entry to the spirit planes. Maybe it's like training with a weight vest - you feel faster once it's off than you would have been otherwise. Maybe these energies, so fragile and useless here below, are actually the coin of the realm there above. Maybe the whole *point* of strapping on a physical jumpsuit in the first place is that the physical is the one realm where it's possible to cultivate certain special energies that can later be harvested for fun and profit in the afterlife. So I continue with it. I wouldn't wanna get back up there without having maxed out my energy opportunities down here to the best of my ability. Otherwise, when I get back through the door, I might have some astral shift boss explain to me that this kind of cultivation can only be done on the physical Earth plane, and that's why I was sent down in the first place. Maybe s/he'll inform me that if I'd come back with a good harvest, I could have bought my permanent freedom, paid my way off the press gang. I don't want to have to say *I screwed up. I want a do-over.*

Actually, alchemic Daoism has a concept somewhat similar to Point (3) above. Of course they've iced the cake with a lot more dogs and ponies than my bare metal version. In fact, alchemical Daoism is not so very unlike Transhumanism in its goal of transcending and transforming the *carbon substrate*... Isn't all just about the same thing? It seems we just can't take reality raw. As-It-Is. Nature has kicked our butt too hard for too long. Yet, I can't help believing that no amount of hi-tech development will solve the underlying problem of suffering. It's basically a mistake to incarnate physically, whether as carbon or silicon or what have you. Leads to nothing but trouble. Every time we do it, it'll just be another twist of the same old screw in this predatory world. Bottom line will never change, from the ancient Pharaohs to pre-or-post Singularity: *some power elite wants to ride you.* Thus has it ever been, thus shall it always be. Probably just as humans first controlled and then eliminated most wildlife from the planet, so we in our turn will be first controlled, and then extinguished by our machines.

Suffering has been called out as a fundamental issue by philosopher David Benatar, in his book *Better Never to Have Been: The Harm of Coming Into Existence*:

> *Conscious life, although but a blip on the radar of cosmic time, is laden with suffering - suffering that is directed to no end other than its own perpetuation.*

Likewise, in his book *The Conspiracy Against the Human Race*, Thomas Ligotti summarizes what to me is the only rational conclusion about human life:

> *For the pessimist, everything considered in isolation from human suffering or any cognition that does not have as its motive the origins, nature, and elimination of human suffering is at base recreational, whether it takes the form of conceptual probing or physical action in the world - for example, delving into game theory or traveling in outer space, respectively. But human suffering will remain insoluble as long as human beings exist. The pessimist's credo, or one of them, is that nonexistence never hurt anyone and existence hurts everyone. Although our selves may be illusory creations of consciousness, our pain is nonetheless real.*

Astral projection pioneer Robert Monroe discovered that physical reality is a hologram type of illusion, one hundred percent mentally created and imagined. Along the same lines, scholar W. Y. Evans-Wentz observed that the spirit realms are also mostly fantasy:

> *The Bible of the Christians, like the Koran of the Moslems, never seems to consider that the spiritual experiences in the form of hallucinatory visions by prophet or devotee, reported therein, may, in the last analysis, not be real. But the Bardo Thodol is so sweeping in its assertions that it leaves its reader with the clear-cut impression that every vision, without any exception whatsoever, in which spiritual beings, gods or demons, or paradises or places of torment and purgation play a part, in a Bardo or any Bardo-like dream or ecstasy, is purely illusionary, being based upon sangsaric phenomena.*

So what does that leave? It's *all* fake all the way down. But the problem remains – we don't experience it that way. No matter how fake it all is, it seems real while it's happening to us. Henry Havelock Ellis said it best: *Dreams are real while they last, can we say more of life?* In his classic poem *Here Dead We Lie*, Alfred Housman wrote of the recent war dead:

> *Life, to be sure,*
> *Is nothing much to lose,*
> *But young men think it is,*
> *And we were young.*

But we could tweak it to say: *Life, to be sure, is nothing much to lose, but humans think it is. And we were human.* We have to take life semi-seriously. So while I'm here and I'm in it, I want to make sure I squeeze whatever there is to get out of it. Therefore, in preference to the darkness invoked by Ligotti above, I need to go with Carlos Castaneda's more poetically soaring version of the same basic point:

271

All paths are the same – they lead nowhere. For me there is only the traveling on the paths that have a heart, on any path that may have a heart. There I travel, and the only worthwhile challenge for me is to traverse its full length. And there I travel – looking, looking, breathlessly.

I'll see you out there, on the road to Ixtlan.

APPENDIX A:
ARE YOU EXPERIENCED?
(THE TRAINING TESTIMONY OF SUN LUTANG)

This seminal essay is written in semi-classical Chinese, the hybrid style of writing that came into being during an interim attempt to bridge the lingering attachment to the ancient imperial exam canon (millennia-old founding canon of Chinese civilization) and the early 20th century movement to modernize and standardize the written and spoken language (heavily influenced by Western grammarians). This piece leans more toward the really hard-core ancient style. Thus, if you run this original through Google translate, the result is total garbage and gibberish.

I've done my best to render the most complete, thorough, and accurate translation possible. But this piece talks about things far beyond most people's experience and uses terms that philosophers and linguists have debated for centuries. There is no way to avoid endless quibbles about whether every mysterious word and phrase is accurately rendered. Therefore it's best to avoid tedious legalism. Despite some differences in terminology, the process Master Sun describes is something I have personally undergone in most details. Take it as merely a finger pointing to up to the night sky, whose sole purpose is to show you the moon.

Ever since I began training boxing in childhood, my teachers always told me *Boxing embodies the Dao*. I was skeptical about it. But when I learned 'concealed energy', and the unification of hard and soft, my movements became lively and swift and then I understood the truth of it. When I got together with fellow trainees, we shared our personal experiences and results. But as I progressed to understanding the next level of 'mysterious energy', although I remained willing to talk about it with classmates, I didn't want to share my experiences with outsiders. But now I want to write my personal experience for people who have started on the same path, in the hope that we can all improve together.

As I began the progression to 'mysterious energy', after practicing a formal sequence (of Xingyiquan) I would finish with upright standing, trying to unify my spirit and energy. Every time I did that, I'd feel some slight subtle movement in my perineal area. At first it was barely perceptible. When doing my quiet standing after each day's practice, I'd sometimes feel it and sometimes not. But over time, the movement became stronger and more frequent, until it got to the point that as soon as I returned to standing at the conclusion of any formal drill, all I had to do was concentrate for a moment, and I would feel a vectored energy discharge. I realized that this was the spontaneous energetic movement of the true *yang*-power, which is described in classical works on Daoist static meditation.

The ancient Daoist meditation masters thoroughly understood this process, which they referred to as movement arising from the stillness of their seated practice methods. What I was doing was the inverse of that - I had been entering stillness (the upright standing) after the movements of my boxing practice. It's hard to understand. This state is also described in the ancient boxing classics with the phrase 'motionless omnipresence'. Anyway I persisted relentlessly in my daily practice.

Finally I reached the point that immediately on assuming the upright standing posture, my entire body entered a state of absolute emptiness, within which the true *yang* power resonated and flowed. This condition has been characterized by Daoist Master Liu Hua Yang as re-experiencing one's original nature. In this state, if I moved even slightly the real *yang* resonance would immediately discharge. I realized I could use the boxing method itself to transform this raw potential. I used my mind to sink my insubstantial spirit, filling my *dantian*. At the same time I used the insubstantial spirit to slightly elevate the energy accumulation of the perineal area [Translator Note 1], which resulted in full coordination of inner and outer activity.

Thereafter, when I merely directed my mind briefly to my *dantian*, even for just a moment, the real *yang* resonance would immediately concentrate itself and rise up into that area. At that time my body would experience a sensation of absolute ease. At that time I hadn't yet heard of the doctrine of ** [Translator Note 2], but anyway I felt as though two powerful forces were interacting within my *dantian*. After standing in this state for up to four or five hours, I would gradually come back to my normal self.

I believe that this immobile state was the result of my gradual accumulation, through the formal boxing practice, of two kinds of breath that were retained in my *dantian* after that practice finished. These internally retained breath elements were entirely different from the breathing of daily life. I had not intentionally created or retained these internal breath elements, but after a practice session I would have persistent experience of them. Zhuangzi wrote that the superior man breathes from his feet, and my experience was consistent with this basic idea. I was then able to use these elements of internal breath to smooth and refine the movement of the real *yang* resonance so that it uniformly suffused my entire body.

Thus I continued as I have already written, with the process of raising the resonance up to my *dantian*, and every time I practiced a boxing sequence my inner and outer movements were absolutely coordinated and unified. I would practice gently and slowly, always careful to maintain my balance. When I practiced the formal sequences, I would take care to keep my limbs relaxed, my movements soft and harmonious, maintaining that feeling of emptiness.

Over time, my dynamic boxing practice came to generate exactly the same state as the static work I described above. Sometimes I would stand after performing only one sequence, sometimes after two, and then begin moving again. No matter what, I would always elevate the internal *yang* resonance to my *dantian*, and leverage the internal breath elements generated by the boxing practice as feedstock for the internal flow. The flow begins at the coccyx [Translator Note 3] and rises through the vertebrae points [Cf. Translator Note 4], then to the upper gate/Jade Pillow [Translator Note 5], then to the crown of the head, before lowering down the front, exactly as taught in seated meditation methods, back to the *dantian*.

Sometimes the flow would circulate two or three times before settling into the uniform state of full-body permeation, while at other times it would make three or four orbits before suffusing into the uniform state. There seemed to be a correlation between the number of circulation orbits and the number of prior practice sets. But that was only in the beginning. Later, even without any prior practice at all, whenever I would merely sit down, or take any action whatsoever, I could use the internal breath elements to achieve the same preliminary circulation.

Finally I could achieve it even while asleep. I'd be sleeping soundly when the internal *yang* resonance would suddenly activate itself, immediately awakening me. Again I was able to use the breath elements derived from the boxing practice to transform this into the uniform state of energetic suffusion. Finally the *yang* resonance no longer spontaneously activated itself during my sleep, and my entire body inside and out, as well as all four limbs, would suddenly transform from the state of full suffusion to the ultimate state of complete emptiness. I experienced this as a kind of shower of complete bliss. I could apply this internal breath to achieve this ultimate state even while dreaming. When I awakened, I would realize that I had experienced that while dreaming. Later I experienced a final abbreviation of this process so that as soon as I fell into deep sleep, I would enter the state of ultimate emptiness.

In daily waking life, while walking or sitting, my limbs would suddenly feel absolutely light or empty, and my body would enter a state of absolute comfort. After each evening's practice of the boxing sequences, when I went to sleep each night, I would almost always experience this transformation to ultimate emptiness. But if I went to sleep without practicing, I would be less likely to experience the shift.

Finally I understood that the internal practice as described here strengthened my internal state to the point of warding off any illness of body, mind, or spirit. I also realized that the process I had gone through in my boxing practice was identical to that taught in classical Daoist meditation, thus these two arts have exactly the same theoretical basis. What I've written about here, above, is my own personal experience of internal and external transformation. I've laid it out openly for the benefit of all fellow practitioners.

TRANSLATOR NOTES:

1. For you academic quibblers out there: I am fully aware of the fact that: 中醫古稱肛門為「谷道」, and therefore this can be alternately translated as 'anal,' but 'perineal' is more faithful to the felt nature of the actual experience.
2. Citation missing from original text
3. 尾閭 Wei Lu Guan
4. 夾脊 Jia Ji Guan
5. 玉枕 Yu Zhen Guan

FREQUENTLY ASKED QUESTIONS

Q: Your model of internal energy and associated practices seems kind of shallow and simple compared to highly elaborated Daoist ontologies and related training disciplines I've seen elsewhere. Couldn't it be dangerous to fool around with qi and other internal energies without encyclopedic knowledge of classical Daoist practices and theories?

A: Yes, the model of energy cultivation presented in this book, and by implication attributed to Taiji overall (perhaps unfairly), is radically simpler than the systems you cite. I admit I'm a bit of a cheerleader for "my thing" – a little parochial on the point. You really have to be somewhat prejudiced in favor of your own stuff to muster the energy to write a book on it. Since we'll never know whose Brand X is really, really the *One True Way* (everyone has unlimited testimonials for their own thing), for now we should be mainly concerned with two things: the *safety* and the *effectiveness* of any given practice.

Most important is safety of course. About that, the first thing I have to re-emphasize is: re-read the Disclaimer at the start of this book. There are no guarantees of absolute safety for anything. Even if you hide under your bed all day, a plane may crash through your roof, or an earthquake may shake you out. I wonder whether any internal or physical cultivation system can be *guaranteed* absolutely safe by its teachers and adherents. We just can't be certain of the health and sanity and suitability for a given practice of everybody who's exposed to our materials. I hope that any teacher of anything would agree with me on that. That's why I have the Disclaimer: *This material is for entertainment purposes only.*

But I think I see where you really want to go with this question. There's a whole tradition of queasiness around mystical internal practices. You hear vague stuff about people going nuts or overstraining their heart or spleen or whatever by rousing the dark side of the Force too soon, or in the wrong order, or at the wrong time of day, and so on. If you're thinking specifically of the NEXUS Point concept in this book, then you should recall that this teaching comes from Professor Zheng's writings where he talks about the niwan head point. So no use crying over spilt milk, the cat's already out of the bag. More broadly though, there's some suggestive literature on this question. For example, there's something called Kundalini Syndrome, a disorder attributed to the workings of the internal energy called Kundalini in Sanskrit.

Wiki says this on it:

> The Kundalini syndrome is a set of sensory, motor, mental and affective symptoms associated with the concept of Kundalini. It has been reported predominantly by people who have had a near-death experience, or by practitioners of Asian spiritual practices. If the accompanying symptoms unfold in an intense manner that destabilizes the person, the process is usually interpreted as a spiritual emergency.

Symptoms are said to somewhat resemble psychosis. It's too big a topic to get into here, but I fully understand that the discussion of energy points in this book, particularly those along the microcosmic orbit, might seem to be straying into the danger zone. However, I've not had this problem (as far as I can tell), nor have I known anybody who has suffered serious Kundalini symptoms brought on by either Taiji or Daoist meditation. Nevertheless, I admit that, as Donald Rumsfeld reminded us about Iraq nukes: *absence of evidence is not evidence of absence*. I have stated repeatedly in this book that you want to approach all aspects of the practice lightly and naturally, without excessive or obsessive concentration.

Professor Zheng Manqing wrote and spoke for decades on the concept of the *qi* energy rising along the spinal column to the head (some of his material is quoted in this book). To my knowledge, his students and readers who were exposed to those teachings have not suffered severe symptoms of Kundalini Syndrome or internal organ failure, etc. Generally Taiji, with its emphasis on connecting to the earth, relaxation, and gentle movement can be thought of more plausibly as a prophylactic or therapy for these problems, rather than a trigger. But I can't speak from personal experience. In any case, the whole discussion is vast and utterly beyond the scope of this book. I suggest you begin your research with the excellent Wiki article quoted above.

More broadly, I'm aware that it's often said you should never attempt to learn any inner work from a book. That you must always seek and work under the guidance of a fully qualified master teacher. I believe that too. That's why *this book doesn't actually teach Taiji* (in case you hadn't noticed). It just offers guidelines and tips to consider for the practice you already have, or may be considering taking up. Obviously *you must have a teacher* to learn the basic dynamic framework of the art. So that aspect is completely covered by the operating premise of the book.

It brings up an interesting philosophical (and practical) question however – how do we know who's a "fully qualified master teacher" in the first place? Most of us go by either general acclimation (big rep) or personal feeling (pure gut). And that's probably all we'll ever have. Because over and again you find that the Exalted Grandmaster of System X is considered a pathetic charlatan by the High Poobah of System Y and vice versa. It reinforces the truth of the old adage: *two of a trade never agree*. And I'm as guilty as the next on that charge. I intensively trained in several highly complex systems of Daoist meditation for years. Stuff way wilder than anything in this book. My teachers had good reputations – but can I be *absolutely sure* they were *totally qualified*? That they knew *everything* - not only about the practice but about *me* too, how it could affect me? Questionable. It's an uncertain world out there. I also found over time that many people claiming or even demonstrating high mastery of the most esoteric energies in some respects, still had exactly the same baggage of unconscious physical tension as anybody else. I admit that shocked me a little, and sent me deeper into the radical relaxation emphasis of the ZMQ37 system. But maybe I was wrong to be so deeply affected by that? Who knows.

So that's safety. As for effectiveness, that's 100% relative to *goals*. Please refer to the exhaustive discussion of Taiji in relation to different kinds of goals in Chapter 1. I think that's all I can say. The choice of how to invest your time and energy is totally up to you. Research, ponder the options, and then lay your money down wherever you think best. Or keep it in your pocket.

Q: Is Taiji radically different from the other Chinese internal martial arts, such as Xingyiquan, Baguazhang, etc.?

A: They cultivate the same energies, so in that sense they're identical. The baseline energy taxonomy I present in this book, and apply to my own development, was elaborated by a Xingyiquan master (Guo Yunshen, see Chapter 2). The outer movements differ, and I personally, having trained all three under a variety of qualified teachers, found that ZMQ37 Taiji work helped me strip off my basic tension better than any of them. Your mileage will differ, so give them a try. They're fun.

Q: You've discussed different kinds of Taiji push hands SHELL interactions, delivered with just a triggering touch. But in addition to all that, is there such a thing as a Taiji strike (punch, slap, or kick)?

No. Taiji is not a *striking* art. But then, what *is* it? Some people would give the shallow answer that it's a *grappling* art. In fact, the combative drills of one venerable style of Taiji largely amount to a kind of primitive standup grappling. But real Taiji isn't a grappling art either, as grappling is accomplished through the use of ordinary leverage and strength. And before you even ask it, no, real Taiji isn't even a *pushing* art either. Because *pushing* at the end of the day is yet another physical modality that is susceptible to having more than four ounces applied.

286

Real Taiji is neither a striking nor grappling nor a pushing art – it's a pure *contact* art. In other arts, the *way* you come into contact with an opponent is paramount. Most people would assume that striking is different from grappling etc. But in Taiji, none of that matters. Real Taiji operates in a higher dimensionality where all that's needed is merely to establish *contact.* When I say 'contact' I'm not talking about 'full contact fighting'. I'm just talking about plain *touch.* In Taiji, a simple touch is the only delivery mechanism needed. If you ever see *qi* masters or Taiji pushers using any degree of mechanical leverage, momentum, struggle for physical position, anything like that, they either aren't Taiji masters or else for whatever reason they aren't using their Taiji. Because real Taiji is based on delivering the trigger effect in the gentlest, easiest way possible. And that's just touching.

An unsheathed live electric wire will zap you regardless of the shape it may happen to be in when you touch it (coiled, straight, curvy, angled, etc.). Taiji is the same. Only *contact* is needed to transfer the energy shock, it doesn't have to be a particular body or method of contact. It's a contact art. Certainly there are movements that *appear* to be strikes, in the superficial sense of forming a loose fist or striking palm shape, but in fact all movements of Taiji are the same - just a touch to transmit the triggering energy delivered from the feet via the FLASHOUT. That's all there is. No strikes in any normal recognized sense. Those who think Taiji is a striking art just because some of the form movements externally mimic a strike configuration are like somebody who sees a man's face on TV and assumes there must be a little man hiding in the TV cabinet or behind the screen.

Q: If I get heavily into Taiji, must I or should I give up ordinary athletics and fitness workouts?

A: No way. Athletics are fun and fitness is important. The key thing is your mindset. Just don't do other athletics or martial arts with the mistaken idea that it's somehow isomorphic to Taiji or the same thing in different clothing, all the same physical principles, etc. If it involves any kind of tension whatsoever, it is emphatically not real Taiji - whatever it may be called. It will only harm, slow, or stop and reverse your development if you mistake it as such. But I am *not* inveighing here against any other form of athletic practice or development whatsoever! I know it's a tough point but try to understand: practicing any kind of athletics or combative or anything physical at all will *not* harm your Taiji development in the least - unless you are doing those other things w*ith the idea that they are enhancing or substituting for real (relaxed) Taiji work.*

Only Taiji is Taiji. For example there are lots of *qi* and martial arts development systems nowadays that incorporate various kinds of tension drills, sometimes intentionally, and sometimes unaware of the tension they're fostering, sometimes as solo work, sometimes as partner work. If you believe that that kind of thing is somehow getting you towards the mind-blowing cosmic bliss of the real Taiji energy, you are mistaken. Those practices aren't harmful due to their physical actions *per se*, but because of the mental block they introduce and the misinterpretation they reinforce. You'll do that stuff thinking you've covered Taiji or "internal" daily practice when actually, because either you were tense, or else you'd been focused on anatomy, physics, or theatrics - you haven't even been on the same planet. We all have only a few ticks on the daily clock to use for this stuff, and just a few pages on the calendar. Be careful with them.

There are mosquito eradication programs where they capture some bugs live, neuter them, and release them back to the wild. Without actually killing a single insect, they can eliminate the entire wild population by deploying fakes that look and appear like the real thing but which lack the essential developmental quality. The decoys end up distracting and depleting the resources of the entire community to the point of total collapse.

I like boxing, Ashtanga yoga, and other such tough physical stuff. But none of that has any connection with the true Taiji path. I don't mistake fool's gold for gold. But I can enjoy the glitter of costume jewelry for the campy fun that it is. And you don't want to end up having mastered the true Taiji energy someday only to find yourself imprisoned in a ugly, unfit, crummy, old physical body. Well ok, *old* we can't do much about, but. So get out there and dance, hike, rock climb, parkour, crossfit, kettlebell, tumbling, rumbling - anything. Just don't ever confuse those with the true Taiji energy work.

Q: OK then, if Taiji is compatible with ordinary athletics, would you go further and say Taiji could actually contribute to athletic development in any way?

A: Yes, I think so, because most sports are based on the same prime tenet of Taiji: relaxation. In boxing for instance, all aspects of the sport demand relaxation, from the stamina you need to make it through a hardcore 3-minute round in the ring, not to mention punching speed, even doing a good jump rope session out of the ring, the sport is all about functional relaxation, all the way down. You also hear occasional stories about the amazing physical (non-combative) abilities of some internal masters. In my own case, the slow evolution of my Taiji attributes has enhanced my boxing skills – power, speed, stamina, etc. - far beyond what they were when I was much younger (youth normally being regarded as the absolute pre-condition for any kind of boxing ability).

Q: I hold a brown belt in Brazilian Jiu-jitsu, and/or I'm a Thailand-trained Muay Thai boxer, and/or I have a black belt in Judo, and/or I'm an instructor of Tae Kwan Do, and/or I work as a professional doorman, etc. Will you meet up with me to spar and test out your Taiji for real?

A: What?! You think I'm nuts? No way. I've already got *one* front tooth knocked out, can't afford to lose any *more*. And I've told you throughout this book that Taiji is not real fighting anyway. However, there are two things I've done down the years that are somewhat – remotely - similar to what you propose.

1. I sometimes accept, or even solicit, freestyle *kuzushi* meet up session requests. I differ from most Taiji teachers in that I allow free play. What I mean is that though I'm into boxing and other things, my preferred vehicle for demonstrating the deeper concepts is Taiji basic fixed-step push hands. Within a broad scope under that umbrella you can try what you will with me, unlike bigger-name Taiji teachers who can't allow free play in this fashion, because they have too much to lose if somebody cell-cams them getting shoved around. But I've had a long-standing offer to meet up with anybody from any style to work on the restricted Taiji push-hands game board. It is *kuzushi* (unbalancing) as defined in the chapter 'PUSH'. This format of meet up is interesting to many people because it helps them diagnose tension in their body and mind. In hundreds of such meetups over many years my art has hardly ever failed me. But some people resist this kind of engagement, claiming that would be "playing my game" and thus they naturally fear losing out. That's sad in a way, because they are letting fear rob them of a rare chance to safely feel their own unconscious tension, but for some of those kinds of cases (unwilling to do *kuzushi* format), I have also sometimes offered boxing meetups (see next item). However, I may not offer free *kuzushi* meetup sessions for very much longer.

2. Western boxing is the only other alternative meetup framework that I do. I'll generally spar a few rounds under MOQ rules with any reasonable person (of any weight class, because most adult USA males outweigh me by minimum 40 lbs.), but in that case it must be: mouth guards, regulation 14 or 16 oz. gloves, standard ring, three (or fewer as agreed) timed 3-minute rounds, and under

some kind of ref or 3rd party supervision. Generally those restrictions are prohibitive for casual meetups in the park. And since boxing is only indirectly related to Taiji, through the *attributes* that Taiji can foster, it doesn't really prove much. But it can occasionally be fun. I may be cutting down on this type of meetup soon though, so you may have missed your chance already.

Q: Why don't you name your Taiji teacher?

A: My teacher is a great master, famous for his love of privacy, his lack of self-promotional ego, and for generally keeping a low profile. Famous for trying not to be famous! His personal standards are too high for a fun but kind of *wild* book like this. He also wouldn't necessarily agree with everything (or anything) I've written here. It would have been way too much of a burden to ask him to review and approve it all. This book is actually more of a *notebook* anyway – it's mostly meant as casual training notes for my Japanese students. It just needs to be translated over to Japanese language, when I get the time. But to answer your question – my teacher's name *does* appear several times in this book (be very very quiet).

APPENDIX C:
SAGAWA YUKIYOSHI'S CORE TEACHINGS WITH TAIJI ANNOTATION

Sagawa Yukiyoshi　(佐川幸義 1902–1998)　was the late great absolutely phenomenal representative of Takeda Sokaku's (武田惣角 1859–1943) Daitou Ryuu　style of Japanese Jiu-Jitsu. Takeda was the seminal master whose trunk teachings blossomed out into modern synthetic styles such as Aikido and Hapkido. But the real essence was carried on with minimal fanfare by one Takeda's main disciples, Sagawa Yukiyoshi.

Among the thousands of martial artists living and dead, people I've met or not, the ones I've always placed in my highest pantheon are few. In no particular order: Li Yaxuan, Benjamin Lo, Musashi Miyamoto, Mikhail Ryabko, Ueshiba Morihei, Vladimir Vasiliev, Yamaoka Tesshu, Yang Chengfu, Yang Luchan, Zheng Manqing - those were my Top Ten. But when I began researching Sagawa Yukiyoshi a few years ago, I had to make it my Top Eleven. He's special for three reasons:

1. He consistently demonstrated unvarying martial arts performance at the absolute highest level.
2. We have numerous reliable contemporary accounts of his skill, primarily thanks to one of Sagawa's own top students, Kimura Tatsuo (among many others who have contributed short pieces and anecdotes).
3. His teachings map perfectly onto the most sophisticated Taiji principles

This Appendix uses ten brief fair-use quotations from Kimura's book 'Transparent Power' (透明な力, hereafter TP) to establish the basic equivalence: the mystical-seeming Aiki power is Taiji power. Even though an English language translation of Transparent Power now exists, in this document I give my own original translations of each teaching selection. While in some cases there isn't huge variation between the book's version and mine, non-readers of Japanese may still be interested to read an alternative translation of key points, to see if it provides any additional insight into this great man and his art. *Transparent Power* covers a wide swath of Sagawa's life and times, including anecdotes about Takeda and much else. Here I've selected only a few brief quotes that illuminate most specifically the technical foundation of Sagawa's approach, and how he advised his students to cultivate and express Aiki - the apparently mysterious and elusive element which, more than any specific set of Daitou Ryuu physical drills, tricks, or techniques, was the heart and soul of Sagawa's total mastery.

I also want to highlight how closely Sagawa's teachings align to the highest of Taiji teachings, primarily from the Zheng Manqing line of thought. If you feel I'm merely cherry-picking the quotes to force-fit the comparisons, then you can skip the Taiji annotations that appear after each translation and simply savor each of Sagawa's teaching nuggets for its own inherent brilliance in isolation. When reading *Transparent Power* it's too easy to lose the essential thread of Sagawa's take on the essence of internal martial arts, and to miss how exactly that maps onto the Taiji principles. This Appendix is the only place you'll find the two lined up side by side for you on a silver platter.

本当の合い氣はゆっくり静かに倒すのだ。

The real aiki power unbalances the opponent softly and quietly.

> I mentioned above that Sagawa makes frequent and crucial reference to a mysterious power (or sometimes 'technique' 技) called 'aiki' 合気. Although the Chinese characters for this are the same as those of the more popular martial art of Japanese Aikido, Sagawa's use of this term doesn't use the word as it's commonly understood in that art. In Aikido, 'aiki' would most commonly refer to a kind of physical and spiritual joining with an attacker's aggressive motions, an attempt to blend with violence and turn it out of harm's way. Sagawa doesn't use the term in this way, and his art was conceptually different.

Sagawa had the ability to neutralize an attacker's power on contact, leaving the attacker absolutely exposed to any response he might choose to apply. The result (absolute neutralization and pacification) is thus compatible with Aikido's highest non-violent aspirations, but through an entirely different mechanism that is much closer (in fact identical to) the highest levels of Taiji function than to Aikido as normally understood.

The "soft, quiet" unbalancing referred to by Sagawa above is the micro-fajing practice described in this book.

私の技は全て瞬間に合気が入って崩ししてしまっている。崩してから技をかけるから自由自在だ。

My entire technique consists of instantaneous application of Aiki power to an opponent, causing unbalancing which sets him up for any technique I may freely choose to apply.

This relates closely to the first quote above. The real Taiji master can always display his power by merely unbalancing softly and quietly - as evidenced by forcing the opponent to take a re-balancing step (one or both feet must move involuntarily). No need for a flamboyant slamming throw down or a crippling power punch or anything at that stage. In reality there would be second stage, as stated in the selection, and an actual opponent can be destroyed at either of the two stages:

(i) the unbalancing itself can easily boosted to cause a heavy slam to a wall or the floor.

(ii) alternatively, once an opponent's balance is taken, any kind of finishing technique - such as a strike or hold - can be readily applied.

だいたい人を投げて息が乱れるということは、力でやっているということだ。合気で正しくやれば息が乱れる筈がない。

When attempting to throw or jolt an opponent, an average practitioner will become short of breath. But when real aiki power is used, there is no disruption of the breath whatsoever.

Here again we have a profound Sagawa teaching that could have been lifted straight from the tongue or pen of Zheng Manqing. Time and again he has enjoined us that any panting or puffing while working with push hands is a sign of relying on ordinary strength and physical force. The same goes for excessive sweating. Even if you move or throw the opponent, if you find yourself out of breath and/or sweating as a result, you are very far from the true power, and your art will fail you as soon as you meet up with a stronger/heavier opponent.

身体の力を全く抜いているから敵の弱い点すぐわかるのです。敵の力に逆らわない。

When you absolutely eliminate all strength from your body, you will instantly realize your opponent's weak spots. Do not oppose your opponent's power.

This is an absolutely pure 24-karat Taiji core teaching. At a high level of Taiji, as described in the writings of Zheng Manqing and Li Yaxuan, and personally experienced and demonstrated by their best students, as soon as your hands come into the slightest contact with an opponent, you can instantly "lock on" to just the right spot to leverage with your internal power (Aiki). This is the SPIKE described in this book.

Li Yaxuan wrote: "[your opponent's] faults will unfailingly be immediately apparent to you and the opportunity to deal with his movement will spring naturally to your hands.... As I follow, before he knows it my presence has infiltrated his body. From this point onward, the slightest movement of my spirit energy and activation of my dantian's qi store will immediately send him reeling as though he's touched a live electric wire. What we call emptiness contains everything, and what we call liveliness feels all, so that whenever the right opportunity comes to your hands your internal energy's automatic reaction instantly sends him sprawling out." This Li Yaxuan quote could have come straight from Sagawa's Transparent Power. Keep this quote in mind as you read the remaining Sagawa quotes further below.

Also, notice that the Sagawa quote above uses the standard Japanese term for "understand" （わかる）for this (though I translated it as "realize" in context), and the Taiji label for this ability is identical, as "understanding energy" (懂勁). The key idea is that when you reach the level of instantaneous and spontaneous identification of the opponent's key strength points, you won't need to oppose your own physical strength or mass or structure to overcome that - a wholly different kind of element will move through you, directly to/through his 'weak spot' (or, spot of tension) and get the job done for you. That's real Aiki/Taiji.

合気がわかったらどんあ者に対しても力を使わずにできる。力が強い者はやりにくいというのでは合気ではない。

When you understand Aiki, you can overcome anybody without using any strength. If you have more trouble against somebody physically stronger, then you haven't mastered Aiki.

Again I can only re-iterate another core Taiji teaching that size, weight, mass, strength of the physical body is totally irrelevant. Only internal tension and internal power are relevant. Nothing physical matters very much in this, including all the current chatter about perfect posture/ structure and anatomical fetishization etc.

肩書の力を抜いて力まない身体を作ることが重要なのだから最初の
うち相手が倒れなくてもきにするな。

*Because your body must be properly conditioned over time to relax and
loosen the shoulders, therefore if you find that at first you have trouble
taking your opponent's balance, don't fret about it.*

Here we have yet another core teaching of Zheng Manqing.
Zheng also emphasized that when you engage in push
hands with a partner/opponent in practice mode, the goal
is emphatically NOT to "win" that particular encounter.
It would mean nothing. The goal is to learn more about
relaxing your body under a bit of psychological and
physical pressure. The real Aiki/Taiji power is cultivated
slowly over a long time via both solo body work and
partner kuzushi sessions. No hurry. Zheng Manqing's
expression of the Sagawa quote above would be his most
famous line: "Invest in loss" （学吃亏）

稽古は繰り返すことによってただしいことを習慣づけ身体に染み込
ませようというわけだから、倒すことばかりに夢中になっていると
力む習慣や悪いくせが体に染み込んでしまう。

*It takes a long period of repeated practice to imbue your body with the
ability to do kuzushi correctly. If you get too hung up on just winning the
encounter, you'll pick up the bad habit of relying on tense physical strength.*

See above comment, it's the same point, again.

腹が大事だと言っても腹に力を入れるわけではない。下腹ウツと力
をいれたら前へ出られなく成ってつてしまう。

*Although the tanden (lower abdomen point) is important, it's not a matter
of hardening it with physical force. If you suddenly tense up your lower
abdomen with a hard breath action you'll find yourself unable to move freely.*

Both Japanese and Chinese culture traditionally
emphasize the importance of the lower abdomen as an
accumulation and staging point for internal energy. But

Taiji, and Daitou Ryuu as stated above, do not attempt to force the issue by any kind of controlled breathing or aggressive breath control or abdominal strengthening. In Zheng style Taiji, breath (and with it, the Aiki/Taiji energy) settles naturally into the lower abdomen as the lower body is stabilized over time. It is often said in this context that you don't attempt to poke down tea leaves floating in a new brew, you wait and allow the heat to do the work naturally over time.

足腰のできていない人はかたの力に頼るようになってしまう。柔らかい動きをする人はうまくなる可能性があるのだが、力んで硬い人はもうそこでダメになってしまう。

People who haven't prepared their lower bodies properly will end up relying on shoulder strength. Only people who practice soft movement have the potential to become skilled. People who use tense up and use strength are hopeless.

Taiji can pretty much be defined as essentially just this: soft movement.

私の考えでは氣というのは自分の体に貯めて置いて必要な瞬間にだすものだ。

*In my view, what we call **ki** is [a power that] you accumulate and store in your body to be instantaneously released at the necessary moment.*

This point could be taken straight from any of the writings or interviews of Zheng Manqing, Li Yaxuan, or Yang Chengfu. Notice that while identical to the Taiji conception of internal power, this formulation differs radically from the traditional Aikido notion of ki skill as the ability to integrate yourself with the physical and psychological 'flow' of an opponent's motion and intent. True aiki/Taiji power is not "joining", but neither is it "opposition" - it is instead *instantaneous absolute neutralization*, which is something radically different.

Taiji is known for emphasizing *relaxation* above all, whereas Sagawa was famous for his extreme *physical conditioning routine*, involving daily performance of hundreds of reps of pushups, squats, hammer and heavy sword swings, etc. Does Sagawa's enormous physical strength (both the strength required to perform this regimen and the strength resulting from it) somehow shoot a fatal hole in the Aiki = Taiji equivalence argued for here?

Not at all. But you need to understand some deeper points to see why not. First, we must distinguish between two related but distinct areas of energy training: *cultivation* vs. *deployment*. The quotes above (which are fully representative of Sagawa's teaching repeated countless times throughout the entire book) leave absolutely no doubt that in deployment, in actual use of the Aiki with a live opponent or partner, *relaxation* was the primary requirement - fundamental and non-negotiable. I shouldn't need to belabor that any further. If you have the slightest doubt on that score, reread the quotes above as many times as you need to convince yourself. He couldn't have been any clearer or more emphatic on that point. In this, his teachings overlap perfectly with Taiji.

Now, what about energy *cultivation*? Is *relaxation* an absolute unchanging requirement for all cultivation schemes? Here's where I've taken a terrible gamble by including this Appendix on Sagawa, because the potential for misunderstanding is so huge that it's almost certain to come back and bite me hard somehow. Yet the topic is too fascinating to ignore. Taiji's cultivation side is consistent with its deployment side, insisting on absolute relaxation as the foundation of both. But quite apart from Sagawa's Daitou Ryuu there are systems that attempt to cultivate the energy through alternation between tense/relaxed states, or that even privilege methods based on physical tension as their royal road to internal energy. An example of a discipline that emphasizes alternation between relaxed and tense states in its cultivation work would be

Russian Systema (see *Let Every Breath: Secrets of the Russian Breath Masters* for details). A discipline that privileges physically tense work in energy cultivation would be various forms of Okinawan karate, with their *sanchin* methods, or some Chinese styles such as *Bajiquan*.

It's a broad scale, and results vary, depending on individual student preference and aptitude. Obviously Sagawa felt that his hard solo training contributed to his mastery of the Aiki force/technique. He is quoted repeatedly throughout the book saying that "creating the proper body" and "conditioning/training the body" and "strengthening the legs and hips" are essential prerequisites to his method. But he makes it equally clear that he isn't talking about ordinary muscle and physical strength cultivation. Here's the punch line: Sagawa was using tension methods to deepen his ability to relax, by sharpening the contrast.

So, even though Sagawa's method on the cultivation side differed radically from Taiji's cultivation work, the end goal of not only the overall martial art but specifically the cultivation portion of his training was geared to developing superior ability to relax. Aiki/Taiji power can *only* function through a maximally relaxed body - that's simply the way things are. Any apparent contradiction will be revealed on closer look to be some kind of misunderstanding. The misunderstanding in this case would be to look at Sagawa's hard physical cultivation work and assume that he must have intended to strengthen tendons or muscles or the physical structure in some way. Not so, it was obviously cultivation of a body that could accept the non-physical Aiki/Taiji energy, and the main condition for that is relaxation, always. Just as Yang Chengfu and other Taiji greats have taught.

Note that Taiji endurance training (such as that offered by some teachers in the Yang/Zheng lineage) is noted for being extremely tough physical practice, involving holding awkward Taiji postures as low to the ground as possible for as long as possible. This work is undeniably physical in its immediate manifestation (we'd have to pull our legs into bed with our arms in the evening after a training session). Does such muscle fatigue mean that this kind of training contradicts the Prime Directive of both Taiji and Daitou, which is relaxation above all? No, that's just the correct Taiji approach to developing "strong legs and hips" (足腰) as proper vessels for the relaxed Aiki/Taiji energy.

So - should you start 1000 daily swings of a 30-pound iron hammer or hundreds of fingertip pushups, like Sagawa? Possibly. But be very careful, because while it's true that geniuses such as Sagawa succeeded in using "tense" methods of cultivation to realize the ultimate state of relaxation required to apply the non-physical energy, the statistical chance that *you* are such a genius is vanishingly small. So maybe you should stick to the consistently relaxed methods of Taiji for optimal cultivation.

Virtually everyone, other than a genius such as Sagawa, who attempts to use the tension methods of *cultivation* will end up binding in additional physical tension ever more deeply and then, unable to shed it or even perceive it, will carry it straight over to the *deployment* side, thereby dooming any chance of ever mastering the Aiki/Taiji energy in actual use. But that's fine for other arts, They have their methods and goals and all are perfectly valid in their own terms, or they wouldn't have any adherents. But it isn't the Taiji way so if higher Taiji power isi your goal, steer clear of it.

APPENDIX D:
GLOSSARY

This glossary includes words I've custom-created for my explanation of Taiji energetics, or which I've used in specific technical ways that aren't obvious to a native speaker of English. The abbreviations and acronyms are capitalized. No Chinese terms are included, because I'd have to re-write the entire book here in the glossary to define and explain them again. Refer to the main text for explanation of all Chinese terms.

ARC	Accumulate, Rebound, Catch - the full-body activation path
accelerant	methods for enhancing the effect of the ARC practice
air element pushing	push hands effect of slow push
BLH	Beautiful Lady's Hand, distinctive hand shape of ZMQ37 Taiji system
BRUTE	lowest level of superficial qi sensations
earth accelerant	category of energy enhancement methods for the feet
earth element pushing	push hands effect of rooting for stability
FAB	Fully Activated Body, the result of ARC training in Taiji form
fire element pushing	push hands effect of instant rebounding
FLASHOUT	The instantaneous transfer of STEEL energy from the NEXUS Point to the hands or SHELL
form	the fixed sequence of Taiji practice postures
heaven accelerant	category of energy enhancement methods for the head
kuzushi	unbalancing exercise similar to Taiji push hands

macro fajing	total energy control of a partner
man accelerant	category of energy enhancement methods for the body
metal element pushing	push hands effect of blending energy to control a partner
micro fajing	partial energy control of a partner
MIRR	premonition of others' motion without physical contact
NEXUS	main head point for energy intake
NUDGE	gentle physical gesture that unbalances a push hands partner
ORE	Original Raw Energy of the external environment
SHELL	human body's energy overlay structure
SLIDE	defensive method for energy deflection
SPIKE	simple direct application of energy to unbalance a push hands partner
Spotlight	imaginary lighting contrasts for emphasizing yin-yang power alternation
STATE	unified energy conditions
STEEL	The ultra-refined predominately yin energy resulting from the ARC internal tempering loop
STREAMOUT	The smooth flow of STEEL energy from the NEXUS Point to the hands or SHELL
SURGE	cyclic power experience in the body
water element pushing	push hands effect of yielding to incoming force
yinfusion	melding of one's energy SHELL with that of a partner

APPENDIX E:
THE CROWN JEWELS

All you need to go forward in your Taiji research from here:

1. The Essence of T'ai Chi Ch'uan - The Literary Tradition
Martin Inn, Robert Amacker, Susan Foe Benjamin Pang Jeng Lo (Translator), Calligraphy by Benjamin Pang Jeng Lo (Illustrator); IRI Press (2008)

2. Cheng Tzu's Thirteen Treatises on T'ai Chi Ch'uan
Cheng Man Ch'Ing (Author), Benjamin Pang Jeng Lo (Translator), Martin Inn (Translator); Blue Snake Books (1993)

3. T'ai Chi Ch'uan Ta Wen: Questions and Answers on T'ai Chi Ch'uan
Chen Wei-Ming (Author), Benjamin Pang Jeng Lo (Translator), Robert W. Smith (Translator); Blue Snake Books (1993)

4. The Lectures with Benjamin Pang Jeng Lo - 4 DVD Set [DVD-ROM]
Benjamin Pang Jeng Lo
IRI Press; 1ST edition (2010)

ACKNOWLEDGEMENTS
AND THANKS

These some of the TAIJI people (teachers, classmates, senior role models, partners, friends, students, and fellow travelers) who've made a dramatic difference in my development as a Taiji enthusiast. There have been hundreds of others over the decades who've helped me immeasurably in every other conceivable way, but this list is the hard-core Taiji people alone – the ones who've tried to lead me to the light. If I start listing everybody who's done so much for me, I'll end up writing a blubbering 500-page personal memoir instead of this lean and mean Taiji floor-shop manual.

Inclusion on this list does not in any way imply the slightest knowledge of, agreement with, endorsement of, involvement with, or responsibility for, any part of what I've written. Nevertheless, even though they run screaming to sign 12-month black-belt contracts at the nearest strip-mall Tae Kwan Do academy every time they hear me say it, here's another huge thank you to the Taiji heart-masters below who've brought it to life:

Benjamin Lo, Wayne Abramson, Burt Brown, Tom Campbell, Ed Chan, Pak Chan, Garrett Chinn, Patricia Corrigan Culotti, Robert Davis, Tana Farnsworth, Marvin Feldman, Don Gillaspie, Anthony Ho, Chien-Liang Huang, Michael Jang, Alan Kempner, Peter Kwok, Terry Li, Daniel Lo, Kayo Robertson, Al Sambuco, Lee Scheele, Robert W. Smith, Lenzie Williams, Carol Yamasaki, Henry Yu.

Made in the USA
San Bernardino, CA
15 June 2014